Dover Opera Guide and Libretto Series

DON GIOVANNI

By   1 3 4 4

WOLFGANG AMADEUS MOZART

Translated and Introduced

By

ELLEN H. BLEILER

DOVER PUBLICATIONS, INC.

New York

This new Dover edition, first published in 1964, contains the following material:

The standard authorized Italian libretto of *Don Giovanni*, as published by G. Schirmer, Inc.

A new English translation of the libretto and supplementary material by Ellen H. Bleiler.

Library of Congress Catalog Card Number: 63-17912

Manufactured in the United States of America

Dover Publications, Inc.
180 Varick Street
New York 14, N.Y.

CONTENTS

	PAGE
Wolfgang Amadeus Mozart	5
Lorenzo Da Ponte, the Librettist	29
Literary Background	42
Plot Summary	52
Musical Background	65
Ludwig Köchel	79

Don Giovanni

Act One
Scene One	85
Scene Two	94
Scene Three	103
Scene Four	124
Scene Five	133

Act Two
Scene One	149
Scene Two	164
Scene Three	173
Scene Four	180
Scene Five	187
Scene Six	189
Epilogue	200

Bibliography	207

WOLFGANG AMADEUS MOZART

About 1740, Johann Georg Leopold Mozart decided he preferred music to jurisprudence. A bookbinder's son from Augsburg in Southern Germany, Leopold Mozart had first been sent to the University of Salzburg to study for the priesthood. As a boy he had sung in church choirs and had sought to learn as much about religious and secular music as he could. By 1737, when he entered the University of Salzburg, he was a proficient violinist; he continued his musical studies at the university (having already given up his preparations for the priesthood in favor of logic and law). Thus, when he determined to make music his career, he was able to enter the services of the Dean of the Salzburg Cathedral as a musician and personal servant—a common combination of chores at eighteenth-century courts.

In 1743 Leopold Mozart became a violinist in the Archbishop of Salzburg's court orchestra. He gave violin lessons to the Archbishop's choirboys and composed music when it was required for religious services. In 1747, when he was twenty-eight years old, Leopold married Anna Maria Pertl (or Bertl), the daughter of a petty official. They were called the handsomest couple in Salzburg and had seven children, of whom only two survived.

In 1756 Leopold Mozart published his "Versuch einer gründlichen Violinschule" ("Essay at a Fundamental Violin School"), which remained for years a standard manual for violinists. This work alone would have ensured its author a certain fame in musical posterity. Earlier that same year, however, an event took place which made Leopold Mozart immortal, regardless of his other achievements. On January 27, 1756, Joannes Chrysostomus Wolfgangus Theophilus* Mozart was born—the only son of Leopold to survive, and quite possibly the greatest musical genius that ever lived.

Wolfgang's sister Maria Anna, nicknamed Nannerl, was four and a half years older than he. When Wolfgang was still a baby,

* German: "Gottlieb"; Latin: "Amadeus."

her assiduous papa began to give Nannerl clavier lessons. The little girl's undoubted talent pleased Leopold, and it must have been amusing for the whole family when Wolfgang, barely three years old, climbed on the clavier stool in imitation of his sister and began picking out chords on the keyboard. Delighted at the little boy's interest, Leopold indulgently gave him clavier lessons too. A year or so later, Wolfgang could learn his little musical exercises to perfection almost on first reading. Before his fifth birthday, Wolfgang was dictating his own compositions to Leopold, who wrote them down in the music books that he was compiling for his children.

By the beginning of 1762 Wolfgang's ability was so extraordinary that Leopold Mozart obtained leaves of absence from his employer, the Archbishop, in order to take the children on concert tours of South Germany and Austria and let their prodigious talent be observed by the resident nobility. Leopold Mozart has been scathingly condemned for exposing a child of Wolfgang's age to the rigors involved in this and subsequent tours. Some say the long, grueling travels, the strain of the numerous exhibitions and performances, and the illnesses the boy contracted away from home did much to weaken his constitution and cause his pitifully early death. But Leopold Mozart must not be judged too harshly: besides having a father's natural pride in his gifted child, he was musically astute enough to realize that Wolfgang's talent was unusual, to say the least; and since the best livelihood for an eighteenth-century musician came from noble patronage, it would be well if Wolfgang's possible future benefactors were made aware of his existence as early as possible. In fact Leopold jeopardized his own career for the sake of his son's. As for Wolfgang, he never thought anything amiss about the whole business. For years Leopold's judgment was practically law to his son ("After God, Papa" is an often-quoted statement of Wolfgang Amadeus). Besides, he was a friendly, vivacious and totally unaffected child, who took his own talents completely for granted and enjoyed performing before an audience—provided only that the audience had proper respect for music.

During 1762 the children went first to Munich; later in the year they traveled to Vienna. En route, Wolfgang's bubbling personality and charm delighted everyone he met, from Franciscan monks to customs officers. The little boy's organ playing so amazed the

Franciscan fathers that they left their lunch to listen. A customs inspector was so enchanted when Wolfgang played his violin for him that he let the Mozarts' baggage through free of charge.

In Vienna the children were well received; they were summoned to Schönbrunn Palace to play for the Empress Maria Theresa, her family and court. There, resplendent in bright velvet attire given them by the royal family, Nannerl and Wolfgang astounded the Hapsburgs with their music making. The Empress and her family were themselves musical and perhaps inclined to be skeptical when they first heard the glowing descriptions of the two little Mozarts. But when the wiry little boy showed that he could play the clavier equally well with the keyboard concealed under a cloth, skepticism vanished. The exuberant and affectionate Wolfgang hugged and kissed the Empress; and it is said that when he fell on the slippery floor, he informed the young Archduchess Marie Antoinette, who helped him up, that he was so grateful, he would marry her when he grew up.

The tour to Vienna was quite remunerative—more so than later tours, which were often rewarded with praise and souvenirs rather than hard cash. But just at the peak of his success, Wolfgang came down with scarlet fever. And so in January 1763, after one more short trip (to Hungary), Leopold Mozart and his remarkable children came home to Salzburg.

By this time the scope of Wolfgang's ability must have been almost frightening. He could play the violin well enough—nobody had taught him—to accompany adult musicians at chamber music, sight-reading the score. His ear was so fine that he could distinguish a difference in pitch of $\frac{1}{8}$ tone. The most exacting clavier music held no difficulties for him; he could improvise or accompany at sight. Without using an instrument, he could set a bass to any melody that was given him. His memory was phenomenal (later, Wolfgang Amadeus Mozart would compose entire symphonies and concertos and keep them in his mind sometimes for weeks until he found time to write them down, complete and fully orchestrated). In short, his talent was so remarkable that Leopold decided to lose no time in acquainting yet further places with his unusual child. (Nannerl, herself a fine performer, seems generally to have been overshadowed by her younger brother; she did not develop beyond a child prodigy.)

In the meantime, the Archbishop of Salzburg's Kapellmeister

had died, and a successor was appointed. Leopold Mozart was
made Vice-Kapellmeister. He never did advance beyond this
rank and grudgingly remained a Vice-Kapellmeister until his
death in 1787.

In June, 1763, the whole Mozart family set out for Germany,
intending eventually to reach Paris. On one of their trips in
Southern Germany, the coach broke down. While it was being re-
paired, Leopold took his children to see a local organ. This was
Wolfgang's first encounter with a pedal organ; being too small to
reach the pedals sitting down, he played the instrument standing
up—and played it beautifully. A letter of Leopold mentions that
on one occasion the little boy was homesick; but even this did not
prevent his talents from astounding all who heard him. The
children performed in Frankfurt-am-Main, where the poet Goethe
recalled them long afterwards. One of Wolfgang's most widely
advertised feats was his ability to play when the keyboard was
covered by a cloth, Leopold using this test of his son's prowess to
good advantage. Finally they arrived in Paris, where Leopold
expressed dismay because the French ladies used cosmetics, and
high hopes because his children had been invited to the Court of
Versailles.

Four violin sonatas by Wolfgang (who at that time signed himself "J. G. Wolfgang Mozart") were engraved in Paris. They were
the first of his works to be printed; he was seven years old.

The Paris venture was successful enough to encourage Leopold
to bring his children on to England, where they arrived in April,
1764. King George III had them play for him several times, and a
public concert at which the prodigies later performed attracted
such notice that people were being turned away on the day
before it. In London Wolfgang became acquainted with Johann
Christian Bach, youngest son of the great Johann Sebastian. J. C.
Bach taught music at the royal court; he played clavier duets with
Wolfgang, and his style of composition made a lasting impression
on the boy.

The family remained in England until the following summer.
Leopold was ill for several weeks, and during the resulting in-
activity Wolfgang composed his first symphonies. When a renowned English lawyer and scholar, the Honorable Daines
Barrington, wished to assure himself that Wolfgang's abilities
were genuine, the boy passed with ease all the tests to which

Anna Maria Pertl Mozart, Wolfgang's mother.

Leopold Mozart, Wolfgang's father.

The town and citadel of Salzburg at the beginning of the nineteenth century. Lithograph by Johann Franke, after a drawing by Hubert Satler.

The Löchelplatz in Salzburg; at the far end of the square, the house where Mozart was born.

Mozart at the age of eight. Oil painting by John Zoffany.

Nannerl Mozart in 1762, aged eleven.

Letter sent by Mozart to his sister from Milan, a week before the first performance of *Lucio Silla* in 1772.

Leopold Mozart and his children in 1763. Engraving by Delafosse after
a water color by Carmontelle.

Barrington subjected him. Again the children were summoned to perform for the royal family, but presently even such prodigies lost their novelty, and Leopold decided to leave England and present his children in Holland.

Prince William of Orange and his sister had invited the Mozart children to play for them at The Hague. Wolfgang gave this concert by himself, for Nannerl was so gravely ill that she had been given extreme unction. The Dutch royal family sent one of its own doctors to the girl; she began to get well, but hardly was she up and around when Wolfgang too fell ill for almost a month. After his recovery he gave more concerts and composed various pieces which were published in Holland. The family left Holland and returned to Paris, where Wolfgang and Nannerl had again been invited to perform at Versailles. But in July, 1766, Leopold Mozart—well aware that the Archbishop was becoming impatient at the absence of his Vice-Kapellmeister—took his wonder children on the last lap of their tour. Side trips to France, Switzerland and Germany filled another four months; it was in November that the Mozarts, after three years, found themselves once more at home in Salzburg.

Wolfgang remained in Salzburg until September, 1767. His father was still his only tutor, and now Leopold put the boy to an earnest study of the rules of composition. Wolfgang became absorbed in whatever he was taught; when learning arithmetic, he covered floor and furniture with chalked sums; when studying Latin, he wrote eager notes to a friend to demonstrate his progress in that language.

The Archbishop of Salzburg ordered several compositions from the boy, among them one for the first part of a three-part oratorio. (The second part was composed by Michael Haydn, brother of Franz Joseph.) In September, 1767, the Mozart family again went to Vienna, where they hoped a forthcoming royal marriage would give Wolfgang a chance to demonstrate his talents before an influential audience. Shortly after the Mozarts' arrival a smallpox epidemic broke out in Vienna. Leopold, preferring to leave such matters in the hands of God, had declined to have his children vaccinated (with matter from an active case of smallpox, as was sometimes done), whereupon they caught the smallpox; Wolfgang was blinded by the disease for over a week. The family had left Vienna when the epidemic broke out, but presently returned to the city.

The children again appeared at the court, and the Emperor helped Wolfgang get a commission to compose his first opera. This was *La finta semplice* ("The Pretended Innocent"); intrigues on the part of the impresario and several courtiers prevented its Viennese performance. But in the following year the Archbishop of Salzburg had it presented at his own court.

Nonetheless, 1768 did mark the first performance of an opera by the twelve-year-old Wolfgang Amadeus Mozart, *Bastien und Bastienne.* It was commissioned by Doctor Anton Mesmer, who, having married a rich wife, had recently built a private theater in his garden. Later in the year Mozart also received a commission for a Mass to be sung at an orphanage sponsored by the royal family. The Emperor was present when the Mass was sung, and marveled at the precision with which the youngster conducted his own work. All in all, the year 1768 was a successful one. But now Leopold Mozart became increasingly eager to take his son to Italy, for no eighteenth-century musical education was considered complete without a study of the immense and important Italian tradition.

Again the Mozarts returned to Salzburg where Wolfgang had been appointed concertmaster of the Archbishop's orchestra (a post which remained for some years unsalaried). By the end of 1769 Leopold was able to leave again, and he and his son set out for Italy. Wolfgang began the journey in high spirits; they arrived at Verona and Mantua in January, 1770. In both these cities Wolfgang attended the opera. Happily, he wrote lively accounts of the performances to his sister in Salzburg. Among the first of Wolfgang Amadeus Mozart's many letters to have survived, they are couched in an amusing and misspelled mishmash of dialect German, as well as Italian and French. They already contain the profusion of puns and off-color comments which are so outstanding in Mozart's later correspondence. From Mantua, he wrote:

"The opera . . . was fine. . . . The *prima donna* sings well, but quietly. . . . The *seconda donna* looks like a grenadier and also has a big voice, and doesn't sing at all badly for all that she's acting it for the first time. . . . *Prima ballerina* good, and it's said she's no dog; but I haven't seen her from close up. . . . I can't really write you much about Milan: we haven't been to the opera yet." The letter is signed pompously "Nobleman of the Highvalley, Friend of the Numerical Society." Apparently Mozart was still studying mathematics before his departure.

Astute as they are in musical observations and comments, none of Mozart's letters contain any reference to the magnificent Italian countryside through which he and his father were traveling. Keenly observant to anything concerned with music, delighted by physical activity (he enjoyed dancing and fencing all his life), Mozart seemed quite oblivious to natural beauty.

In Milan, Wolfgang received a commission to compose an opera for the following autumn. From Milan, he and his father traveled to Bologna, where Wolfgang met Giovanni Battista Martini, known as Padre Martini, one of Italy's foremost scholars and composers. Martini tested the boy's ability to write fugues and was astounded at the proficiency displayed by this fourteen-year-old genius. Next, Leopold and Wolfgang went to Florence, and presently to Rome, where they arrived on the Wednesday before Easter. One of the first things father and son did in Rome was to attend a performance of the seventeenth-century composer Gregorio Allegri's *Miserere*, which was sung annually in the Sistine Chapel by the Papal Choir.

Allegri's *Miserere* was a treasured possession of the Church. The penalty for making its score public was excommunication. After hearing it once on the Wednesday before Easter, Wolfgang returned to his hostel and wrote out the whole piece from memory. On Good Friday the Papal Choir repeated its performance. Wolfgang smuggled his manuscript into the Sistine Chapel and made a few corrections on it. Somehow the matter was found out, but instead of creating consternation, it seemed only to increase the awe and admiration with which young Mozart was regarded.

In Naples, where Wolfgang and Leopold then went, a superstitious audience attributed the boy's virtuosity to a supposedly magical ring he wore. When Wolfgang removed the ring and performed just as well, his audience became even more enthusiastic.

In midsummer of 1770, the travelers returned to Rome, where Wolfgang was decorated by the Pope with an order which years before had also been awarded to the venerated composer Gluck. This decoration gave Wolfgang the right to call himself a knight or chevalier; but despite Leopold's urging to the contrary, Wolfgang dropped the title after a few years and never used it again. From Rome Leopold wrote that his son's voice was changing, a

fact which annoyed the boy because it made him unable to sing
the music he was composing.

The rest of that summer was spent in Bologna, where Wolfgang
studied music with Padre Martini and continued composing. The
Philharmonic Society of Bologna elected the boy to membership,
though its rules specifically stated that members had to be at least
twenty years of age; Wolfgang had passed the composition test in
a fraction of the time it usually took applicants for admission to
the Society. Despite his studies and dazzling achievements, his
mischievous high spirits remained undimmed. To his mother and
sister in Salzburg he wrote:

> Today I had the urge to ride on a donkey, for this is the custom in Italy, and
> so I thought that I ought to try it too. We have the honor to go about with a
> certain Dominican monk, who is considered very holy. But I don't really
> believe that, because he often takes a cup of chocolate for breakfast, and then
> right afterwards a good glass of strong Spanish wine; and I myself have had the
> honor of dining with this holy man, who gamely drank wine, and then finished
> the meal with a whole glass of strong wine, two good slices of melon, peaches,
> pears, five cups of coffee, a whole plate of cloves, two full plates of milk with
> lemons. He could indeed do this if he really applied himself, but I don't think
> so, it was too much, and besides he takes a lot of things for afternoon snacks.

In October Wolfgang and his father returned to Milan where
the boy worked at the opera he had been asked to compose. This
work, *Mitridate, Re di Ponto* ("Mithridates, King of Pontus"), was
performed in December with such success that it was repeated
twenty times that season. Further honors were heaped on Wolfgang, and more commissions given him, including an order for
another opera, to be performed in Milan two years hence. And so,
well satisfied with their first tour of Italy, father and son once
more went home to Salzburg—it was March, 1771.

Back in Salzburg, Wolfgang began composing the music
which had been commissioned, including a *serenata* to celebrate
a royal wedding in Milan the coming October. By August the
verbal text for this *serenata* had still not arrived at Salzburg; the
young composer could not begin work on it until September, by
which time he and his father were again in Milan. After they had
arrived there, Wolfgang, busy fulfilling his commissions, wrote to
his sister: "There's a violinist above us, underneath us another
one, next door to us a singing master who gives lessons, in the last
room opposite us is an oboist. That's jolly for composing! . . ."

He completed the *serenata* for the royal wedding within an almost incredible three weeks. The work was well received (Leopold proudly reported that it had completely stolen the limelight from another composer's opera, written for the same occasion), and in December of 1771 the two travelers came back to Salzburg. Wolfgang Amadeus Mozart was not quite sixteen years old. His musical output would have been a credit to a composer twice his age. Europe's learned men had marveled at his genius, and royalty had welcomed him in its palaces. If he thought at all about the future, it could hardly have been with foreboding. He had already made a name for himself in a highly competitive profession; the great composers of his day admired and respected him. Surely nothing could lie ahead but further fame and laurels.

The day after Leopold and Wolfgang arrived in Salzburg, their employer, the easygoing Archbishop, died. His successor, Count Hieronymus Colloredo, was not popular in Salzburg. He ordered Wolfgang to write a dramatic *serenata* for his investiture. Before Wolfgang could begin this piece, he again became very ill. After his recovery he composed rapidly; besides the Archbishop's *serenata*, he completed more than a score of other works. He was reappointed concertmaster in the new Archbishop's orchestra—this time with a salary. Best of all, in autumn he and his father were again granted leave to go to Milan, where Wolfgang's previously commissioned opera was to be performed. This was the third and last of Wolfgang's Italian journeys.

The second Milan opera, *Lucio Silla*, was also composed with amazing speed. Mozart continued supplying the singers with arias even after the work was put into rehearsal. Despite the pace at which he was working, Wolfgang remained full of nonsense. He brightened Nannerl's life with the following, of which alternate lines were written upside-down:

I hope this finds you well, my dear sister. On the same evening that you will receive this letter, my dear sister, my opera, my dear sister, will be put on the stage. Think of me, my dear sister, and imagine hard, my dear sister, that you are seeing and hearing it too, my dear sister. . . . My dear sister, tomorrow we are dining with Herr von Mayer, and why, do you think? Guess. Because he invited us. The rehearsal tomorrow is at the theater. But the impresario . . . begged me not to tell anyone about it, otherwise everybody will come to it, and this we don't want. So, my child, I beg you, don't tell anyone about it, my child, for otherwise too many people will come, my child. . . . Do you already know the story of what has happened here? Now I'll tell it to you. Today we left Count Firmian's in order to go home, and as we came to our street and opened the door of our house, just what do you think occurred? We entered. Stay well, my little lung. I kiss you, my liver, and remain as ever, my stomach, your unworthy brother (*frater*) Wolfgang. Please, please, my dear sister, something's biting me, scratch me.

Lucio Silla was a success; Leopold hoped fervently that his son would receive a permanent appointment to a Tuscan court. But nothing came of the negotiations for this post, and in the early months of 1773 Wolfgang Mozart was back in Salzburg, a place he was beginning to detest.

Wolfgang Amadeus Mozart spent most of the next four years in Salzburg. The new Archbishop was more critical and exacting than his predecessor. Moreover, he was almost certainly jealous of his famous and widely praised concertmaster. His jealousy took the form of trying to keep Wolfgang's talents exclusively to himself, while making sure that the young man "knew his place." Mozart was able to spend some months in Vienna, while the Archbishop moved to his summer residence. Leopold's hopes for a permanent appointment and royal patronage for his son again came to nothing. The stay in Vienna, however, did affect Wolfgang's musical development, for at this time he seems to have become familiar with the music of Franz Joseph Haydn, whose work influenced his own (and vice versa).

After Wolfgang returned to Salzburg, one task which occupied him was the composition of an opera which had been ordered for Munich's carnival season. Since the order came from the Elector of Bavaria, Archbishop Hieronymus could not very well refuse Wolfgang a leave of absence to supervise his opera, nor Leopold a leave of absence to supervise Wolfgang. It was the last journey father and son took together; Nannerl also came to Munich to attend the première of Wolfgang's *La Finta Giardiniera* ("The Pretended Gardener"). The work was successful, but unfortunately no further commission followed it. In March, 1775, Wolfgang returned to Salzburg, where he remained for the next two and one half years, composing, playing the clavier—and fretting.

By the middle of 1777 the fortunes of Wolfgang Amadeus Mozart seemed to be at a standstill. Leopold, still disappointed that no royal patron had offered Wolfgang a sinecure, decided that a final grand tour was necessary to assure his son's future. But the Archbishop thought differently, and refused both father

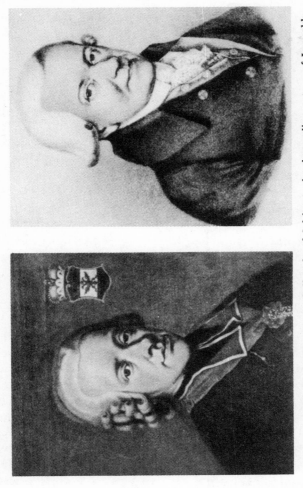

LEFT: Archbishop Hieronymus Colloredo of Salzburg, the demanding patron of Leopold and Wolfgang Mozart. RIGHT: Michael Haydn, composer, younger brother of Franz Joseph, and a Salzburg friend of the Mozarts. Wolfgang composed two duets to help him out of a predicament.

Maria Anna Thekla Mozart, known as the "Bäsle."

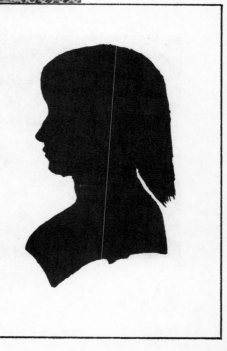

Aloysia Weber, with whom Mozart fell madly in love, only to be rejected.

Mozart about 1782. Unfinished portrait by Joseph Lange.

Constanze Mozart in 1782, the year in which she and Wolfgang were married.

Mozart in 1780. Detail of a painting of the Mozart family by J. N. della Croce.

and son the leave of absence they requested. Angrily, Wolfgang resigned his post; to mollify the ruffled churchman, Leopold stayed behind, and it was in his mother's company that Wolfgang left Salzburg in September, 1777. Paris was his ultimate goal; he intended to visit various German cities on the way.

Augsburg—Mannheim—wherever Wolfgang appeared, he was admired, he was praised, sometimes he was even paid. He hoped constantly that some influential courtier or aristocrat would help him obtain a permanent post, but his hopes were just as constantly shattered. In Augsburg he met relatives—his father's family—and among them his cousin Maria Anna Thekla Mozart, who is better known to posterity as "Mozart's Bäsle" ("Bäsle" is a German dialect term for "girl cousin"). She was an earthy sort of girl and provided Wolfgang with a refreshing change from the strain of traveling, performing and job-seeking. It was to her that he wrote the famous "Letters to the Bäsle" which still cause the worldly to snicker, the prudish to shudder and psychoanalysts to chortle. Their content, incidentally, is usually nonsense; this is frequently couched in meaningless rhyme and sprinkled liberally with terms relating to the hindmost portion of the anatomy as well as certain excretory functions, and not generally used in polite society.

In autumn Wolfgang and his mother came to Mannheim, a city of much musical activity. It was a princely seat, and again Mozart hoped for an appointment. While waiting to see if his hopes would materialize, he gave clavier lessons, attended concerts, and made the acquaintance of Fridolin Weber, a music copyist who had four gifted daughters.

The second of Herr Weber's daughters was sixteen-year-old Aloysia, a pretty girl with a promising voice. Mozart fell head over heels in love with her. He composed songs and arias for her and decided to spend the winter in Mannheim. From Salzburg, Leopold at first agreed to this plan; so far as he knew, his son's chief reason for staying in Mannheim was to await an appointment to the court. But when Wolfgang proposed abandoning the whole Paris trip in favor of accompanying the Webers to Italy, Leopold reacted sharply. In no uncertain terms he ordered his son off to Paris; nor did he neglect to mention the sacrifices he and Nannerl were making in Salzburg for the sake of Wolfgang and his career. Dutifully, the son acknowledged his error, and in March, 1778, he and his mother arrived in Paris. Once again

Wolfgang was optimistic about his prospects; although he corresponded with Aloysia Weber, he postponed his dreams of the success she would bring them both by singing his beautiful songs with her beautiful voice. Later, when Wolfgang met her again, Aloysia's interest in him had died. Even so, Wolfgang Amadeus Mozart's association with the daughters of Herr Weber was far from ended.

The Paris venture began well but grew steadily more disappointing. Mozart gave music lessons; he composed his only ballet *Les Petits Riens* ("The Little Nothings") and many other works as well, and he was offered a job at Versailles, which he refused because the pay was insufficient. But Paris was a city of pronounced musical tradition as well as spirited claques and cliques. Wolfgang was not enough the sycophant or the politician to overcome these obstacles.

In July Wolfgang's mother died, a grave shock to the young man more or less alone in a foreign city and discouraged about his prospects there. By greatly exaggerating the demand for his son's talents in other places, Leopold skillfully contrived to get Wolfgang reinstated in the Salzburg Archbishop's service. Wolfgang was less than delighted at the prospect of returning to Salzburg, but at least a post awaited him there. In the last months of 1778 he began the journey back. He traveled via Mannheim (to the despair of Leopold) but found that the Webers had moved to Munich. Still hoping to press his suit to Aloysia, Wolfgang also went to Munich. But by this time Aloysia was a successful singer and had no more use for a struggling musician. And so Wolfgang returned to Salzburg, unwillingly, but with little other choice.

For the next year Wolfgang Amadeus Mozart chafed as concertmaster and organist to the Cathedral and Court of Salzburg. Despite his discontent, he continued composing. By this time he had already produced more than half his entire musical output (in number of compositions). In 1780 he became acquainted with Emanuel Schikaneder, impresario of a theatrical troupe which was appearing in Salzburg. Schikaneder strengthened Wolfgang's desire to compose for the stage, and a stroke of good fortune came to him from Munich in the form of another order for an opera. The work Wolfgang composed was *Idomeneo*; its success made him feel his true metier was that of "dramatic composer." When Archbishop Hieronymus, still not impressed by his concertmaster's extracurricular achievements, summoned him from Munich to join the archiepiscopal entourage in Vienna, Wolfgang was all too ready to precipitate a final break with his employer.

Wolfgang Amadeus Mozart wished to remain in Vienna; when the Archbishop ordered him to return to Salzburg, he made a flimsy excuse for being unable to do so. Having thus aroused Colloredo's ire, Mozart lost no time in submitting his resignation from the Archbishop's employ. In fact he submitted it three times, and it was refused three times, the refusals being accompanied by insults; on the third occasion the Archbishop's steward emphasized the refusal by literally kicking Mozart out the door. Leopold learned of this affair from his son's letters and was horrified at Wolfgang's rashness; he begged Wolfgang to reconsider and to return to Salzburg. For once the son remained adamant: he was through with the Archbishop, he was finished with Salzburg, henceforth Vienna was to be his home.

To his indignant father Wolfgang wrote that he would have quit the Archbishop's employment even apart from the injuries done him. "[In Vienna] I have the best and most useful acquaintances in the world, I am liked and respected in the best houses, all possible honors are given me, and moreover I get paid for it—and I'm supposed to languish in Salzburg for 400 florins—languish without pay, without encouragement, and be of no use to you in any fashion, as I certainly can be here. What would be the result of all that? Always the same—either I'd have to let myself be vexed to death, or go away again. . . . I guarantee you I'll be successful. . . ." Furthermore, he wrote, if the Archbishop gave Leopold any cause for anger on his son's account, he and Nannerl should also move to Vienna. Wolfgang's letters were confident and optimistic. He was certain that in Vienna he would at last find the good fortune which had so long eluded him.

At the start of his feud with Archbishop Hieronymus, Wolfgang had taken a room in the house of Frau Weber, the mother of his Mannheim-love, Aloysia. The Webers had moved to Vienna a year before; Herr Weber had died, Aloysia had married, and Frau Weber was left with three unmarried daughters. Frau Weber was something of a schemer. She was quite delighted when the unsuspecting Wolfgang Amadeus Mozart took up residence in her menage.

Leopold was far from pleased at this additional turn of events.

Wolfgang, however, ignored the insistent fatherly admonitions to find other living quarters. To Frau Weber's joy, people soon began to gossip about her lodger and her eighteen-year-old daughter Constanze. Wolfgang blithely reassured his father of the total innocence of the situation. Hypocritically Frau Weber advised Wolfgang to move out. Wolfgang obliged, but visited the Webers daily. Frau Weber was now able to convince him that in the eyes of the public he had thoroughly ruined Constanze's reputation by these attentions. A contract was drawn up for Wolfgang to sign: either he would marry Constanze within three years or he would pay damages. Wolfgang, assuring Frau Weber that his intentions were honorable, signed the document. (Constanze tore it up immediately afterwards, he reported to his father.) Frau Weber now turned her efforts to getting rid of Constanze quickly and proceeded to treat the girl as unkindly as possible. Constanze fled to the protection of one of Wolfgang's patrons; Frau Weber threatened to call out the police to bring the girl home. The situation was impossible. Leopold's objections—that the Webers were not respectable, that Wolfgang could not support a wife and family—were in vain. On August 4, 1782, Wolfgang Amadeus Mozart and Constanze Weber were married.

Wolfgang's letters leave no doubt that he did indeed love Constanze and saw in her the qualities of a good mate. But historians have not been very kind to her, often making her the scapegoat for Mozart's later misfortunes. Constanze is accused of infidelity to Mozart, but this was hardly likely since she was pregnant during much of their eight and one-half years of marriage. Similar accusations against Mozart would seem equally unfounded. While admittedly flirtatious, he had a strong sense of morality. It is said Constanze neither fully understood nor appreciated Mozart's genius; this may have been true, but it was a shortcoming she shared with her husband's most learned and brilliant contemporaries. (Constanze herself was a capable singer, though not in the class of her older sisters Aloysia and Josepha.) She was not a good manager of money, but he himself provided her with very little incentive to be. Although he sank more and more deeply into debt during his later years, Mozart's careless generosity made him the continual prey of spongers and leeches, regardless of whether the little money he had was his own or someone else's. As a result of her many pregnancies and the loss of four of the six children she bore, Constanze's health was poor and she frequently had to take costly cures at health resorts, causing a further drain on her husband's emotional and financial resources. Of their six children only two lived: Karl Thomas, who was born in 1784 and died in 1858; and Franz Xaver Wolfgang, who was born in 1791, less than five months before his father's death, and died in 1844. In spite of all tragic events, Constanze's marriage with Wolfgang Amadeus Mozart was nevertheless a happy one.

Meantime, Wolfgang's pen had not been idle. At the wish of the Emperor, Vienna's Imperial Theater had some years before abandoned traditional Italian opera in favor of the German Singspiel (a form of musical drama in which the dialogue is spoken as well as sung). An official of the Imperial Theater gave Mozart a libretto to set to music, and this became *Die Entführung aus dem Serail* ("The Abduction from the Seraglio"), the first of his five most famous operas. The heroine's name was Constanze. Its première in July, 1782, was well received; even the aging composer Gluck, best remembered for his own operas *Orfeo ed Euridice* and *Alceste*, congratulated Mozart on the work. Nevertheless, Mozart was still without permanent employment. What money he earned came from commissions for musical compositions, pupils, and public subscription concerts. The latter were especially grueling; once, in a period of six weeks, Mozart gave twenty-two such concerts. He complained that the German lands were not good to their musicians. He had heard it said of himself that "such people only come into the world once every hundred years," yet no one would hire him. He was almost ready to leave Vienna and try his luck abroad once more. Leopold duly chastised his son for such fickleness of purpose; Wolfgang remained in Vienna, composed, gave recitals for the aristocracy, and hoped for the opportunity to write another opera.

About this time Mozart became well acquainted with Franz Joseph Haydn, one of the few persons who recognized his true musical stature. Mozart dedicated six string quartets to Haydn and had them published, although the publisher complained they were too difficult for most of his customers. The two great composers remained friendly until 1790, when Haydn went to London. When he returned, Mozart was dead. Once, while visiting Salzburg, Wolfgang rescued Michael Haydn, brother of Franz Joseph, from a predicament. Mozart admired the music of Michael

Haydn, who was an organist in Salzburg. Archbishop Hieronymus
Colloredo had ordered six violin–viola duets from Michael Haydn,
but the latter fell sick after composing only four of the duets. When
the Archbishop refused to pay until all six were completed,
Mozart wrote the final two duets and let Michael Haydn submit
them under his own name, unknown to the Archbishop.

In 1784 Wolfgang Amadeus Mozart joined the Freemasons and
later persuaded his father to do the same. The Mozarts were good
Catholics and remained so, although Wolfgang seems to have
placed less emphasis on outward form than his father could sometimes desire. At that time the Masonic lodges in Vienna were
gathering places for the intelligentsia, and from 1784, references
to Masonic philosophy and beliefs occur in many of Wolfgang's
letters. He composed several pieces of music for the Masons' rites;
the most famous "Masonic music" occurs in *Die Zauberflöte* ("The
Magic Flute"), much of whose plot is an allegory about Free-
masonry, the State and the Church.

After Wolfgang and Constanze visited Leopold Mozart in Salzburg, the father returned their visit. But he was apparently never
quite reconciled to his son's marriage; their later letters to each
other, though affectionate in tone, are more formal and con-
strained than the many earlier ones.

By 1785 Mozart was in debt, despite all his hard work. He
began, but never finished, two comic operas. By that time, however, he had been introduced to the Abbé Lorenzo Da Ponte, a
lively and rather remarkable Italian who was a poet for the
Imperial Theater. Da Ponte had recently written the libretto for
an opera which turned out to be a failure. The composer, blaming
Da Ponte for this, had turned elsewhere for his next libretto, leaving Da Ponte available for other work. When Mozart asked him
for a libretto based on the second of the French playwright Beaumarchais' trilogy about a Sevillian barber, Da Ponte consented to
do the work.

Beaumarchais' plays were controversial in France because of
their egalitarian social sentiments. But the first one, *Le Barbier de
Séville* ("The Barber of Seville"), had in 1782 been turned into a
successful Italian opera by Giovanni Paisiello.* Da Ponte was able

* Mozart's letters show that he knew this work. Before Paisiello, two other composers
had also made operas of *Le Barbier de Séville*; but what has become the most famous
opera based on the play—Rossini's—was composed in 1816.

to convince the Emperor and his officials that he had transformed the second Beaumarchais play, *Le Mariage de Figaro* ("The Marriage of Figaro"), into a harmless, uncontroversial Italian libretto. Mozart now devoted himself to composing music for the opera, whose Italian title became *Le Nozze di Figaro*. In February, 1786, less than three months before the completion of *Figaro*, he also wrote a little one-act *pastiche, Der Schauspieldirektor* (usually translated "The Impresario"), which was presented at the Schönbrunn Palace for the entertainment of a visiting dignitary; and he composed three piano concertos and numerous other works as well while working on *Figaro*.

Le Nozze di Figaro received its première in Vienna on May 1, 1786, before an enthusiastic audience. Michael Kelly, an Irish tenor who was a friend of Mozart and sang in *Figaro's* première, said that the Emperor himself had to prohibit encores in subsequent performances, because their inclusion made the opera last almost twice its scheduled time. The music Mozart wrote for the characters in *Le Nozze di Figaro* has been called so perfectly descriptive that a listener can tell who is supposed to sing each aria or *canzonetta* just by hearing the music. Despite its acclaim, *Le Nozze di Figaro* was performed in Vienna only nine times that season. Da Ponte and Michael Kelly both blamed the intrigues and cabals of Mozart's rivals for this. And regardless of its immediate popularity, *Figaro* did nothing to enhance the state of Mozart's finances.

Again, Wolfgang considered making a musical tour through Europe and England; but when his father emphatically refused to look after the grandchildren during their parents' absence, this idea was dropped. At the end of 1786 Wolfgang was invited to Prague to attend the first performances of *Le Nozze di Figaro* in the Bohemian capital. He and Constanze arrived there in January, 1787, and it must have gladdened Mozart to find his work so well-liked that its music had even been arranged for dances. Everything in Prague was *Figaro*, he wrote to a friend. When he himself was recognized in the audience of his opera, he was wildly applauded and had to conduct some subsequent performances of it.

At the end of the month, Wolfgang and Constanze prepared to return to Vienna. Pasquale Bondini, the impresario of the Prague opera, was eager to capitalize on Mozart's success in Bohemia. Before Mozart left, Bondini commissioned him to write another opera which would be performed in Prague the next season. On returning to Vienna, Mozart again asked Lorenzo Da Ponte to provide him with a libretto. Da Ponte, who was working on two other librettos at the time, suggested Mozart make a new opera out of the familiar old story of the libertine blasphemer who is taken to hell by the statue of one of his victims. This story was a stand-by in repertory theaters. It had provided Molière and others with the matter for a drama, and had already been turned into an opera at least twice in recent years, as well as into a ballet by Gluck. Mozart was undisturbed by the familiarity (not to say triteness) of the subject. And so he began to compose *Don Giovanni*.

Don Giovanni had been called the greatest opera ever composed, a well-nigh perfect work. In 1787, however, it was very likely only one more commission to be completed by the thirty-one-year-old Mozart, who was becoming ever more harassed and depressed by financial difficulties, personal tragedies and professional setbacks. Interest in Mozart's subscription concerts was waning; it was difficult to find enough time to compose while continuing to take pupils; Mozart was badly in debt and had to appeal again and again to a brother Mason for money. A son had died just a few months before, and already Constanze was pregnant again. Leopold Mozart, ailing for some time, died in May of 1787. His had been the guiding hand, and he had made the decisions which shaped most of Wolfgang's life. Father and son had at length disagreed to the extent that Wolfgang finally shook off the parental traces. But the news of Leopold Mozart's death was tragic to his son.

Despite all his troubles, Mozart managed to compose most of *Don Giovanni* that summer in Vienna. Early in October he went to Prague and finished the opera, working chiefly at the villa of some friends there. A week or so later Da Ponte came to Prague. The singers who were to take part in the première of *Don Giovanni* proved hard to please; Luigi Bassi, the young baritone who appeared in the title role, complained that Mozart had not provided him with sufficient opportunity to display his vocal prowess. Bassi was supposed to have made Mozart revise the duet "Là ci darem la mano" five times (though the state of the manuscript shows this to be an exaggeration). Mozart was rumored to be carrying on flirtations with all three leading sopranos in the cast (probably exaggeration, too). Gossip had it that when the lady who was to sing the part of Donna Anna showed herself disappointed at the composer's appearance—Mozart was short and rather slight, with a long nose—he supposedly withdrew his favors from her and bestowed them elsewhere. The première of *Don Giovanni* was first scheduled for October 14, in honor of visiting royalty. But the cast was not prepared by this date, and instead of the new opera, *Le Nozze di Figaro* was given for the guests. The first performance of *Don Giovanni* was postponed until October 29.

By October 27—two days before the première—Mozart still had not composed an overture to his opera. That is to say, he had not written down the overture; as was his custom, he had probably thought it out completely and was simply carrying the finished version in his mind. The story goes that late in the evening he began transcribing his thoughts to paper, while Constanze helped him to stay awake by giving him punch to drink and telling him amusing stories.*

Trombonists were specially hired for the Prague performances of *Don Giovanni*; they did not otherwise form a regular section of the orchestra. Following the custom of his day, Mozart himself conducted the première of *Don Giovanni* from the clavier, and accompanied the recitatives. After the overture, he said to someone, "Quite a few notes did fall under the podium, but [it] came off rather well." The Prague audience warmly applauded both the music and the composer; critics recognized that *Don Giovanni* was more than just a difficult work, it was unique.

Just after the Mozarts returned to Vienna, the aged and revered composer Christoph Willibald von Gluck died. Gluck had been a well-paid court composer to the Emperor Joseph II. The news of *Don Giovanni's* success in Prague induced the Emperor to give Gluck's post to Mozart—at a fraction of Gluck's salary. Even this small fixed income did not help Mozart's finances, any more than did the growing fame of his operas. His situation was becoming desperate. In his letters to creditors he still expressed hope of eventually paying back what he had borrowed; but even his optimism sometimes waned.

Don Giovanni was not given in Vienna until May, 1788, partly because of the opposition of Antonio Salieri, a rival composer of

---

* The better-known version of the overture's composition says that Mozart only barely finished composing it on the night before the performance, so that the copyists' ink was still wet on the paper when the orchestra played the overture at sight the next evening. Mozart's own catalogue of his works, however, lists the entire opera as completed on October 28, the day of the final rehearsal, rather than the day of the première.

operas, who was the conductor at the Imperial Theater. Salieri had worked against Mozart before; this time he was anxious for his own works to take precedence in Vienna. Mozart made various alterations in the score of *Don Giovanni*, some to suit the new singers, some to please the Viennese public. The solo arias which he added are still generally performed, but a new low-comedy scene he wrote for the first Viennese performances has usually been dropped from modern productions of the opera. To allow for the time this additional scene would take, Mozart cut *Don Giovanni's* epilogue from the Vienna première. This is still left out in many European productions of the opera. Its original omission forms one of the principal arguments of those who insist—contrary to Mozart's own description of his work—that *Don Giovanni* is an opera of tragic romance.

Only fifteen performances of *Don Giovanni* were given in Vienna that year, and the next season it was dropped from the repertory. After the first performance, according to Da Ponte, the Emperor Joseph II remarked that it was a fine work, but hardly food for his Viennese subjects' teeth. To which Mozart commented, "Well, give them time to chew it."

Wolfgang and Constanze moved to cheaper lodgings on the outskirts of the city. At the request of a patron, Mozart revised some of Handel's choral works, and in fulfillment of his chores as a court composer he wrote dance music for Viennese balls. He composed the final three of his forty-one symphonies. But his pressing difficulties began to cause his inspiration to lag. When a pupil sought his company on a journey to Berlin, Mozart accepted the invitation, wistfully hoping to earn a little money by giving concerts on the way. He left Vienna in the spring of 1789 and returned three months later. A story that the King of Prussia offered Mozart a post which the composer refused out of loyalty to his own Emperor seems to be apocryphal. The Prussian king, however, did order several string quartets from Mozart. An enthusiastic amateur musician, he allegedly asked Mozart what he thought of the court orchestra. Mozart, who was prone to forget that other humans were not possessed of his exceedingly sensitive ear, replied with ruthless honesty that the king's orchestra was good but would be better if it played in unison. Tact was never one of Wolfgang Amadeus Mozart's strong points. From Berlin he ruefully wrote to Constanze:

LEFT: Franz Joseph Haydn, the friend and mentor of Mozart. The younger composer dedicated six of his greatest quartets to Haydn. RIGHT: The composer Antonio Salieri, jealous rival of Mozart in Vienna.

LEFT: Joseph II, Emperor of Austria, 1780–1790, patron of Mozart and Da Ponte. RIGHT: Leopold II, Emperor of Austria, 1790–1792, who looked upon Mozart with less favor than did his predecessor on the throne.

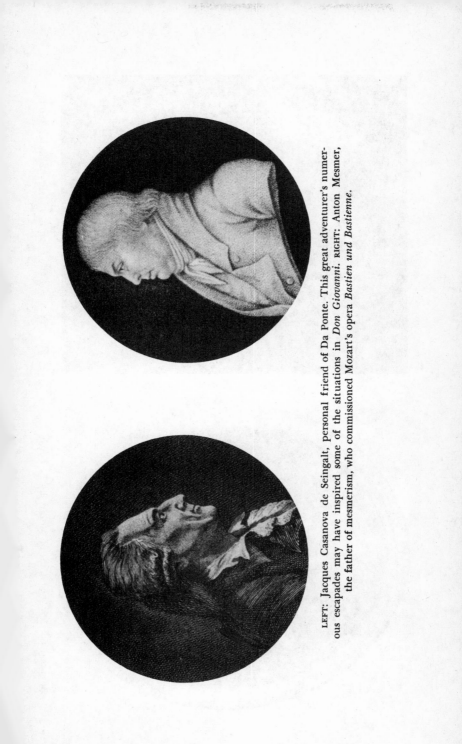

LEFT: Jacques Casanova de Seingalt, personal friend of Da Ponte. This great adventurer's numerous escapades may have inspired some of the situations in *Don Giovanni*. RIGHT: Anton Mesmer, the father of mesmerism, who commissioned Mozart's opera *Bastien und Bastienne*.

Mozart's sons Karl Thomas and Franz Xaver Wolfgang in 1798.

Boxwood portrait medallion of Mozart by L. Posch, 1789.

The Queen wants to hear me on Tuesday; but I won't be able to earn much there. I only accepted the summons because it's the custom here, and she would be offended otherwise. My dearest little wife, you'll have to be more happy about my coming home than about the money. . . .

One of Mozart's creditors was Michael Puchberg, a well-to-do Viennese merchant who belonged to the same Masonic Lodge as Mozart. After his return from Berlin the composer's entreaties to Puchberg became more frequent and more pathetic. He begged for extensions on his loans, and for yet more loans. Constanze was ill again . . . only one person had subscribed to his next public concert. . . . "God!" he wrote to Puchberg, "I'm in a situation that I wouldn't wish on my worst enemy." Surely, he ended his letter, matters couldn't get any worse; in a few months he must certainly be able to pay his debts.

In 1789 *Le Nozze di Figaro* was successfully revived in Vienna. The Emperor promptly ordered Mozart to compose a new opera and Da Ponte to write the libretto for it. The subject was to be a wager which had actually been made in Vienna not too long before, concerning the faithfulness of two ladies to their fiancés. The result was *Così fan Tutte* ("Thus Do All Women"), which received its first performance at the end of January, 1790. The public was moderately pleased by the new opera, but the death of the Emperor Joseph II a few weeks later curtailed further performances for some months. The new Emperor, Leopold II, had serious political difficulties to contend with. He was apparently little interested in music, and moreover seemed to harbor a personal dislike for Wolfgang Amadeus Mozart—who now found himself not only penniless, but for all practical purposes without a patron as well.

Antonio Salieri left his conductorship at the Theater and became Kapellmeister to the new Emperor. Though Salieri was a jealous rival, Mozart swallowed his pride and applied to the Emperor for the post of Assistant Kapellmeister. The application was rejected, and when the Emperor went to Frankfurt-am-Main to be crowned, Mozart was not one of the musicians who was asked to go with the royal party.

Because the guests at the coronation might include some who remembered his abilities, Mozart decided to go to Frankfurt on his own. To pay for the trip he pawned his personal valuables and, accompanied by his equally poverty-stricken brother-in-law (a

violinist who had also been snubbed by the royal party), left for
Frankfurt in September, 1790. Mozart gave concerts in several
German cities, playing his own compositions. He was received
with considerable acclaim, which for a time buoyed his spirits, but
presently he had to write to his wife: ". . . it's all boasting, what
one can earn in the cities of the Empire—famous, admired, and
well-liked I certainly am here; but in other respects, the people
are even more pinchpennies than in Vienna." A short time later
Mozart returned to Vienna; he was just as badly off as when he
had left. Years later, an acquaintance remembered going to
Mozart's house that winter and finding the composer and his wife
dancing energetically. Mozart explained they were only doing
this to keep warm, being too poor to buy firewood.

On returning to Vienna, Mozart found that he had been invited
to England by a London impresario. But he was unable to accept
what must have been a tempting offer. Aside from his financial
obligations in Vienna, his health was none too good; Constanze's
was worse—she was expecting a child and taking expensive treat-
ments at a spa outside the city. His musical output had fallen off
during the previous troubled and hectic year; at the beginning of
1791, Mozart again devoted himself to composition.

In the spring he was asked by his old acquaintance, the actor-
director Emanuel Schikaneder, to set to music a German libretto
which Schikaneder had written.* Schikaneder's story was derived
from an improbable fairy tale, and the finished opera would be
presented in Schikaneder's rather disreputable theater, not at the
Imperial Opera. Mozart consented to compose the music, partly
because he had long wanted to write another German Singspiel,
partly because his wife's sister Josepha, a gifted soprano, belonged
to Schikaneder's troupe, but mostly because Schikaneder himself
was a fellow Mason. Schikaneder provided Mozart with a place
near the theater where he could compose the music. The impresario also induced Mozart to share his rather Bohemian style of living; and the composer, lonely in the absence of Constanze,
complied, to the further detriment of his own health.

By the summer of 1791 a rough version of *Die Zauberflöte* ("The
Magic Flute") was ready. Now there occurred two interruptions
which temporarily delayed its completion. The first came in the

* In 1803 Schikaneder also commissioned Ludwig van Beethoven's only opera,
Fidelio.

form of a man dressed completely in gray, who brought Mozart an anonymous letter commissioning him to compose a Requiem Mass for the sender. The author of the letter has long been identified as a widowed Count, who often paid different composers for music which he then passed off as his own. The strangely dressed letter-bearer was merely the Count's steward. Mozart did not know this, however; nervous and ill, he slowly became convinced that he had been visited by a messenger of death, and was really going to write the Requiem for himself.

The second interruption was an order from Prague for a new opera, to celebrate the Austrian Emperor's installation in that city as King of Bohemia. Hastily, Mozart prepared to travel to Prague with his wife and a devoted friend and pupil, Franz Süssmayr. For the occasion, he planned to compose *La Clemenza di Tito* ("The Clemency of Titus"), using an old, hastily revised libretto as his text. Just as Mozart and his companions were about to enter the coach for Prague, the gray-clad messenger of the Requiem appeared and asked what had become of this commission. Mozart explained and apologized, promising to finish the Requiem immediately after his return from Prague. His conviction about the stranger's identity now became a fixation: Wolfgang Amadeus Mozart was certain he would die soon.

Though quite ill on the whole journey, Mozart composed *La Clemenza di Tito* in the coach and at the inns where they stopped at night. His pupil Süssmayr helped him copy out the music. The whole work was finished and rehearsed in just eighteen days. It failed to please at its première. (Later it became better-liked.) Mozart hurried back to Vienna to complete *Die Zauberflöte*, which was first performed on September 30, 1791. Schikaneder, who sang in the opera, was able gradually to make the public like the work more and more; but Mozart's pleasure in its growing popularity was short-lived.

After finishing *Die Zauberflöte*, Mozart devoted his remaining energies to composing the Requiem Mass. In his own mind, as well as in reality, he was racing death to finish the work. Someone urged him to come to England—most likely Lorenzo Da Ponte, who is thought to have been planning a journey to London at the time—and the composer replied:

I would like to follow your advice, but what would be the use of it? My head is troubled. . . . I cannot remove from my eyes the picture of this unknown person . . . he impatiently demands the work from me. I continue, because composing tires me less than resting. I feel . . . I am about to die; I have finished before having enjoyed my talent. Yet life was so beautiful, my career began under so many good omens, but one cannot change one's own destiny. . . . I am finishing . . . my funeral song, I must not leave it unfinished.*

When he felt a little better, Mozart managed to compose a Masonic cantata to words again supplied by Schikaneder, and he himself conducted its first performance. But to Constanze he confided his premonition of death; he was afraid someone was poisoning him.† Toward the end of November, his Requiem still incomplete, Mozart was too sick to leave his bed. Each evening he looked at his watch and timed the performance of *Die Zauberflöte*, now hugely successful. With cruel irony, news arrived that his money troubles would soon be ended: in both Holland and Hungary annuities were being collected for him. On the evening of December 4 he was still preoccupied with the Requiem, now knowing well that he would never finish it. Feverishly he gave Süssmayr directions for its completion. Presently Mozart fell asleep; even in his sleep, witnesses said, he seemed concerned with music. Early the following morning—December 5, 1791—he died.

Constanze broke down completely on her husband's death. One of Mozart's patrons arranged for a funeral, taking care not to overextend himself financially: Mozart was buried in a pauper's grave. As the weather was stormy, the few mourners who attended the final services did not follow Mozart's coffin to the cemetery. By the time Constanze recovered her health, the location of his grave was quite forgotten. It has never been found.

Constanze Mozart, née Weber, survived her husband by more than half a century. After his death she made a considerable sum from the sale of his manuscripts, and also gave benefit concerts in his memory. In 1809 she married a Danish diplomat Georg von Nissen, who presently resigned from the diplomatic corps to devote himself to writing a biography of Mozart, published in 1828. Constanze died in 1842, knowing that Wolfgang Amadeus Mozart had long since become immortal.

* Authenticity of this letter of September 7, 1791, is doubted by Friedrich Blume (*Musik in Geschichte und Gegenwart*, v. 9, col. 730) and rejected by Emily Anderson.

† After Mozart's death rumor spread that he had indeed been poisoned by his old rival Salieri. This suspicion must have hounded Salieri—he denied the deed on his deathbed. Pushkin wrote a dramatic poem about this supposed crime, which Rimsky-Korsakoff turned into the opera *Mozart and Salieri*.

LORENZO DA PONTE, THE LIBRETTIST

Like his esteemed friend Giacomo Casanova, Lorenzo Da Ponte graced posterity by writing his memoirs. These reminiscences offer some fascinating sidelights on eighteenth-century conventions, and are especially worthwhile literature for parlor psychologists, since the author has innocently bared his inner soul while ostensibly revealing only his outer travels. Unfortunately, Da Ponte's memoirs are not always strictly candid or accurate in their discussion of mere historical facts.

Mozart's best-known librettist was a gifted rogue, adventurer and mountebank—the product of an age which produced such other talented rascals as Beaumarchais, Cagliostro and, of course, Casanova himself. Da Ponte was born on March 10, 1749, in Ceneda, a small town north of Venice. He was the oldest son of a Jewish tanner named Conegliano; his mother died when he was five years old. Fully occupied with scraping together a living for himself and three small sons, his father had little time for him. At any rate, in his memoirs, Da Ponte modestly recalls having been an exceptionally bright child whose knowledge of his own ignorance proved a source of continual mortification to him. In 1763 the widower Conegliano planned to marry a Catholic girl, and had himself and the three sons of his first wife converted to the Christian faith. The Bishop of Ceneda baptized them, and following an established custom the oldest Conegliano boy took the Bishop's name. Thus Emmanuele Conegliano became Lorenzo Da Ponte.

Under the Bishop's sponsorship, young Lorenzo was sent to Ceneda's seminary, where he did so well in his studies that his father thought he should become a priest. Lorenzo already had an inkling that this profession might not suit his natural inclinations, but he acquiesced anyway. He continued to study at another seminary and was appointed to its teaching staff. In 1773 he was ordained and celebrated his first Mass. But the petty feuds of

faculty life did not please Lorenzo; soon he resigned his post and
went to Venice.

· In Venice, Da Ponte found employment as a tutor in an aristocratic household, and enjoyment among the city's gambling halls
and *demimonde*. In fact he enjoyed himself so much that his employer heard rumors about his extracurricular activities and dis-
missed him. Fortunately, Lorenzo was soon appointed a teacher
at the seminary of Treviso, north of Venice. Here he remained
until the end of 1776, when he became fired by Rousseau's philosophy, which he declaimed in verse at a sort of early-day P.T.A.
meeting. Rousseau was regarded with disfavor by the Venetian
authorities, and Lorenzo Da Ponte had to resign from the seminary in disgrace. In his memoirs he insists that this affair and a
similar episode following it caused him in 1777 to be banished
from Venice for fifteen years; but an enterprising scholar later
discovered that Da Ponte's banishment did not occur until 1779,
nor was it precisely occasioned by his political views.

The real reason for his banishment was this. Upon returning to
Venice from the Treviso seminary, Da Ponte had attempted to
resume his former activities even more enthusiastically than before.
He became friendly with Casanova and his circle. He also seduced
his landlady's daughter-in-law and tried to elope with her. When
the matter was discovered, Da Ponte was denounced, and a formal
trial was scheduled. Da Ponte escaped across the Austrian border
to Gorizia (Görz) before the trial could take place. The young lady
eventually returned to her husband.

The Abbé Da Ponte remained over a year in Gorizia, where he
was befriended by acquaintances of Casanova and made his first
attempts at writing for the stage. When a literary acquaintance
passed through Gorizia en route to a post as court poet in Dresden,
Da Ponte asked his help in finding a similar job. Receiving word
that his prospects in the Saxon capital were good, Da Ponte left
Gorizia for Dresden. On arriving, he discovered he was the victim
of a ruse: a rival, feeling Da Ponte's presence in Gorizia to be
superfluous, had substituted a forgery for the original discouraging
letter from Dresden. Da Ponte made the best of the matter, earn-
ing what he could by his pen. Soon he found himself in a new
dilemma: he was deeply in love with both of two sisters and could
not decide between them (he was also friendly with their mother).

Not wishing to hurt anyone's feelings, Da Ponte left Dresden and went to Vienna.

Da Ponte's friend in Dresden had given him letters of introduction to several well-known literary men and musicians in Vienna, among them the poet Metastasio (who died shortly after Da Ponte's arrival) and the composer Salieri. About the time Da Ponte reached Vienna in 1782, the new Emperor Joseph II decided again to use the Imperial Theater for traditional Italian opera rather than German Singspiel, which had been in vogue there. With Salieri's help, Da Ponte was chosen as the new Theater Poet.

He was now kept busy writing new librettos, revising old ones, and aspiring to the post of Caesarian Poet—Chief Imperial Poet —which Metastasio had held. For this post Da Ponte was opposed by the Abbé Casti, a famous dramatist and librettist, who had just returned to Vienna from the Russian court. Casti did not immediately receive the coveted appointment either, but avenged himself on the wildly jealous Da Ponte by modeling after him a comic character in his next libretto. Michael Kelly, the same Irish tenor who sang in the première of *Figaro*, took the role, and in his *Reminiscences* recalled how he mimicked Da Ponte's peculiar walk and stance (Da Ponte, a tall man, liked to lean so far backwards that he had to support himself on a cane which he held behind him), his dandified attire and slight lisp. Kelly said Da Ponte took the satire in better nature than the latter's memoirs would indicate.

To professional rivalry was added personal rivalry. A surgeon, secretly resenting Da Ponte's attentions to a certain lady, caused the poet to lose nearly all his teeth by giving him a medicine that was only supposed to cure a sore gum. For some time Da Ponte was beside himself at this blow to his vanity (and appetite). Years later he was delighted at seeing his old enemy suffer an accident and lose several of his own teeth. At length Da Ponte recovered his spirits and returned to his work with renewed zeal. He collaborated on an opera with Salieri, who was one of the Emperor's favorite composers. When the work failed, Salieri blamed Da Ponte and turned elsewhere for his next libretto. Da Ponte then offered his services to Salieri's rival, Wolfgang Amadeus Mozart.

When he wrote his memoirs, Da Ponte knew Mozart's true genius was at last recognized, and he doubtless exaggerated in asserting that he too had seen in Mozart a jewel whose real worth was tragically unappreciated. (In fact Da Ponte consistently mis-spelled Mozart's name in his writings.) He seems at any rate to have felt no particular professional loyalty to Mozart. He was pleased at the success of *Le Nozze di Figaro*, the first completed work to result from his collaboration with Mozart, but at the same time he also wrote the libretto for the opera that eclipsed *Figaro* in Vienna, *Una Cosa Rara* by Vicente Martín y Solar. Oddly enough, it was Mozart himself who gave *Cosa Rara* lasting fame—by using a selection from it in *Don Giovanni*.

It was Mozart's idea to make an opera of *Le Mariage de Figaro*, and it was Da Ponte's suggestion to use *Don Giovanni* for their next collaboration. Da Ponte's reason for proposing this subject was that it had been turned into an opera only a few months earlier; the libretto of this work was available, and Da Ponte, who was busy with other commissions besides Mozart's, found it a conveni-ent source of inspiration. The idea of copyright did not yet exist, and Da Ponte, like most authors of the time, felt few qualms about improving a previous author's ideas. Da Ponte forgot, however, to mention this source material in his memoirs, and describes the creation of *Don Giovanni* as follows:

I thought it was perhaps time to reanimate the poetic spirit, which had seemed to be quite dried up when I wrote for Reghini and Peticchio. The three much-praised composers Martini,* Mozart, and Salieri, who all came to me at once and asked me for a play, presented me with the opportunity. I liked and respected all three of them, and from all three hoped for a remedy of past fail-ures and for some increase of my small theatrical fame. I wondered if it might not be possible to please all three, and to write three operas at once. Salieri did not demand an original play from me. In Paris he had written the music to an opera of *Tarar*, and wanted to change play and music to the Italian style, and only asked me for a free translation of it; Mozart and Martini left the choice entirely up to me. I chose *Don Giovanni* for the former, a subject that was infi-nitely pleasing to him, and *L'Arbore di Diana* for Martini, to whom I wanted to give a genteel topic, suitable for his sweetest melodies, which are heard in one's soul, but which very few can imitate. Having found these subjects, I went to the Emperor, stated my ideas to him, and told him that my intention was to write three operas simultaneously. You won't be able to do it! he answered me. Perhaps not, I replied: but I shall try. At night I shall write for Mozart, and make believe I am reading Dante's *Inferno*; in the morning I shall write for Martini and think I am studying Petrarch. In the evening for Salieri, and he will be my Tasso. He found my simile pretty enough, and I immediately re-turned home and devoted myself to writing. I went to my writing table and

* Vicente Martín y Solar (1756–1806), composer of *Una Cosa Rara*.

remained there continuously for twelve hours. A bottle of Tokay on the right, the inkstand in the middle, and a box of Seville tobacco to the left. A pretty girl of sixteen years, whom I would have liked to love only as a daughter, but . . . was staying in my house with her mother, who had charge of the family, and would come into my room at the sound of a bell which, in truth, I used to ring often enough, and especially when it seemed to me that my inspiration was beginning to wane; she would bring me a biscuit, or a cup of coffee, or nothing except her pretty face, always gay, always smiling, and just made to inspire poetic thoughts and lively ideas. I continued to work twelve hours every day, with brief pauses, for two months on end, and for that entire time she remained in the next room, now with a book in her hand, and now with a needle and her embroidery, in order to be ready to come at my first touch of the bell. At such times she would sit down beside me without moving, without opening her mouth, without blinking, she would watch me steadily, steadily, she would smile most softly, she would sigh, and sometimes it seemed she would weep: in short, this girl was my Calliope for those three operas, and afterwards she was the same for all the verses that I wrote in the entire course of another six years. At the beginning I used to permit such visits very often; finally I had to make them less frequent in order not to lose too much time in loving caresses, of which she was a perfect mistress. On the first day, meanwhile, between the Tokay, the Seville tobacco, the coffee, and the young Muse, I wrote the first two scenes of *Don Giovanni*, another two of *L'Arbore di Diana*, and more than half of the first act of *Tarar*, whose title was changed by me to *Assur*. In the morning I brought these scenes to the three composers, who could hardly believe that what they were reading with their own eyes was possible; and in sixty-three days the first two operas were all finished, and almost two thirds of the last. . . .

Da Ponte himself thought that *L'Arbore di Diana* was the best of all his efforts but today only his work for Mozart is remembered. Mozart, who said very little about his philosophy of music, once wrote that in an opera "the poetry should be the obedient daughter of the music." But as a dramatic composer Mozart is peerless, and his music can exact obedience from any "daughter," however wayward. It is to Da Ponte's credit that he complemented Mozart's music with three well-disciplined librettos. The libretto for *Le Nozze di Figaro* is praised because Da Ponte's careful translation caught the comic spirit of Beaumarchais' original even while it did away with the play's political overtones. On the other hand, Da Ponte's version of *Don Giovanni* is so witty, its dramatic interest so well sustained, that one seldom notices how much of the action consists of incidents which are really only tenuously connected to the main plot.

The last opera Da Ponte wrote for Mozart was *Così fan Tutte*. This is the only one of the Mozart–Da Ponte trilogy for which the

librettist wrote an original scenario. Da Ponte claimed to have
written the work for a particular soprano whose beguiling eyes
and smile caused him regretfully to forsake an old vow not to have
any amours with ladies of the theater. Some consider *Così fan Tutte*
his best libretto.

The year 1790 marked the turning point of Da Ponte's fortunes
in Vienna. He quarreled with the influential composer Salieri. The
cause of the quarrel, according to Da Ponte, was the spirited com-
petition between Salieri's mistress and his own, who were rival
singers at the Opera. Worse yet, Da Ponte's protector, the
Emperor Joseph II, died. Joseph had found Da Ponte's quick wit
amusing, tolerated the poet's personal idiosyncrasies, and kept
him around as a sort of palace pet; but his successor, Leopold II,
did not particularly like the erratic Italian. Leopold grew cooler
and cooler toward Da Ponte, who in June, 1791, found himself
with exactly twenty-four hours to get out of Vienna. Da Ponte
blamed this second banishment of his life on some exceedingly
complex intrigues among his professional rivals in Vienna; in
truth, he was probably exiled for printing a scandalous satire
about Emperor Leopold.

The poet now hastened to Trieste, hoping to appeal the banishment to Leopold, who was also expected in that city. Da Ponte's
first request for an audience with the Emperor was refused, and in
despair he considered approaching His Majesty a second time,
accompanied by eleven members of his family whom his salary in
Vienna had helped to support. (It would have taken too long to
bring them from Ceneda, so Da Ponte gave up this idea.) The
Emperor first saw Da Ponte at a distance and called him a scoundrel; presently, however, he granted the poet an audience. Just
what transpired at this interview is not known; Da Ponte claimed
the Emperor admitted treating him unjustly, but declared it
was not yet safe for the former Theater Poet to return to Vienna.
Da Ponte also recalled that the Emperor offered him money,
which he was too proud (though impoverished) to accept. Possibly
Da Ponte volunteered his services as a spy in Trieste.

For almost a whole month after leaving Vienna, Da Ponte
burned with unrequited passion for the soprano whom he had
loved there. By his own admission, his was a nature which needed
to love and be loved; his memoirs sadly admit that despite the
horrid ingratitude shown to him by women, he could not

remember even six months of his life when he was not desperately in love with somebody or other, and always with perfect fidelity. Now, having snuffed the final glow of his previous romance, Da Ponte thought it quite likely he would never love again. Soon after making this despairing decision, he got married.

The woman for whom Da Ponte yielded to the lure of domesticity for almost forty years was Anna Celestina (Nancy) Grahl, the daughter of a rich merchant. She was born in England, but her father was German and her mother French. Da Ponte was friendly with Nancy's father and offered his services as a go-between in arranging the marriage of Nancy to a wealthy Viennese. He also gave Nancy Italian lessons, in return for which she taught him French. Lovingly the pair parsed verbs and discussed syntax while casting longing glances at one another. The plans for Nancy's marriage were almost settled when the prospective bridegroom indelicately raised the question of dowry. Furious that someone might wish to marry his daughter for her money, Nancy's father rather unceremoniously offered her to Da Ponte. They were married on August 12, 1792. She was twenty years younger than he; until her death in 1832 she shared with Da Ponte a hectic existence. But she remained a devoted helpmate to him, and he a protective and faithful husband to her. Nobody has ever explained why Lorenzo Da Ponte, a gifted linguist who knew the plays of Molière and had translated those of Beaumarchais, felt it necessary to take French lessons.

After his interview with Leopold II, Da Ponte waited in Trieste for a summons from the Emperor. When no summons came, and his letters to Leopold remained unanswered, Da Ponte decided to go to Vienna and renew his appeals in person. On the very day of his arrival in Vienna, Leopold II died. The new Emperor would not see Da Ponte, though he did send the poet money and a promise to publish a repeal of his banishment. At this time Da Ponte also called on the Imperial Theater's new poet, Giovanni Bertati, whose earlier *Don Giovanni* libretto Da Ponte had found so helpful. Regrettably, Da Ponte came away with a very low opinion of Bertati's talents, though he had availed himself of them so freely only a few years before. In his memoirs he called Bertati a "windbag."

Finding no employment in Vienna, Da Ponte returned to Trieste and set out with Nancy for Paris. En route they lost their money; they reported the loss to a priest who promised to forward their cash to them as soon as it was found. Da Ponte and Nancy stopped in Prague, where they vainly hoped to receive the money and where Da Ponte was delighted to find all three of "his" operas (not to mention Mozart's) being performed for an appreciative public. He also remembered that his old friend Giacomo Casanova lived nearby and decided to visit him. The two men had not met for several years, and Da Ponte's regard for his compatriot warmed at his recollecting that Casanova owed him some money.

The aging Casanova was librarian to Count Waldstein in Dux, Bohemia. Da Ponte, wishing to retain his friend's esteem, introduced Nancy as his mistress, and left Casanova in such a fever of curiosity that he actually wrote to the Chief of Police in Trieste to find out whether Da Ponte really *was* married. Casanova had even less money than Da Ponte, but kindly helped the latter to sell his equipage and helped himself to a commission for this service. The old adventurer expressed regret at being unable to pay the money he owed; in lieu of it, he gave Da Ponte advice, and ironically enough good advice. Da Ponte later admitted ruefully that had he followed Casanova's counsel, he would have been better off. Casanova had told Da Ponte that he should not go to Paris but to London instead, that he must never go the the Italian Café in London, and, above all, that once in London he must never sign his name to any financial notes.

Cheerfully disregarding the first item of Casanova's advice, Da Ponte and his wife set out for Paris. News of the French Revolution made them uneasy and finally caused them after all to change their destination to London. London at this time had a lively interest in Italian opera, which was centered at the King's Theater in the Haymarket. With speed and ease (aided by his visits to the Italian Café), Da Ponte thoroughly enmeshed himself in the King's Theater's rivalries and intrigues.

Although in 1792 King's Theater was managed by Mozart's old friend Michael Kelly, Da Ponte did not succeed in becoming its resident poet. When after some time the post was offered to him, Da Ponte refused it in favor of a literary rival, whom he hoped to appease by this gesture. The rival became Theater Poet, and Da Ponte promptly tried to undermine the Theater's management and policies by publishing a hostile magazine. The action led to a violent literary brawl. Da Ponte was the loser, and decided to find a better outlet for his talents. Scraping together a little money, he left Nancy in London and went first to Belgium and then to Holland, hoping to establish an Italian opera in these places.

Da Ponte's sojourn in the Low Countries failed; the Dutch had been defeated in battle and were in no mood for frivolity like opera. Da Ponte wrote Nancy to join him in Holland, but lacked money to pay her passage. She was able to join him only when she received, almost miraculously, their lost money which had followed them across half of Europe.

In Holland matters got so bad that Da Ponte had to appeal, again, to Casanova for money. In order to increase Casanova's sympathy for his plight, Da Ponte made the request in verse; Casanova answered in graceful prose: No. Da Ponte and Nancy were on the verge of starvation and eviction from their lodgings when word came that the new owner of the King's Theater, William Taylor, wished Da Ponte to return to London and become Theater Poet.

William Taylor was a slightly shady and financially disreputable person who found Da Ponte's engaging charm useful in helping to raise the money that the King's Theater seemed perpetually to lack. On assuming his new job, Da Ponte found himself in the middle of a whole new series of jealous plots, revenges and counter-revenges. The arrival in London of two famous rival prima donnas precipitated the first storms. One, an *opera seria* soprano, demanded that Da Ponte write a new libretto for her, and became William Taylor's mistress; the other, an *opera buffa* soprano, demanded that Da Ponte write a new libretto for *her*, and became the mistress of the composer Vicente Martín y Solar, whom Da Ponte had meanwhile brought to England. Martín was staying at Da Ponte's house; when one of the servants became pregnant, the composer falsely announced that Da Ponte and not he was the parent of this indiscretion. The friendship cooled; Da Ponte joined the camp of the soprano *seria*, with the result that he rose in William Taylor's esteem and became his general assistant and confidant.

This association lasted five years, during the course of which Da Ponte disregarded the final part of Casanova's advice and blithely countersigned notes and loans for his free-spending employer. In 1798 Taylor sent him to Italy to bring back fresh operatic talent. Da Ponte had a last happy reunion with his family on this journey,

but on going to Venice he was again requested by the authorities
to leave the city. He returned to England in early spring of 1799,
bringing back singers who proved totally unsatisfactory (one of
them was more or less hissed off the King's Theater's stage), and
Taylor summarily fired his librettist.

Worse misfortunes followed. The many notes Da Ponte had
signed for Taylor now fell due, one after another. Taylor had
cannily gotten himself elected to Parliament, thereby securing
himself against arrest for debt. Da Ponte was held responsible for
Taylor's liabilities; in three months he was arrested thirty times
by Taylor's creditors, and finally had no choice but to declare
himself bankrupt.

As always, Da Ponte's resilience was remarkable. He no sooner
had a few guineas again than he opened an Italian bookstore and
energetically began to acquaint Englishmen with his native
literature. This enterprise flourished and compensated for various
unsuccessful schemes and sidelines into which the restless poet was
forever venturing. In 1802 Parliament was dissolved; Taylor sold
his share in the King's Theater and fled to France to escape arrest
for his debts. Da Ponte was reinstated as Theater Poet by the new
management, a post he held until leaving England in 1805. He
wrote the last of his forty or so librettos during this period.

William Taylor returned to England and was promptly thrown
into debtor's prison. Da Ponte did all he could to free Taylor from
prison and himself from Taylor's debts. His own finances, however, were beyond repair. In August, 1804, he sent Nancy and
their four children (ages eleven, five, four, and one) to the United
States. In April, 1805, Da Ponte himself hastily left England. He
reached Philadelphia in June, and for the twenty-three remaining
years of his life made his home in America.

Da Ponte's life in the United States was a series of small successes
punctuated by large streaks of misfortune. He had lost neither his
restlessness nor his buoyancy. Undaunted by failure, he leaped
from one enterprise to another, always certain that the most
recent undertaking was the surest means to a quick fortune. Un-
luckily for him, Da Ponte was a poet, not a businessman; and
despite his ever-scheming brain and suspicious nature, he remained a thinker, not a trader.

On disembarking, Da Ponte joined his family in New York and
opened a grocery store. A yellow-fever epidemic forced him to

move to Elizabeth, New Jersey. After two years there, the grocery store failed—a spendthrift partner hastened its collapse—and in 1807 Da Ponte took his family back to New York. One day, while browsing in a bookstore, he struck up a friendship with Clement Moore, who was the founder of New York's General Theological Seminary but is better remembered as the author of "A Visit from St. Nicholas" ("'Twas the night before Christmas . . ."). Moore belonged to a prominent and cultivated New York family; he suggested Da Ponte give Italian lessons and helped him get students for the first classes. Da Ponte is said to have been an excellent teacher, and for a few years his Manhattan Academy for Young Gentlemen flourished. His wife assisted him by establishing the Manhattan Academy for Young Ladies, a feminine counterpart of his own school.

By 1811 the number of the Da Pontes' pupils began to dwindle. Packing up his family of five children and one son-in-law, Da Ponte moved them to Sunbury, Pennsylvania, where his wife's well-to-do family had settled. Here Da Ponte's fortunes fluctuated wildly. He was by turns distiller, seller of medicines, owner of a dry-goods and millinery store, teamster of market produce, and teacher of languages to the somewhat reluctant local citizenry. At one point the Da Pontes could afford to build themselves a three-story brick house, the tallest in Sunbury; soon afterwards they were in such straits that the county sheriff seized their furniture. Local merchants took advantage of Da Ponte's inexperience as a trader, and he was especially hard hit during the slump after the War of 1812. Da Ponte, by now an American citizen, took several of his complaints to court, but his complex litigations dragged on and on and yielded him little but the feeling of moral righteousness.

Da Ponte's physical strength was as remarkable as his untiring mental agility. When he was past sixty-five, he suffered within a year two serious carriage accidents that could easily have killed a weaker man; but Da Ponte refused to be laid low, and as soon as he could again hobble about, he returned to his various complex enterprises, in the course of which he often made 250-mile round trips between Sunbury and Philadelphia. Despite all his efforts, his affairs in Sunbury grew more tangled and hopeless. In 1818 he left the town in disgust and moved to Philadelphia, hoping to support his family there by again teaching Italian. This plan also failed, and a year later Da Ponte returned to New York.

Clement Moore again helped the seventy-year-old Da Ponte organize Italian classes. This time the classes were successful, and Da Ponte lived to see some of his students distinguish themselves. When his oldest son died at the age of twenty, Da Ponte resumed his literary activities in order to divert his mind from this tragedy. He translated Byron's "Prophecy of Dante" into Italian, and published various works, including a dictionary of Italian literature; on occasion he also entered into written combat with authors of magazine articles on Italian literature. In 1823 Da Ponte again opened a store of Italian books. That year the first edition of his *Memorie* ("Memoirs") appeared. Da Ponte had been planning to write his reminiscences since 1807; the project very probably received an impetus when Da Ponte saw Casanova's *Memoirs*, which began to appear in 1822.

For some years, Da Ponte's life ran with surprising smoothness. He seems to have participated neither in wildcat speculations nor in vengeful plots. In 1825 Clement Moore, himself a Trustee of Columbia College, helped Da Ponte to be appointed Professor of Italian Literature to the college. The post was unsalaried—Da Ponte's students were supposed to pay him a fee. Unfortunately, he had hardly any students. He remained nominally a member of Columbia's faculty the rest of his life, but in actuality had little connection with the college after 1826. Later on, his efforts to have Italian made a required subject of the curriculum proved fruitless, and his professorship remained unremunerative.

In the autumn of 1825 the famous singer Manuel Garcia and his opera troupe arrived in New York. With nostalgic enthusiasm Da Ponte attended the troupe's performances of Italian opera and introduced himself to Garcia, who was so delig'.ted to meet the librettist of *Don Giovanni* that he grabbed the elderly Da Ponte and danced him around the room, singing the Don's "champagne aria." Da Ponte suggested the Garcia troupe present *Don Giovanni* and himself hired a tenor for the part of Don Ottavio. (Garcia, officially a tenor, preferred to sing the title role, which he handled capably.) May 23, 1826, marked the first performance of *Don Giovanni* in America. Da Ponte had previously permitted his second son, Lorenzo, to translate the libretto into English, and Garcia was sufficiently pleased by New York's reception of the opera to let Da Ponte sell printed copies of the translation in the theater. When a bookseller ordered the translations for his store, Da Ponte

Lorenzo Da Ponte, librettist
of *Don Giovanni*.

Manuel Garcia, the first
Don Giovanni in America.

Tirso de Molina (Gabriel Téllez), author of *El Burlador de Sevilla.*

Molière, whose version of the Don Juan story was written in 1665.

bought a lottery ticket with the proceeds. To his delight, he won $500, and used it to purchase select Italian literary classics which he gave to Columbia.

The Garcia troupe's visit, plus his good luck in the lottery, re-animated Da Ponte's interest in opera. He brought his niece, a singer, from Europe to New York and at his own expense arranged a series of concerts to introduce her to the American public. The concerts were failures, and the niece soon retired to private life. Da Ponte opened another bookstore and devoted himself to writing his memoirs, which break off in September, 1830. He originally planned to continue them; but other events intervened.

In December, 1831, Nancy Da Ponte died of pneumonia. She had had a private income, money which was always useful and sometimes indispensable when one of Da Ponte's enterprises collapsed. After her death Da Ponte was in continual financial difficulties which grew worse at his renewed speculations in operatic ventures. In 1832, associating himself with the French tenor Montresor and his troupe, he became, at eighty-three, an energetic impresario, managing the Montresor Company's opera performances in New York and Philadelphia. After the usual intrigues, Da Ponte was eased out of the company's managership. Next he went into partnership with an old acquaintance and built a luxurious Italian Opera House in New York. The theater opened in November, 1833; its repertoire included Cimarosa and Rossini. After one year, the partner disappeared, Da Ponte ran out of money, and the Italian Opera House was sold.

In 1835, at the age of eighty-six, Da Ponte published a new book of verses and in an English preface stated his intention of returning to Italy to die. But an anonymous admirer of his poetry sent him $50, and Da Ponte decided to remain in America after all. For his last three years he lived in the home of his son. He became reconciled to the Catholic Church and received absolution from the Bishop of New York. On the day before his death, Da Ponte composed verses to his doctor, to demonstrate that he still had his mental powers. On August 17, 1838, Lorenzo Da Ponte died, "surrounded by his friends and compatriots, his only regret . . . being no doubt that he could not himself describe the pompous funeral accorded him."* He owed his most lasting fame to Mozart, whom he mentioned so casually and briefly in the *Memoirs*; and like Mozart, Da Ponte was buried in an unmarked and long since forgotten grave.

---

* L. A. Sheppard in his introduction to *The Memoirs of Lorenzo Da Ponte*.

LITERARY BACKGROUND

I

One of the more noteworthy recurrent themes in Western literature is that of Don Juan, the lustful nobleman, who insults the dead and as punishment is dragged alive to hell. This story was once a popular folk tale; it has been rewritten scores of times by lesser authors; and it has been used by important authors of every European literary tradition, including Byron, Molière, Goldoni, Shaw, Dumas, and Alexei Tolstoi.

In its modern form, the story first appeared in seventeenth-century Spain. Between 1613 and 1630, Gabriel Téllez, a Spanish monk better known as Tirso de Molina, wrote a play called *El Burlador de Sevilla y Convidado de Piedra* ("The Prankster of Seville and His Stone Guest"). It was a rather straggling work about the exploits of a lascivious nobleman, Don Juan Tenorio. In the play, one of Don Juan's victims is Doña Ana, daughter of the knight Don Gonzalo de Ulloa. Don Juan seduces Doña Ana by a ruse; the trick is discovered, and while escaping, Juan duels with and kills Don Gonzalo. Later, others whom Don Juan has deceived search for him, hoping to avenge themselves. Accompanied by his servant Catalinón, Don Juan is forced to take temporary refuge in a church near Seville. Here he finds a statue of Don Gonzalo de Ulloa, jokingly pulls its stone beard, and invites it to sup with him. The statue accepts the invitation and asks Don Juan to dine with it in the church. Don Juan and Catalinón go to Don Gonzalo's tomb, where they are served a gruesome repast. After the meal, Don Juan gives his hand to the statue, and together they sink into the earth. Catalinón alone escapes from the wreckage of the church.

El Burlador is considered the common ancestor of the many Don Juan stories and dramas which followed it. Because Tirso gave his characters historical names, a belief grew that the Don Juan story was based on fact. Actually, the old legend of a blasphemer who meets a supernatural end had already been used in several plays before Tirso's. Furthermore, there seems little reason to believe that the legend was ultimately true: though the Tenorios and Ulloas were ancient and esteemed Spanish families, there is nothing in their histories to connect them with the Don Juan legend. Tirso was probably only following the common practice of giving dramatic characters real names to make the play more plausible. In any case, Tirso's play provided the foundation for later versions of the Don Juan story, and his characters, incidents, sometimes his very words were borrowed by later authors, among whom Mozart's librettist Lorenzo Da Ponte was by no means the last.

The sources from which Tirso derived *El Burlador* have been lost, but some scholars have surmised that the two main themes—the libertine, and the statue which comes to dinner—reached Spain from other parts of Europe. The earliest Spanish Don Juan figure seems to appear in Juan de la Cueva's play *El Infamador* ("The Defamer"), performed in 1581. Here the main character, Leucino, tries to rape a girl and kills her father; Leucino is punished by a supernatural appearance of the goddess Diana, who makes the earth swallow him. Another Spaniard, Lope de Vega, based at least two plays on the Don Juan theme. Tirso was familiar with one of these, *Dineros Son Calidad* ("Money Makes the Man"), in which the hero Octavio duels with a statue.

As early as 1615 there was also a German drama containing the Don Juan motif. The text of this work is lost, but the plot is known. The central figure, a duke named Leontio, reads the works of Machiavelli and becomes a scoffing atheist. In his folly Leontio invites the skull of an ancestor to dine with him; the skull appears, kills Leontio, and takes him to hell. This play became widely known in Europe.

A second Don Juan play by Tirso de Molina, *Tan Largo Me Lo Fiáis* ("You Keep Me Waiting So Long"), was discovered in 1878. In this work the characters have different names and speak somewhat different lines than in *El Burlador*, but the plot is basically that of the earlier work.

Soon after its production in Spain, *El Burlador de Sevilla* was brought to Italy, probably by strolling actors. By 1652 the play had already been translated twice into Italian as *Il Convitato di Pietra* ("The Stone Guest"), the name by which it became best known. The second translation—that of Onofrio Giliberto—may have been performed by an Italian troupe in France, where it also met with success. It was translated and adapted into French several times, and finally, in 1665, completely rewritten as *Don Juan, ou le Festin de Pierre* ("Don Juan, or the Feast of Stone") by Molière.

By Molière's time the Don Juan drama had become a hackneyed vehicle for buffoonery; Molière tried to rewrite it in a high-comedy vein. In the first performance Molière himself played the part of Don Juan's servant whom he named Sganarelle. Molière's play has almost as many characters as Tirso's (which has twenty-one), although neither Doña Ana nor Duke Octavio appear in the work, and the Commandant's murder is mentioned only casually in a passing reference. Molière did originate the part of Donna Elvira, who was a novice in a convent when Don Juan seduced her, married her and left her. Two brothers of Elvira appear in the play, seeking to avenge her betrayal. Don Juan also promises marriage to two peasant girls; these two confront each other, each claiming to be his betrothed, and he cleverly convinces each of them that she is right and the other is mad. The statue appears rather casually at the very end (he was invited two acts earlier), Don Juan defiantly goes to hell, and Sganarelle is finally left to wail about his unpaid back wages. Molière's play was versified by Thomas Corneille in 1677; the Corneille version was performed until 1847, when it was again replaced by Molière's prose drama.

By 1662, a statue which comes to dinner had appeared in the English playwright Aston Cockayne's *Tragedy of Ovid*. In 1676 the dramatist Thomas Shadwell used an early French version of *Le Festin de Pierre* as the source for his "Don Juan" play, *The Libertine Destroyed*. (At this time, the term "libertine" was used more commonly to describe a religious freethinker than a sexual profligate.) Henry Purcell wrote some music for Shadwell's play. Shadwell's Don John was very villainous, and the drama enjoyed considerable success.

By the beginning of the eighteenth century Don Juan had also become part of the standard German theater repertory as *Das Steinerne Gastmahl* ("The Stone Banquet"). The Don Juan drama was so well known throughout Europe that a legend about it spread, claiming that the original author had bargained with the devil to keep the work on the stage. Playwrights scoffed at it and declared that their only reason for producing yet another version of such a trite, silly (and immensely popular) tale was to improve on the wretched preceding ones. In 1736 the famous Italian playwright Carlo Goldoni wrote a Don Juan play called *Don Giovanni Tenorio ossia Il Dissoluto* ("Don Juan Tenorio, or the Dissolute One"). This was to some extent a *drame à clef*—Goldoni used some of the characters to portray himself and his rivals—but it was a work which Da Ponte probably knew and possibly drew on. Perhaps Mozart too was familiar with Goldoni's drama; his early opera *La Finta Semplice* was based on another work of Goldoni's.

One of the first musical versions of the Don Juan legend seems to have been a Parisian comic opera, *Le Festin de Pierre*, composed by Le Tellier in 1713. Pious civic authorities were at first dismayed that the last scene took place in hell, and forbade further performances; but this sentence was soon revoked. Gluck's ballet *Don Juan* was performed in Vienna in 1761; and a full-length opera "tragicomico," *Il Convitato di Pietra ossia Il Dissoluto* by Vincenzo Righini, was performed in Vienna and Prague in 1777, ten years before Mozart's *Don Giovanni*.

Several other operas followed Righini's work. The most famous was *Don Giovanni Tenorio ossia Il Convitato di Pietra*, with music by Giuseppe Gazzaniga and libretto by Giovanni Bertati. This work was produced in Italy in 1787. Goethe saw it in Rome and attested to its great popularity, which led several others to imitate it.

Gazzaniga's and Bertati's opera is really a play within a play. The framework concerns a touring opera company which is facing bankruptcy because it cannot seem to please its audiences. In desperation the manager overrides his singers' protests and decides to stage that dreadful but always pleasing old war-horse *Il Convitato di Pietra*. Bertati's libretto included an additional lady for the Don, Donna Ximena, whom he is pursuing when Donna Elvira unexpectedly confronts him. Besides Don Giovanni's servant Pasquariello, there is also a comic cook, Lanterna, who participates in the last scene's supper party and, after the Don's descent to hell, fetches the other characters for a final sextet. Donna Anna does not appear after Bertati's first scene, in which Don Giovanni kills the Commendatore.

Gazzaniga's opera remained in favor even after Mozart's work was known. When Da Ponte was in London, he urged Michael Kelly, then manager of the King's Theater, to stage Mozart's *Don Giovanni*. Kelly refused, preferring to present the Gazzaniga work instead (with some of Mozart's and Da Ponte's arias interpolated). Since Mozart, more than a dozen musical works about Don Juan have been composed. Some of them are practically unknown today. One, *The Stone Guest*, was based on a poem by Pushkin with music composed by Dargomijsky and orchestrated by Rimsky-Korsakoff. It was performed in St. Petersburg in 1872. Another, *La Statue du Commandeur* ("The Commandant's Statue"), was given in Paris in 1892. This work is a cheerful satire in pantomime. The statue comes to dinner, gets splendidly drunk, dances a cancan, and has to be helped back onto his pedestal by Don Juan. Other prose writers and poets who used the Don Juan story include Alexandre Dumas père, Byron, Alexei Tolstoy and G. B. Shaw.

II

In general, Da Ponte followed Bertati's libretto quite closely. He did have to drop some of Bertati's characters, since the Prague opera company could provide only seven singers. (In the première of Mozart's *Don Giovanni* one basso had to double as the Commendatore and Masetto.) Tirso de Molina brings together some of the characters wronged by Don Juan only at the end of his play, Molière not at all. But Da Ponte, borrowing various incidents from his predecessors and inventing others, introduces his *dramatis personae* rapidly, one after the other; cleverly, he makes their reactions to one another reflect their highly individual personalities.

Leporello, who appears first, is descended from a long tradition of comic servants. Like Falstaff, he is a stock comic character; and like Falstaff, he so epitomizes the general qualities of which he is formed that he rises above generalities to become a unique personality. He is customarily greedy, cowardly and buffoonish. In an early version of the drama one of his functions was to let fall into the pit the end of the long scroll on which were listed the Don's conquests; members of the audience would amuse themselves by looking for familiar names. The idea of having the Don's servant reel off a catalogue of his master's conquests was old long before Da Ponte used it, which may explain the offhand way it is first mentioned in Mozart's opera. No previous author, though, seems to have included Turkey in the Don's itinerary. Da Ponte was seeing Casanova not long before writing the *Don Giovanni* libretto, and Casanova (truly or falsely) claimed to have visited Turkey. Perhaps Casanova's boast remained in Da Ponte's mind when he wrote the "catalogue aria."

Casanova had another small but strange connection with *Don Giovanni*. A few decades ago there were found among his papers in Bohemia some tentative verses for Leporello and the other four characters who remain on the stage after Donna Anna's exit in Scene 2 of Act II. The situation these verses fit is plainly that conceived by Mozart and Da Ponte: Leporello has revealed his identity and is pleading for mercy, and the others are denying his plea.

Why Casanova sketched out this scene is not really known, but various guesses have been made. Casanova was in Prague shortly before *Don Giovanni's* première, and quite likely attended the performance. Da Ponte, however, had previously been summoned back to Vienna. It is possible that there was trouble with the continuity and scene divisions of the second half of the opera. Da Ponte, unable to help out himself, perhaps asked his old friend Casanova to work with Mozart if necessary. If this is so, it may have been Casanova and not Da Ponte who wrote Leporello's aria "Ah, pietà, signori miei," and the text directly before and after it. The unexplained verses that were found are perhaps a rejected draft for the same scene.

Others surmise that Casanova wrote the verses idly after attending the performance, just to try his hand at producing one of the buffo "extemporizations" common at the time. The stage managers in both Prague and Vienna are known to have added "improvisations" to their singers' roles, sometimes to the extent of inserting practically a whole new scene into the opera. Possibly Casanova wrote the verses to prove to himself that he could have "improvised" better stuff than the stage manager of the Prague opera.

Why Da Ponte chose to name his character "Leporello" has caused some speculation. Some authorities claim the name is derived from a diminutive of "lepus," the Latin word for "hare," thus indicating its owner's cowardice. Edward Dent, whose book *Mozart's Operas* is regarded as definitive on the subject, is of a different opinion. Professor Dent thinks that "Leporello" is an Italianization of "Lipperl" (Austrian diminutive of Philipp), which in turn is an alternate name for Kasperl, the Harlequin of the German stage.

The Commendatore's name also has a curious history. Tirso de Molina called him "Don Gonzalo." Da Ponte in his curt stage directions for the Prague performance referred to him only as "Il Commendatore." Years later, however, Da Ponte authorized his son to make an English translation of *Don Giovanni*; in this he gave fuller stage directions and referred to the Commendatore as "Don Pedro." The metamorphosis of "Gonzalo" to "Pedro" did not originate with Da Ponte; it seems to have been due to the old French title *Le Festin de Pierre*, where "Pierre" was mistakenly thought to mean "Peter" rather than "stone." Da Ponte's translation of the libretto, incidentally, omitted the epilogue.

III

Surely no opera has occasioned so much discussion as *Don Giovanni*. Various questions left unanswered by Mozart and Da Ponte still cause as much controversy as if they dealt with knotty scientific tangibles instead of dramatic abstractions. One argument concerns the Commendatore's statue: If the opera's entire action takes place within twenty-four hours, how on earth could there have been time to make a marble statue (and an equestrian one at that) of Don Giovanni's victim? Where was the Commendatore's tomb actually located anyway?

The answer most often given to the first question is that it was formerly the common custom for Spanish nobles to have statues of themselves erected at their family sepulchres before they died; thus the Commendatore's statue already existed while he was still alive. How, then, did the inscription read off by Leporello get there so fast? Bertati's libretto has a neat answer to this query: Don Ottavio appears with some stonemasons who chisel the inscription onto the base of the statue as Don Giovanni and his servant watch secretly. An objection to this solution, as one critic points out, is that Don Ottavio's day would have been terribly crowded if he took time to oversee the inscribing of the statue in addition to his other activities.

The question about the location of the Commendatore's grave was of especial interest to those nineteenth-century Romantics who tried to find a factual basis for the whole Don Juan legend. One scholar claimed to have found an account of the Commendatore's murder by Don Juan in the Chronicles of Seville (nobody else ever found it). The Commendatore was supposedly buried in his private family vault at a Franciscan convent in Seville. The Franciscans lured Don Juan into the convent and murdered him near the Commendatore's statue, whence grew the legend that he was taken away by the statue itself. There is no factual support whatsoever for this tale. Tirso de Molina himself, in fact, mentioned a different site for the Commendatore's tomb in each version of his Don Juan play.

Another matter of endless discussion is whether or not Don Giovanni actually managed to seduce Donna Anna before she discovered her mistake and chased him away. Either answer to this question has its heated partisans. Those who favor Donna Anna's chastity claim that in the first place, Tirso's Don Juan himself admitted failure; in the second place, one of the factors that make Mozart's Don Giovanni a comic figure is that in spite of his reputation and catalogue, during the duration of the opera he is entirely unsuccessful in his aims. Dramatic consistency must be carried through. (The problem of Donna Elvira's maid—how did she fare after the Don finished beating up Masetto?—is gracefully skirted. In any case, whatever happened to the maid happened during the sextet of the following scene, when the Don is not present.)

That Don Giovanni *did* seduce Donna Anna is just as seriously claimed by many others. They claim that this deed, rather than Don Giovanni's killing the Commendatore in a duel he tried to avoid, lies behind Donna Anna's passionate desire for revenge. Moreover, she is less than candid in her account to Don Ottavio of her experiences the previous evening, and it is because of her seduction by the Don that she wishes to postpone her marriage to Ottavio. The climax of this argument is that Don Giovanni's success with Donna Anna explains his subsequent lack of interest in her throughout the opera, just as his earlier success with Donna Elvira explains why she no longer attracts him.

E. T. A. Hoffmann, the German Romantic author (*Tales of Hoffmann*), was also an opera composer and impresario, and an admirer of Mozart. In one of the tales, Hoffmann gave his interpretation of the Don Juan–Donna Anna relationship. To Hoffmann, Don Giovanni was a superman with far more than ordinary human talent and perceptiveness, of whose soul Satan had gained possession. Donna Anna was potentially Don Giovanni's counterpart, though she remained as pure as he was evil. Don Giovanni seduced Donna Anna. He was the only man who ever aroused her superhuman passions and sensibilities, but because he was evil and had killed her father, her love was transmuted into hate on an equally exalted plane. Hoffmann claims that Donna Anna's promise to marry Don Ottavio after a year is an empty vow: having been contaminated by Satan himself, an experience both sublime and terrible, she intends to die before the year is ended.

Nineteenth-century intellectuals set themselves earnestly to reinterpreting and explaining *Don Giovanni*. The Romantic school, regarding the opera through Faust-colored glasses, was concerned with finding an explanation for Don Giovanni's inherent "Weltschmerz." The Freudian psychoanalytic school blamed the Don's peccadillos on his mother, who (a) may have loved him too much, or (b) may not have loved him enough. The Don's amours really represent a pathetic search for a mother substitute. An alternative possibility, suggested by others of the psychoanalytic school, is that Don Giovanni is a latent homosexual. His 2,065 conquests were all attempts to assert his masculinity both to himself and to the world.

The late German psychoanalyst Otto Rank wrote a whole book about Don Giovanni, in which he concluded that the more orthodox Freudian interpretations tended, on the whole, to be somewhat extreme. Dr. Rank held that much of Mozart's thought and music for Don Giovanni were influenced by his feelings about the recent death of his father; hence, the constant comic-tragic ambivalence of the music.* In a cultural context, says Dr. Rank, Don Giovanni represents an ancient fertility god or demigod, whom the Christian ideal of continence and sense of guilt have changed into a mere gross sensualist. Leporello is another aspect of the same person, namely his conscience. It is the servant, not the master, who takes the brunt of corporal punishment throughout the opera. These concepts embody an ideological conflict between pagan heroism and Christian spirituality.

The basic situation of the drama, as Dr. Rank sees it, is the episode of the Statue. The Statue itself symbolizes the rigidity of

---

* Professor Dent warns against overly diligent attempts to draw analogies between Mozart's life and his music by reminding readers of *Mozart's Operas* that the composer's slapstick parody, "A Musical Joke," K.522, was written a little over two weeks after his father's death.

death. Its part in the drama is symbolic of the dead who return to earth to destroy the living, a common primitive belief. Don Giovanni is also an early crusader for the equal rights of women. His activities helped to liberate the female sex from the shackles of morality and religion.

Even today, the interpretation of the opera continues to fascinate. Is it a comic opera or a tragic one? Is its plot, as Beethoven thought, an immoral gibe, unworthy of Mozart's music? Is it really a morality play in which the main character is punished for his sins? Or is it a fable of man's pitiful and repetitive efforts to rise above his capacities, only to be continually thwarted and beaten down? Perhaps no story except *Faust* and certainly no other single opera, has had so many interpreters and interpretations. Possibly Mozart and Da Ponte were the last two persons to whom the libretto and score of *Don Giovanni* presented no great philosophical dilemmas.

Composer and librettist called it a "dramma giocoso." The work was, in fact, specifically commissioned to be a comic entertainment which, it was hoped, would succeed the tremendously popular *Le Nozze di Figaro* as Prague's hit of the season. The Italian libretto is witty, most of the characters are humorous, and many of the situations are ludicrous, despite their occasional overtones of supernatural horror. Perhaps the epilogue sets the tone of the whole work in a catchy refrain: Don Giovanni, that seducer, betrayer and evildoer, is casually relegated by his victims to no worse a fate than the domain of Pluto and Persephone.

PLOT SUMMARY

Don Giovanni is written in two acts. Act I is divided into five scenes, although scene breaks and changes of setting now vary with the production. Act II was originally also written in five scenes. Another scene was inserted and the epilogue dropped for the opera's first performance in Vienna. This scene (Scene 3 in the libretto) is no longer performed; the epilogue is sometimes omitted too. Plot and action are episodic—most of the opera is about the Don's misdeeds and attempted misdeeds, and their effect on the other characters.

The exact number of days taken by the action is not stated explicitly, but a time unity is closely observed (indeed, Act II takes place in less than twenty-four hours). Nonetheless, the literal-minded will note that enough time must have elapsed during the opera's events for a life-sized marble statue to be built and erected.*

ACT ONE

Scene One

Characters in order of their appearance : Leporello; Don Giovanni and Donna Anna; the Commendatore; Don Ottavio; servants of Donna Anna.

The opera takes place in seventeenth-century Seville. After an overture the curtain rises on a courtyard or garden outside the palace of the Commendatore (Commander),† a dignified elderly nobleman. It is evening; at the foot of the palace stairs Leporello,

---

* See notes on Literary Background for a refutation of this belief.
† The Da Ponte libretto never specifies what the Commendatore commands; some sources claim him to be Commander of the Knights of Malta.

LEFT: Josepha Duschek, noted singer in whose country house near Prague, The Villa Bertramka, Mozart completed the composition of *Don Giovanni* on October 28, 1787. RIGHT: The Villa Bertramka.

The National Theater in Prague, where *Don Giovanni* was first performed.

Playbill of the first Viennese performance of *Don Giovanni*. Note the spelling "Mozzart."

Mozart's fee for *Don Giovanni* in Vienna. From the ledgers of the Court Theaters.

servant of Don Giovanni, strides back and forth, impatiently awaiting his master's return. As he paces, Leporello complains about his thankless job as servant to the lively Don ("Notte e giorno faticar") ("Toiling night and day"). His tale of woe is interrupted by sounds of an approaching struggle, and he hastily takes cover.

Don Giovanni and Donna Anna lurch down the stairs. With one hand, the Don shields his face behind his cloak; with the other, he attempts to restrain the lady, who is trying to discover his identity as she screams for help. While Leporello, from his hiding place, comments on this scene, the two continue to struggle. Suddenly, Donna Anna's father, the Commendatore, appears, carrying a light and a sword; he challenges Don Giovanni, and Donna Anna flees into the palace. Don Giovanni is at first unwilling to duel with a man so old, but goaded by the Commendatore, finally draws his sword and swiftly kills him while the horror-struck Leporello watches.

When the duel is finished, Don Giovanni calls Leporello, who emerges from his nook with various sarcastic comments on the events he has just seen. Angrily the Don silences him, and they hastily leave together.

Meanwhile, the servants have found Don Ottavio, the betrothed of Donna Anna. Ottavio and Donna Anna come out of the palace. Donna Anna sees her father's body and is dazed with horror and grief. When Don Ottavio tries to console her, she makes him swear solemnly to avenge her father's death. Together they vow vengeance in a duet ("Che giuramento, o Dei") ("What an oath, oh Gods"), which ends Scene 1.

Scene Two

Characters in order of their appearance: Don Giovanni and Leporello; Donna Elvira.

Scene 2 takes place either on the next morning or a few days later, on a road in or near Seville. Leporello and Don Giovanni walk along talking.

Leporello has something very serious to tell the Don and exacts the latter's promise to let him speak freely without punishment.

When the Don agrees, Leporello blurts out that his master's way
of life is scandalous. Don Giovanni is enraged despite his promise,
and the subject is hastily changed to a more familiar one, namely
women. The Don tells his servant of his latest interest, and
Leporello requests further particulars so that he may enter them
in a certain catalogue. The Don's reply is cut short by the
approach of Donna Elvira. Master and servant step into a doorway
in order to survey the scene, and Donna Elvira enters, bewailing
her fate: she has been loved and left, and she would just like to
find the scoundrel that betrayed her ("Ah! chi mi dice mai")
("Ah! who will ever tell me").

As it happens, her betrayer was none other than Don Giovanni,
but the Don does not immediately recognize her and commiserates
with the pretty, unhappy lady, whom he wishes to console.
Mingled with the Don's expressions of sympathy are Leporello's
ironic remarks on his master's peculiar brand of comfort. The Don
gallantly addresses the distressed lady; she recognizes him, and for
once the Don comes off second best. He is forced to retreat hastily
and leaves his servant to handle the situation. Leporello, after a
confused attempt at conversation, produces a long scroll—the
famous catalogue of Don Giovanni's conquests—and in the "catalogue aria," beginning "Madamina" ("Dear lady") proceeds,
in some detail, to enumerate his master's amorous adventures and
preferences. He dwells lovingly on the catholicity of the Don's
taste, and on the numbers of ladies in various lands who have suc-
cumbed to the Don. Having thus buoyed Donna Elvira's spirits,
Leporello departs, leaving Donna Elvira in somewhat worse
shape than before.

Scene Three

Characters in order of their appearance: Zerlina and Masetto; peasant
boys and girls; Don Giovanni and Leporello; Donna Elvira;
Donna Anna and Don Ottavio.

The scene shifts to the open countryside, not far from Don Giovanni's estate or castle. (In actual production, this scene often
takes place in the same setting as the previous one.)

The villagers and peasants are celebrating the wedding of Zerlina and Masetto, which is just about to take place. These two

enter, dancing with village youths and girls. Don Giovanni and Leporello approach and watch from the side.

Don Giovanni comments favorably on the number of pretty girls in the crowd; even Leporello is pleased, hoping that he too may make a conquest here. The Don introduces himself to Zerlina and Masetto, solicitously offering them his lordly protection; he orders Leporello (who is busily offering his own protection to several girls) to take the villagers to his castle and provide them— *especially* Masetto—with food, drink and entertainment. As Leporello and the villagers start off, the Don keeps Zerlina back. Masetto refuses to leave without her. She, however, assures the peasant lad that she is in good hands; when Masetto remains adamant, Don Giovanni touches his sword, and Leporello finally manages to lead away the protesting swain ("Ho capito, Signor, sì") ("I understand, yes, sir").

Don Giovanni now tells Zerlina that she is meant for better stuff than Masetto. Zerlina is coy; Don Giovanni waves a hand in the direction of his castle and suggests that she accompany him there so that they can be married immediately. In the duet "Là ci darem la mano" ("There we shall join our hands") the Don succeeds in persuading Zerlina to come with him, but as they are about to leave, Donna Elvira appears and shatters his expectations. Brushing aside Giovanni's attempted explanations, she warns Zerlina against him ("Ah! fuggi il traditor") ("Ah! fly from the betrayer") and takes the peasant girl away with her.

As Don Giovanni is grumbling about his bad luck, Donna Anna, dressed in mourning, enters with her faithful Ottavio. Donna Anna does not yet realize that Don Giovanni is the man who killed her father, and begs for his aid in finding the culprit. Don Giovanni is happily and hypocritically promising his help when Donna Elvira returns. Furiously she confronts the Don and tries to tell the others what sort of person he really is. The Don calmly explains to Anna and Ottavio that poor Elvira is quite mad; in asides to the latter, he begs her for heaven's sake to exercise a little more restraint. Anna and Ottavio are confused and do not know whom to believe; Elvira sputters; and the Don continues trying suavely to explain everything to everyone. Finally, Giovanni manages to draw Elvira away and hastily follows her.

Now Donna Anna becomes overwrought, for she has recognized Don Giovanni's voice as that of her recent assailant and her father's slayer. She tells the story of her misadventure to the incredulous Don Ottavio; in the aria "Or sai chi l'onore" ("Now you know") she again demands that Ottavio help her obtain vengeance. Donna Anna leaves, and her rather stunned fiancé muses over the situation. In the aria "Dalla sua pace" ("Upon her peace")* he sings of his love for Donna Anna and his desire to please her.

In the score the action now continues without a scene break, although in some performances the setting changes to the garden of Don Giovanni's castle, or to his ballroom, where the next two scenes take place. Leporello and Don Giovanni re-enter from opposite sides. Leporello tells his approving master that instructions have been carried out: the villagers have been nobly entertained, and Donna Elvira, who unexpectedly arrived on the scene, was locked out. The Don cheers, and in high spirits bursts into the "champagne aria"—"Finch'han dal vino" ("Till from the wine")—in which he instructs Leporello to prepare a wild party for all the villagers and any other girls he can find. (When this scene takes place at the Don's castle, it is often the custom for Giovanni to raise a wineglass, which he shatters at the end of the song.)

Scene Four

Characters who appear in this scene: Masetto and Zerlina; Don Giovanni; Leporello and other servants; Donna Anna, Donna Elvira, and Don Ottavio; villagers, peasants, and other guests.

It is evening in the garden outside Don Giovanni's castle. A balcony overlooks various trees and arbors.

Masetto huffily enters the garden, followed by Zerlina, who plucks at his sleeve, and runs behind and beside him, trying to make him listen to her. Masetto accuses his bride of gross infidelity; Zerlina protests her innocence. In the aria "Batti, batti" ("Beat, beat") she urges Masetto to beat her if he will, but then to make peace and forget the whole thing. Masetto relents. They are making up when they hear Don Giovanni approaching. Zerlina becomes agitated, and Masetto suspiciously hides in the

* This aria was not written for the original Prague performance of the opera. Mozart composed it for the tenor who sang the part of Don Ottavio in the Viennese première of *Don Giovanni*, as Ottavio's later aria, "Il mio tesoro," was too difficult for this tenor

shrubbery to see how she greets the Don. As his guests begin to arrive, Don Giovanni renews his attentions to Zerlina. He draws her aside, but unfortunately chooses the very place where Masetto is hiding. When the angry Masetto confronts him, the Don blithely explains that Zerlina was lonely without her bridegroom, and takes the couple into the castle with him.

Now Donna Anna, Donna Elvira, and Don Ottavio enter the garden. They are attired in cloaks and dominoes; they intend to expose Don Giovanni's wickedness before the entire assembly. While a minuet is heard from inside the castle, Leporello appears on the balcony, sees (but does not recognize) the masked trio, and calls to his master to come and look. From the balcony Don Giovanni, also unaware of their identity, invites the masqueraders to come inside. The trio remove their dominoes, again vow vengeance (with the exception of Donna Anna, who has momentary trepidations), replace their masks, and enter the ballroom.

Scene Five

Characters in order of their appearance: Don Giovanni, Leporello, Zerlina, Masetto, guests, servants, and musicians; Donna Anna, Donna Elvira, Don Ottavio.

The scene shifts to the huge, brilliantly lighted and decorated ballroom of Don Giovanni's castle. Three separate orchestras play on the stage, and many guests dance.

To Masetto's dismay, Don Giovanni again makes advances to Zerlina, while nearby, Leporello mimics his master. The masqueraders enter, and Don Giovanni welcomes them, offering them the freedom of his castle. He then begins to dance with Zerlina, while the mocking Leporello forces a most unwilling Masetto to dance with him. Cleverly, Don Giovanni maneuvers Zerlina into a room off to one side. With a loud squeal, Zerlina expresses her indignation at whatever he does there, and confusion ensues.*

Masetto, Don Ottavio, Donna Anna, and Donna Elvira rush

* Legend has it that Mozart was dissatisfied with the timid squeaks his original Zerlina persisted in giving during rehearsals in Prague. To get the effect he wanted, the composer is supposed to have hidden in the wings and appositely pinched the soprano when she came off the stage with Don Giovanni. The result, apparently, was satisfactory.

to the door of the side room and are about to break it down when
Don Giovanni bursts out, holding Leporello and pretending that
the servant is the miscreant. This ruse fools nobody; Don Ottavio
produces a pistol and points it at the Don. The masqueraders,
their dominoes now removed, and the other guests advance
threateningly toward Don Giovanni. For a brief instant the Don
is nonplussed; but he rapidly regains his poise, draws his sword
and, using Leporello as a shield, boldly pushes through the crowd
and escapes.

ACT TWO

Scene One

Characters in order of their appearance: Don Giovanni and Leporello;
Donna Elvira; Masetto and other peasants; Zerlina.

It is a short time later, at dusk near the house where Donna
Elvira now resides. A balcony of the house overlooks a small
square, surrounded by shrubs and trees. Leporello and Don Giovanni appear, arguing.

Once again Leporello wishes to quit the rather hazardous
employ of Don Giovanni, but the Don airily pooh-poohs this desire.
Leporello, who is shrewd enough to anticipate the probable outcome
of the argument, is insistent; to persuade Leporello to remain, the
Don finally tosses him a purse of money. The matter now settled,
Don Giovanni requests Leporello's help in a new enterprise. The
servant consents, provided his master give up women. Don Giovanni explodes: not only are women more important to him than
food and air, but the reason for his so-called inconstancy is that in
being faithful to one lady alone, he would be causing unhappi-
ness to so many others! Furthermore, his notice has recently been
attracted by Donna Elvira's maid; so that he can woo her more
successfully, Giovanni orders Leporello to change cloaks with him.
Leporello, dressed as the Don, is then to decoy Donna Elvira from
the scene, while the Don, in Leporello's garb, attends to the maid.
The servant unwillingly agrees to the scheme, and the exchange
takes place.

When Donna Elvira appears on her balcony, Don Giovanni
pushes Leporello into her sight. Hiding behind his servant, the Don

Luigi Bassi, the first Don Giovanni, performing his second act mandolin serenade.

Catarina Micelli, who created the role of Donna Elvira.

Singers in the première of *Don Giovanni*.

Teresina Bondini, wife of Pasquale Bondini, the Prague opera impresario, who created the role of Zerlina.

Teresa Saporiti, the first Donna Anna.

Stockfischlederlagen aufführten, wie es der hiesige Handelsmann Hr. Wimmer bereits gethan hat.

Die Weinärndte fällt im ganzen Lande über die Erwartung gut aus.

Montags den 29ten wurde von der italienischen Operngesellschaft die mit Sehnsucht erwartete Oper des Meisters Mozard Don Giovani, oder das steinerne Gastmahl gegeben. Kenner und Tonkünstler sagen, daß zu Prag ihres Gleichen noch nicht aufgeführt worden. Hr. Mozard dirigirte selbst, u. als er ins Orchester trat, wurde ihm ein dreymaliger Jubel gegeben, welches auch bey seinem Austritte aus demselben geschah. Die Oper ist übrigens äußerst schwer zu exequiren, und jeder bewundert dem ungeachtet die gute Vorstellung derselben nach so kurzer Studierzelt. Alles, Theater und Orchester bot seine Kräften auf, Mozarden zum Danke mit guter Exequirung zu belohnen. Es werden auch sehr viele Kosten durch mehrere Chöre und Dekorazion erfordert, welches alles Herr Guardasoni glänzend hergestellt hat. Die außerordentliche Menge Zuschauer bürgen für den allgemeinen Beyfall.

(Courtesy Mozarteum, Salzburg)

Review of the first performance of *Don Giovanni* from the Prague *Oberpostamtszeitung* of November 3, 1787. Printed directly beneath articles on stockfish merchants and a bumper vintage, the review reads: "Monday the 29th the Italian Opera Society presented the passionately awaited opera of the composer Mozard *Don Giovani*, or the Stone Feast. Connoisseurs and musicians say that its equal has never been presented in Prague. Herr Mozard himself conducted, and when he entered the orchestra, he was accorded a triple ovation; this occurred when he left the orchestra pit as well. As for the opera, it is extremely difficult to execute, and everyone admires, regardless, the good performance after such a short rehearsal period. Everything, theater and orchestra, offered its all to reward and thank Mozard with a good performance. Moreover, much expense was entailed by the several choruses and the decoration, all of which was splendidly arranged by Herr Guardasoni. The extraordinary number of spectators is evidence for the general approbation."

Title page of the first edition of the score of *Don Giovanni*, published in 1801 by Breitkopf and Härtel in Leipzig.

This scene is laid in a room with a window on one side and one or two chairs for furniture. Zerlina and Leporello burst in; she alternately threatens him with a razor and drags him about by the hair.

With ghoulish glee, Zerlina threatens to carve up Leporello, while he exhibits both fear and a tendency to jest. Presently, Zerlina and a peasant who happens to be near-by tie Leporello to a chair. In a duet "Per queste tue manine" ("By these your hands") Leporello asks for mercy and Zerlina responds that she is now demonstrating the proper way of behaving toward the male sex. After the duet Zerlina goes out, and Leporello piteously begs the peasant for a drink of water. The peasant leaves to oblige; Leporello loosens his bonds enough to drag himself and his chair to the window, through which he escapes.

Zerlina now returns with Donna Elvira, Masetto, and some other peasants. All are convinced that Don Giovanni is responsible for Leporello's escape, and all but Donna Elvira depart to tell Don Ottavio of this latest misdeed. Elvira, left alone, sings the recitative "In quali eccessi, o Numi" ("In what excesses, o Gods!") and aria "Mi tradì" ("That thankless spirit betrayed me"), which reveal her mixed emotions about Don Giovanni: though angered and embittered by his treatment of her, she still feels tenderness and pity for him, and regrets the certain doom she knows is in store for him.

Scene Four

Characters in order of their appearance: Leporello and Don Giovanni; the Statue.

It is very late the same night. The scene is a graveyard, enclosed by a low wall. Among the monuments and statues is one of the late Commendatore. This is sometimes described as an equestrian statue. Leporello crouches by the churchyard wall, over which Don Giovanni leaps as the curtain rises.

Laughing, the Don exclaims how beautiful the night is and how curious he is to learn what finally happened to Leporello and Donna Elvira. When the servant appears, the Don begins to relate his own recent adventures. These, to Leporello's chagrin, concern a young lady who mistook the Don for his servant because of their earlier exchange of cloaks.

As the Don's laughter grows more boisterous, a sepulchral voice suddenly says that his mirth will soon end. Giovanni at first thinks someone is eavesdropping outside the wall; but when the same voice orders him to leave the dead in peace, he notices the Commendatore's statue and tells Leporello to read the inscription engraved on it. This Leporello is most unwilling to do; but when the Don threatens him, he quaveringly reads the inscription: "Here I await vengeance on the wicked man who brought me to my death." Don Giovanni, in higher spirits than before, now commands Leporello to invite the statue to dinner the next evening; Leporello, beside himself with fear, obeys. To his horror, the statue nods acceptance. Don Giovanni himself steps forward and repeats the invitation. The statue replies with the one word "Yes," and Giovanni, dragging along his trembling servant, announces that they will go home to prepare for the meal.

Scene Five

Characters who appear in this scene: Donna Anna and Don Ottavio.

It is the following day, in a room of Donna Anna's house. She and Don Ottavio are conversing.

Don Ottavio, still trying to console Donna Anna for her father's death, pleads with her to let his love atone for the loss. Reproached for his indelicacy, Don Ottavio tells his fiancée that she is cruel to him. Bitterly, Donna Anna tells him not to call her cruel (the recitative "Crudele?" ("Cruel?") followed by the aria "Non mi dir" ("Do not tell me"); her grief is so great that she can cope with no other emotion just yet. Having thus unburdened herself, she leaves the room, and Ottavio, with a dutiful sigh, follows her.

Scene Six

Characters in order of their appearance: Don Giovanni, Leporello, servants, musicians and girls; Donna Elvira; statue of the Commendatore.

It is evening in the banquet hall of Don Giovanni's castle. There are doors on both sides of the hall, and an alcove for musicians

toward the rear. A lavish table is set with wines and delicacies. Beautiful girls flit about flirtatiously. Don Giovanni enters and surveys the scene with pleasure.

Since I'm spending my money, says the Don, I'm going to have fun. The musicians begin to play a selection from an opera popular in Mozart's time; Leporello recognizes the tune and applauds it. As a lavish meal is served to the Don, Leporello watches enviously and hungrily. The musicians strike up another air taken from an opera of the day, and Leporello can contain himself no longer. Thinking himself unobserved, he surreptitiously snatches a piece of pheasant. Now the stage orchestra begins the "Non più andrai" from Mozart's own *Marriage of Figaro*, a great favorite of the time. Don Giovanni mischievously orders Leporello to whistle a bit of the song, and Leporello is forced to admit shamefacedly that the skill of the Don's cook has been too tempting for him. The playful exchange is cut short when Donna Elvira unexpectedly bursts in. Don Giovanni dismisses the musicians and his other lady friends. Donna Elvira kneels; in desperation she begs the Don to mend his ways. Don Giovanni finds the situation humorous and companionably kneels beside her. Donna Elvira, not amused, requests him not to make fun of her. At this, Don Giovanni resumes his seat at the table and invites the lady to dine with him. Donna Elvira denounces his evil ways; Leporello remarks on his master's lack of feeling; and Don Giovanni raises his glass in praise of women and wine.

Her good intentions defeated, Donna Elvira rushes toward one of the doors, opens it, shrieks in dread, and runs out through the opposite door. Don Giovanni orders Leporello to go see why Elvira screamed so. Leporello obeys; on opening the first door, he too yells with terror and stumbles back with a frightened description of the Commendatore's marble statue, which stands just outside the door. Don Giovanni scoffs, and when a knock is heard on the door, tells Leporello to answer. For once the servant's refusal is firm; the Don himself must go to open the door for the visitor. With a dreadful rumbling of kettledrums, the statue of the Commendatore now enters the room and announces that it has arrived to accept the Don's invitation to dine.

Don Giovanni is at first taken aback by his new guest; but he almost immediately collects himself and prepares to demonstrate hospitality. Leporello, meanwhile, has hidden under a table where he cowers, shivering. The statue refuses the food of mortals, and invites Don Giovanni, in turn, to dinner. Don Giovanni, who is no coward, accepts, while Leporello politely declines on his behalf from beneath the table.

The statue demands Don Giovanni's hand as promise that he accepts its invitation. The Don gives his hand and is appalled by the statue's icy clasp. But he quickly regains his composure, and when the statue orders him to repent of his sins, he haughtily refuses. The statue insists; the Don refuses more stubbornly. At this, the statue announces that the time has come and moves toward the door whence it entered. Smoke and flames begin to envelop Don Giovanni; a chorus of hollow demon voices summons him to hell where yet a worse agony awaits him. While Leporello cringes under the table and watches in horror, Don Giovanni, with a final scream, vanishes amid hellfire and smoke.

Epilogue

Characters who appear in this scene: Leporello; Donna Anna and Don Ottavio, Donna Elvira, Zerlina and Masetto, policemen.

This final brief scene is sometimes omitted so that the performance ends with Don Giovanni's disappearance. When presented, it takes place only a few minutes later, in the same room as before. Donna Anna and Don Ottavio, Donna Elvira, Zerlina, and Masetto enter, followed by various minions of the law.

As the quintet look about for Don Giovanni, Leporello shakily emerges from under the table where he has been hiding, and tells them that their efforts to find his late master are futile. The others demand an explanation, which Leporello rather disjointedly offers. Now the newcomers realize the identity of the mysterious shade that passed Donna Elvira on the road shortly before. Don Ottavio turns to Donna Anna and again pleads his suit; she agrees to marry him after one more year of mourning, to which Ottavio graciously assents. Elvira states that she will retire to a convent; Zerlina and Masetto decide to go home to dinner; and Leporello, now recovered from his recent shock, announces that he will go to the inn to find a new employer. All six then join in a final sextet whose point is that the death of the wicked fits the life they have led. And thus ends *Don Giovanni*.

MUSICAL BACKGROUND

By Mozart's time Italian opera fell roughly into two classes: *opera seria* and *opera buffa*. *Opera seria* was the older. Its best-known composers included Alessandro Scarlatti, Handel and Gluck. Mozart composed operas of both genres. *Idomeneo* is considered his best *opera seria*.

To a modern listener, *opera seria* is a curious alternation of recitative, during which the action takes place, and arias, during which everything comes to a standstill. Each aria represented a single, isolated mood or emotion which the action aroused in the character singing it; the same character could express a different mood in another aria. The arias thus provided contemplative comment on the action. *Opera seria* was characterized by florid solo singing, with hardly any true ensembles. It was for their virtuosity in *seria* music that the castrati became renowned. The art of the castrato was already waning in Mozart's time (in fact the composer complained of the dearth of good ones) and soprano roles were again frequently being taken by women.

During the middle of the eighteenth century *opera seria* standards were reformed and redefined. Irrelevant comic elements were eliminated from the libretto, and a tragic ending became almost universal. Intervention by any sort of *deus ex machina* was condemned. *Opera seria* was remolded on austere, classic lines. Gradually, it became so austere and rarefied that comic opera— *opera buffa*—began to replace it in the public's esteem.

Opera buffa began in Naples, when short, light musical works were presented during the intermissions of *seria* performances. These "intermezzo" works, based on comic librettos, were marked by a rapid succession of incident which was furthered rather than suspended by the arias. The settings were contemporary, the emphasis on realism. In keeping with the latter, castrati were replaced by bass voices in *opera buffa*, making possible the "ensemble finale," one of the important features of this new genre. Instead of isolating one emotion at one time, *buffa* librettists and composers

tried to depict the "whole man" with all his conflicting and sometimes contradictory moods and reactions. Furthermore, in the
"ensemble finale" it became possible to present the emotions or
humors of several characters simultaneously.

An offshoot of *opera buffa* was the "commedia per musica." This
was a full-length comic work rather than an "intermezzo."
Mozart and Da Ponte described *Le Nozze di Figaro* as a "commedia
per musica," and it is surely the supreme example of the comic-
opera tradition. Mozart far surpassed any previous composer in
his use of the ensemble finale. Not only do *Figaro's* ensembles
naturally and smoothly further the action; but Mozart's musical
character sketches are at their most uncannily incisive in the ensembles, with their sharply contrasting and interacting vocal parts.

In its original conception *Don Giovanni* was probably closer to
opera buffa structure than it proved to be in actuality, though the epilogue sextet with its unnecessary moral was borrowed by Mozart
from French rather than Italian comic-opera tradition. From a
strictly dramatic standpoint, the arias added by Mozart for the
first Vienna performance of *Don Giovanni* do not further the plot,
though they do provide insight into character motivations. But
even before these additions, *Don Giovanni's* peculiar two-act construction contained enough dramatic anticlimaxes that a renowned scholar and critic, Edward J. Dent, thought Mozart and
Da Ponte originally cast the opera in four acts. Act I, according to
this theory, was supposed to end with Donna Anna's aria "Or sai
chi l'onore"; Act II with the Don's escape from the party in his
castle; Act III with the sextet that follows the revelation of
Leporello's identity. Thus one of the Don's women would domin-
ate each of the first three acts, and the statue the last. Why the
opera was changed to two acts is not known. One of the officials
at Prague's Italian theater may have asked Mozart to follow the
current practice of compressing *buffa* works into fewer acts; or the
singers' demands for additional arias may have made the four-act
construction impracticable.

Several members of the Prague cast are known to have been
dissatisfied because Mozart gave them so few solos. For Luigi
Bassi, the young baritone* who sang the title role, Mozart composed Don Giovanni's serenade, "Deh vieni alla finestra" and the

---

* Mozart designated Don Giovanni as a baritone, but the music lies easily within the
bass range and is often sung by a bass.

"disguise aria," "Metà di voi quà vadano." Leporello was given another patter song, "Ah, pietà, Signori miei"; Masetto's "Ho capito" was also added by Mozart in Prague. Professor Dent's theory that *Don Giovanni* was first meant to be in four acts, plus Leporello's demand for another aria would explain the peculiar drawn-out ending of what is now Scene 2, Act II. According to *opera buffa* tradition, this scene—if it originally ended an act—should have closed with the sextet. Instead, there are first Leporello's aria and escape, which lower the tension built up while his fate hung in the balance during the sextet; then, as a decided anticlimax (again speaking strictly from a dramatic, not from a musical viewpoint) there is Don Ottavio's doubtful logic which culminates in the aria "Il mio tesoro."

The dramatic construction of *Don Giovanni* was further muddled by the additions Mozart had to make when the opera was given in Vienna. There, the Don Ottavio could not manage the extremely difficult "Il mio tesoro," and Mozart gave him "Dalla sua pace" instead. As the text of this aria would have made it completely out of place at the end of Scene 2, Act II, it was sung after Donna Anna's haughty vengeance aria, "Or sai chi l'onore," in Scene 3 of Act I. Here it remained, although "Il mio tesoro" is now also included in most performances. As a result, in contrast to the strong personality Donna Anna shows in her aria, Don Ottavio seems more vacillating than ever.

Katharina Cavalieri,* who sang Elvira in the Viennese première of *Don Giovanni*, demanded a *scena* to herself. Mozart gave her the recitative "In quali eccessi" followed by the aria "Mi tradì." She sang them after a low-comedy scene for Zerlina and Leporello, which Mozart also inserted into the second act to please the Viennese. The scene was dropped from performance long ago, and stage managers have been puzzled what to do with Donna Elvira's aria ever since. Usually it is sung after Don Ottavio's "Il mio tesoro," and adds yet another anticlimax to that catchall, Scene 2 of Act II.

As the Vienna performance of *Don Giovanni* was supposed to last only two and a half hours, something had to be cut to accommodate the various additions. Mozart decided to eliminate the epilogue; but to show that the other characters in the opera knew

---

* Whose friendship with Salieri helped cause Da Ponte's break with this composer.

about the Don's end, the composer requested them to run onto the stage right after the Don's demise and scream in D major. They were unable to do exactly this, so they ran onto the stage and just screamed.

In the final analysis, one is not too concerned with the weak points in the dramatic construction of *Don Giovanni*, because Mozart's music is incomparable. Each character is distinctly realized, and every situation is captivating if not always logical.

Like almost all of Mozart's operas, *Don Giovanni* begins and ends in the same key. The overture begins in D minor and switches to D major; Don Giovanni descends into hell in D minor, and the epilogue ends in D major. The opening chords of the overture hardly presage a comedy; they are the music that accompanies the statue as he arrives for dinner (though the famous trombones associated with the statue are not heard until the cemetery scene in Act II). The overture leads without a break into the first scene. As the curtain rises, the music depicts Leporello's impatient pacing.

From the start, Leporello's music identifies him as a *buffo* character: the sharp syllabification of the words lends itself to the patter-chatter of *buffo* music; the rapid ascents and descents, the large intervals in some of Leporello's arias were traditional devices for *buffo* parts. When the Commendatore appears and challenges Don Giovanni, the predominant mood becomes tragic. During the brief ensuing trio, as the Commendatore lies dying, Leporello is all but paralyzed with dread. His very fright, and the inanities it makes him utter, restore the comic mood which again prevails while master and servant escape. With the appearance of Donna Anna and Don Ottavio, the mood changes again. The almost hysterical grief into which the discovery of her father's body plunges Donna Anna is contrasted by the lyrical smoothness of Don Ottavio's comforting phrases. The gist of Don Ottavio's music here was much copied and imitated by later composers.

Donna Elvira is also immediately identifiable as a comic character. If she were a tragic personality, she would have explained her plight in a solo aria when she first appeared. Instead, Don Giovanni and Leporello are present, unknown to her, and make frivolous remarks in all the places where an ordinary heroine would be pausing for breath while the orchestra played reprises of her aria. Later on, when Don Giovanni tells Anna and Ottavio that Elvira is mad, she herself lends comic substance to his claim by singing, in rapid succession, passages of florid coloratura, rage and pathos.

Leporello's "catalogue aria" is the masterpiece of *basso buffo* songs. It shifts from the rapid patter in which Leporello enumerates the Don's conquests to the slower, salacious phrases in which he describes the ladies; the latter passages reach their climax in Leporello's almost lip-smacking statement about the Don's preference for "beginners." The aria ends with the repeated insinuating and insulting suggestion that Donna Elvira knows exactly how Don Giovanni manages all his affairs.

The music that accompanies the entrance of Zerlina and Masetto—a simple melody with a refrain—shows they are country folk. Masetto's personality is defined in his "Ho capito." Its first rising and falling phrases suggest the fear which has already taken possession of his slow-working mind; the song ends with Masetto's repeated heavy sarcasm, which he wishes frantically to deliver as Leporello tries to drag him away. The deceptive simplicity of "Là ci darem la mano" proves that Don Giovanni has quickly sized up Zerlina and is translating his proposition into her own musical terms. Elvira's warning aria to Zerlina is in an older operatic style. It is sometimes thought Mozart intended it to be either an imitation or a parody of Handel's music.

In contrast to the uninhibited and vacillating Elvira, Donna Anna is impossibly ladylike and noble (though her music grows progressively mellower). And in contrast to the solemn, single-minded Donna Anna, Don Ottavio sometimes becomes positively funny. His ineffectual gasps of relief while Donna Anna forges through the story of her attempted rape often produce giggles in the audience.

Don Giovanni's striking "Finch'han dal vino" seems all the more exuberant as Mozart orchestrated it more fully than any passage since the overture; all the horns and woodwinds play. The Don's subsequent invitation to the peasants to join his party is underlined by trumpet and drum flourishes. These also appear in his welcome to the masked trio and at the beginning of the finale of Act II, when Don Giovanni is in a similarly expansive mood.

The blending of the three on-stage dance orchestras in Don Giovanni's ballroom is a unique example of Mozart's genius. The first orchestra, composed of strings, oboes and horns, plays an aristocratic minuet in 3/4 time; the second orchestra, violins and bass strings, plays a middle-class country dance in 2/4 time; and the third orchestra, also strings, plays a peasant waltz in 3/8 time. Traditionally, Don Ottavio and Donna Anna are supposed to dance the minuet (this must have been Mozart's intention, because it is known that he personally had to teach his first Don Ottavio how to minuet), but some of the scores do not include this in their stage directions. The Schirmer score, from which the libretto in this book is translated, directs that chairs be placed for the masked trio by Don Giovanni's servants. When Zerlina screams, the main orchestra again takes over. The music of the rapid finale conveys the turmoil of the situation.

Act II begins with one of the briefest of operatic introductions—four quarter notes. Don Giovanni and Leporello are in the middle of an argument. That they are arguing on equal terms, not as master and servant, is apparent, since they both sing exactly the same music. The duet's fast patter quality makes it equally apparent that the matter of the argument is none too weighty. (This short duet was also written by Mozart in Prague.)

The sad little tune Elvira sings when she appears on her balcony shows her for the moment not as a vengeful virago, but in a mood of nostalgic longing. With his customary quick perception, Don Giovanni takes advantage of Elvira's frame of mind by repeating and exaggerating the very melody she has been singing. The farce is kept from becoming cruel by the chattering undertone in which Leporello threatens to laugh. One line of the Don's invitation to Elvira anticipates in a different key the serenade which follows; probably the similarity of the situations evoked the similarity of the music in the Don's mind.

Had Mozart wanted to use any Spanish local color in the opera, Don Giovanni's serenade would have been the place for it. The Don, however, uses a mandolin, a very Italian instrument, to accompany himself instead of a guitar. The serenade itself was quite characteristic of the Italian opera of Mozart's time.

When Don Giovanni scatters the peasants, he first remembers his exchange of cloaks with Leporello and sings in the quick patter of his servant; as he grows more pleased with his cleverness, Don Giovanni forgets to imitate Leporello and switches back to his own more leisurely and polished style. Zerlina's aria, "Vedrai, carino," which comes next, ends, as its words suggest, with a "heartbeat effect," a popular device used by several other composers of Mozart's day.

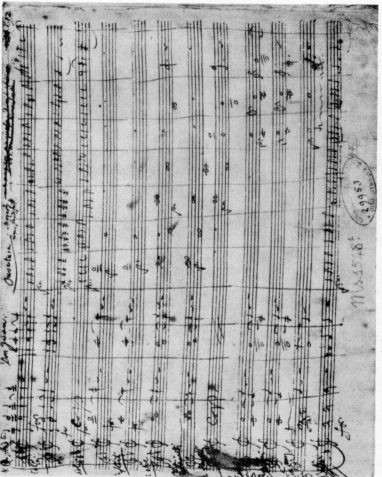

First page of the overture to *Don Giovanni* from the autograph score.

(Courtesy Mozarteum, Salzburg)

Don Giovanni's serenade ("Deh vieni alla finestra") from the autograph score.

(Courtesy Mozarteum, Salzburg)

Beginning of the sextet in Act 2, Scene 2 of
Don Giovanni ("Sola, sola in buio loco") from the
autograph score.

The long sextet of the next scene actually begins with Elvira's plaintive "Sola, sola in buio loco" ("Alone, alone in a dark place"). Donna Anna and Don Ottavio enter and are so surprised to find (as they think) Don Giovanni that they sing a few bars in unison, instead of their more customary harmony. Again, it is Leporello's sustained undertone of patter which gives the sextet a comic flavor. On the other hand, Don Ottavio's aria "Il mio tesoro" is almost a reversion to the musical style of *opera seria*.

In the interpolated *scena* for Elvira, Mozart anticipated Beethoven by using the cellos as a separate bass component instead of combining all the bass strings. This division of the basses helps to prevent the aria's practically unvaried rhythm from becoming obtrusive. But Mozart's most striking unconventionality in *Don Giovanni*—the use of three trombones—comes in the next scene.

In the eighteenth century, trombones were used mainly for religious music. They were seldom played even for *opera seria*, and then only in supernatural scenes. In his incidental music to Shadwell's play *The Libertine*, Henry Purcell emphasized Don John's dreadful fate with off-stage trombones. The trombones in *Don Giovanni* serve the same function. Because there are no dynamics for their cemetery-scene music in the autograph score, Mozart must have meant them to be heard either from in back of the stage or from under it. (Mozart never gave dynamics to the music he wrote for instruments which were separated from the main orchestra, as for example the three stage orchestras of the party scene. To be heard by the audience, such ensembles had to play consistently loudly, and dynamic markings would have been pointless.) The trombones' entrance into a scene that begins comically must have awed Mozart's audiences. It must be remembered at this point that Mozart's orchestra in Prague consisted of twenty-five members playing twenty-six instruments: seven violins, two violas, one cello, two contrabasses, two flutes, two oboes, two clarinets, two bassoons, two horns, two trumpets, two kettledrums. With a group of this size, three trombones would be much more emphatic than in a modern symphony orchestra where, in any case, we are accustomed to their sound.

The trombones accompany the Commendatore's statue during two of the three times it speaks in the cemetery scene. The third time the statue says only one word—"Sì"—and there are no trombones. The players were probably on their way back to the orchestra pit, so that they would be out of the way of the stage-hands (who had to manage two quick scene changes in a row) and back in their seats for the finale. Mozart may have had trouble with the trombonists during rehearsals; in case they failed him, he had the bassoons and basses play the same music, also apart from the orchestra.

Leporello's superstitious panic forms a comic contrast to the solemn statue music. His invitation to the statue, with its sudden drops of sevenths, typifies his *buffo* fear.

The next scene is utterly extraneous to the plot. Apparently Mozart wanted to give Donna Anna one more big solo and inserted the aria "Non mi dir." This is the most nearly light-hearted music sung by Donna Anna in the entire opera. The aria ends with a burst of coloratura, after which Don Ottavio's few lines seem so absurdly anticlimactic that they are often cut, the scene ending with Donna Anna's exit.

The finale begins cheerfully. The audience was probably amused by the inclusion of three popular songs to accompany Don Giovanni's meal; the "Non più andrai" was a great favorite in Prague at the time, and the Don's musicians play it twice. Don Giovanni's private orchestra consists of two oboes, two clarinets, two bassoons, two horns and a cello. It is clear from the libretto that they are supposed to be on the stage during the meal; their music in the autograph score, however, is marked with dynamics, an indication that in Prague they were *not* on-stage but played from the orchestra pit. One explanation may be that the stage was so cluttered with Don Giovanni's supper tables that there was no room for his private orchestra. But, in the preceding act, there was room for *three* orchestras on a stage crowded with people. Some authorities, therefore, think the absence of the Don's musicians on the Prague stage was due not to lack of space, but to lack of extra clarinets. The orchestration here calls for a full complement of clarinets immediately before and after the Don's musicians play. There would have been no time for the clarinetists to get onto the stage and back to the pit without holding up the opera's action, so the first Don Giovanni had to do without musicians in his dining hall.

Donna Elvira, already in a frenzy when she bursts in, is goaded by Don Giovanni to the edge of hysteria. Her repeated shrieks, the Don's loud happy toasts and Leporello's grumbles form a curious trio of contrasting moods. The rest of this scene is also marked by strong contrast. Almost all the deadly serious business between Don Giovanni and the statue is punctuated by Leporello's terrified *buffo* commentary from under the table.

After Leporello's cry on opening the door, there is a change in the tempo of the music. Leporello's disjointed description of what he has seen makes even more hair-raising the great chord which accompanies the statue as it enters.

Now the trombones come into full prominence as part of the orchestra. First they accompany only the statue; but from the moment Don Giovanni seals his doom by giving his hand to the statue, the trombones play almost continuously. Their initial repeated entrances into the dialogue between Don Giovanni and the statue sustain the suspense during the latter's rather repetitious conversation. Later, the trombones emphasize the hollow sound of the demon chorus. Constant alternations of loud and soft add to the music's effectiveness. Don Giovanni's end is marked by a long D minor chord. This shifts to D major, and the epilogue begins.

When one considers that Don Giovanni has just been enveloped and swallowed by flames, the moral viewpoint expressed in the sextet seems a bit lame. But the principals are characterized faithfully to the end. Donna Anna and Don Ottavio sing a serious, old-fashioned duet; Elvira, subdued again, has one sad line in the minor mode; Zerlina and Masetto turn Elvira's phrase into the happier major; and Leporello also shows that he is once more quite himself.

Best-known selections from DON GIOVANNI:

PAGE

"Ah! chi mi dice mai"—sung by Donna Elvira in 96
Act I, Scene 2

Allegro

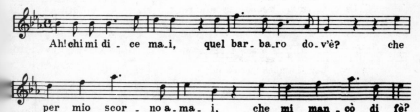

Ah! chi mi di _ ce ma_i, quel bar_ ba_ro do_ v'è? che

per mio scor _ no a_ma_ i, che mi man _ cò di fè?

"Madamina" (Catalogue aria)—sung by Leporello
in Act I, Scene 2

Allegro

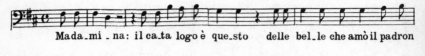

Mada_mi_na: il ca_ta logoè que_sto   delle bel_le che amòil padron

mi_o;

"Ho capito"—sung by Masetto in Act I, Scene 3

Allegro molto

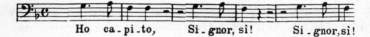

Ho ca_pi_to,   Si_gnor, sì!   Si_gnor,sì!

"Là ci darem la mano"—sung by Don Giovanni
and Zerlina in Act I, Scene 3

Andante

Là ci daremla ma_no, là midi_rai di   sì;   ve_di,nonè lon_

_ta_no, par_tiam,benmio,da qui.

"Ah! fuggi il traditor!"—sung by Donna Elvira in Act I, Scene 3   111

Allegro

"Or sai chi l'onore"—sung by Donna Anna in Act I, Scene 3   119

Andante

"Dalla sua pace"—sung by Don Ottavio in Act I, Scene 3   120

Andantino sostenuto

PAGE

"Finch'han dal vino" (Champagne aria)—sung by   123
    Don Giovanni in Act I, Scene 3

Presto

"Batti, batti, o bel Masetto"—sung by Zerlina in   125
    Act I, Scene 4

Andante grazioso

"Deh vieni alla finestra"—sung by Don Giovanni in   158
    Act II, Scene 1

Allegretto

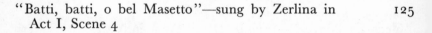

PAGE

"Metà di voi"—sung by Don Giovanni in Act II,   159
Scene 1

Andante con moto

Me‗tà   di voi   quà va ‗ dano,   e gli al‗tri va‗danlà.

"Vedrai, carino"—sung by Zerlina in Act II,   163
Scene 1

Andante

Ve‗drai, ca ‗ ri ‗ no,   se sei buo‗ni ‗ no,   che bel ri ‗

me ‗ dio   ti   vo‗glio   dar.

"Ah, pietà!"—sung by Leporello in Act II, Scene 2   171

Allegro assai

Ah, pie ‗ tà! Si‗gno‗ri miei!ah, pie ‗ tà, pietà, pie‗tà,pie‗tà di

me,   pie ‗ tà!

"Il mio tesoro"—sung by Don Ottavio in Act II,   172
   Scene 2

Andante grazioso

Il mio te_so_ ro in- tan_ to   an_ da   _ te, an_
da _   _ te a _ con_so _ lar!

"Mi tradì"—sung by Donna Elvira in Act II,   179
   Scene 3

Allegretto

Mitradì quel_l'al_ma in_gra_ta,   quel _ l'al _ ma in_gra_ta,

"Non mi dir"—sung by Donna Anna in Act II,   188
   Scene 5

Larghetto

Non mi____ dir,____ bel_ l'i _.dol_mi _ o,   che son i_o cru_
del____ con te,

LUDWIG KÖCHEL

Before Beethoven, only a few composers bothered to make chronological lists of their music based on the opus-number system. ("Opus" indicates a particular work or group of works written during one period; "number" shows the sequence of compositions within the opus.) Chronological classifications were made, if at all, by music publishers, who enumerated only that small proportion of a composer's output which ever reached printed form. That Mozart's 626 musical works have been classified and catalogued in chronological sequence is largely due to Ludwig Köchel, whose surname (often abbreviated to "K.") appears with the title of every Mozart composition.

Köchel was born in Stein, Austria, in 1800, and died in Vienna in 1877. He was educated chiefly in Vienna, where he earned a doctorate at the University, and in 1827 became tutor to the sons of the Archduke Karl. Köchel was knighted for his conscientious work at the Hapsburg Court, and in 1842 retired from teaching to devote himself to his vocation of naturalist and his avocation of musical historian. In 1850, Köchel moved to Mozart's birthplace, Salzburg. He loved Mozart's music and was dismayed to find the composer's works in an utterly chaotic state—the compositions had neither been dated nor enumerated in any sort of sequence. For about the last seven years of his life, Mozart had noted his finished works in a thematic catalogue he personally kept. Köchel resolved to make an orderly listing of the hundreds of compositions Mozart had completed prior to starting this catalogue.

Köchel journeyed widely, retracing Mozart's own travels, in order to gather and inspect every available scrap of material that might help him with his project. Through painstaking examination of contemporary documentary evidence, Mozart's correspondence, and the very paper and ink used by the composer for his music, Köchel was able in 1862 to have his 551-page *Chronological-Thematic Catalogue of the Works of W. A. Mozart* published.

Besides the Mozart catalogue, Köchel published studies on other music and musicians as well. An esteemed naturalist, he traveled much in the course of his scientific investigations and also wrote several books on his findings and theories about mineralogy, meteorology, and botany. In the past hundred years, Köchel's Mozart catalogue has been revised several times, most recently by the musicologist Alfred Einstein. Mozart's music itself has been intrinsically analyzed and classified according to the periods and styles of its composition. Nonetheless, the name "Köchel" remains the identifying clue to a work of Mozart. *Don Giovanni* has Köchel Listing Number 527.

DON GIOVANNI

or

THE LIBERTINE'S PUNISHMENT

Opera in Two Acts
Music by Wolfgang Amadeus Mozart
Libretto by Lorenzo Da Ponte

DON GIOVANNI

DON GIOVANNI, a libertine   Bass or baritone

LEPORELLO, servant to Don Giovanni   Bass

DONNA ANNA, a noblewoman whom Don
     Giovanni unsuccessfully assaults   Soprano

DON OTTAVIO,
     betrothed of Donna Anna   Tenor

THE COMMENDATORE, an elderly nobleman,
     father of Donna Anna   Bass

DONNA ELVIRA, a lady whom Don Giovanni
     loved and left in Burgos   Soprano

ZERLINA, a peasant girl   Soprano

MASETTO, bridegroom of Zerlina   Bass

Servants, peasants, musicians, chorus.

Act One

ACT ONE

Scene One

Seville in the seventeenth century. Late evening, out-side the palace of the Commendatore. At the foot of the stairs which lead from the palace, Leporello, dressed in a cloak, paces back and forth.

LEPORELLO: Notte e giorno faticar, per chi nulla sa gradir; piova e vento sopportar, mangiar male e mal dormir! Voglio far il gentiluomo, e non voglio più servir, e non voglio più servir, no, no, no, no, no, no, non voglio più servir.

LEPORELLO: Toiling night and day, for someone whom nothing can please; withstanding rain and wind, eating poorly and sleeping badly! I want to be a gentleman, and I don't want to serve any longer, and I don't want to serve any longer, no, no, no, no, no, no, I don't want to serve any longer.

He turns towards the palace with an impatient gesture.

Oh che caro galantuomo! Voi star dentro colla bella, ed io far la sentinella, la sentinella, la sentinella! Voglio far il gentiluomo, e non voglio più servir, e non voglio più servir, no, no, no, no, no, no, non voglio più servir.

Oh that dear gentleman! It's for you to stay inside with the pretty lady, and for me to play the sentinel, the sentinel, the sentinel! I want to be a gentleman, and I don't want to serve any longer, and I don't want to serve any longer, no, no, no, no, no, no, I don't want to serve any longer.

He listens attentively.

Ma mi par, che venga gente; ma mi par, che venga gente; non mi voglio far sentir, ah non mi voglio far sentir, non mi voglio far sentir, no, no, no, no, no, non mi voglio far sentir.	But I think that someone is coming; but I think that someone is coming; I don't want to be seen, ah, I don't want to be seen, I don't want to be seen, no, no, no, no, no, I don't want to be seen.

Leporello hides to one side, as Donna Anna and Don Giovanni come down the palace stairs struggling. She attempts to discover the Don's identity, he to hide it.

DONNA ANNA: Non sperar, se non m'uccidi, ch'io ti lasci fuggir mai.

DON GIOVANNI: Donna folle! indarno gridi, chi son io, tu non saprai.

LEPORELLO: Che tumulto! o ciel! che gridi! Il padron in nuovi guai.

DONNA ANNA: Non sperar, se non m'uccidi, ch'io ti lasci fuggir mai, non sperar, ch'io ti lasci fuggir ma.

DON GIOVANNI: Donna folle! indarno gridi, chi son io tu non saprai, no, tu non saprai.

DONNA ANNA: Do not expect me ever to let you escape, unless you kill me.

DON GIOVANNI: Foolish woman! you scream in vain, you shall not know who I am.

LEPORELLO: What a racket! oh heavens! what screams! My master in a fresh scrape.

DONNA ANNA: Do not expect me ever to let you escape, unless you kill me, do not expect me ever to let you escape.

DON GIOVANNI: Foolish woman! you scream in vain, you shall not know who I am, no, you shall not know.

Donna Anna calls for help.

DONNA ANNA: Gente! Servi! al traditore!

DONNA ANNA: Help! Servants! get the traitor!

Don Giovanni tries to stifle Donna Anna's cries.

DON GIOVANNI: Taci, e trema al mio furore!

DONNA ANNA: Scellerato!

DON GIOVANNI: Be quiet, and tremble at my rage!

DONNA ANNA: Villain!

DON GIOVANNI: Sconsigliata!

DON GIOVANNI: Foolish woman!

{ DONNA ANNA: Scellerato!

DONNA ANNA: Villain!

DON GIOVANNI: Sconsigliata!

DON GIOVANNI: Foolish woman!

LEPORELLO: Sta a veder che il libertino mi farà precipitar.

LEPORELLO: I can see that the libertine will be my undoing.

DONNA ANNA: Gente! Servi!

DONNA ANNA: Help! Servants!

DON GIOVANNI: Taci, e trema!

DON GIOVANNI: Be quiet and tremble!

DONNA ANNA: Come furia disperata ti saprò perseguitar. Come furia disperata disperata ti saprò perseguitar. Scellerato!

DONNA ANNA: I shall persecute you like a maddened fury. I shall persecute you like a maddened, maddened fury. Villain!

DON GIOVANNI: Questa furia disperata mi vuol far precipitar, questa furia disperata mi vuol far precipitar. Sconsigliata!

DON GIOVANNI: This desperate fury will be my undoing, this desperate fury will be my undoing. Foolish woman!

LEPORELLO: Che tumulto! oh ciel, che gridi! Sta a veder che il libertino mi farà precipitar, sta a veder che il libertino mi farà precipitar.

LEPORELLO: What a racket! oh heavens, what screams! I can see that the libertine will be my undoing, I can see that the libertine will be my undoing.

DONNA ANNA: Scellerato!

DONNA ANNA: Villain!

DON GIOVANNI: Sconsigliata!

DON GIOVANNI: Foolish woman!

LEPORELLO: Sta a veder che il libertino mi farà precipitar.

LEPORELLO: I can see that the libertine will be my undoing.

DONNA ANNA: Gente! servi!

DONNA ANNA: Help! servants!

DON GIOVANNI: Taci, e trema!

DON GIOVANNI: Be quiet, and tremble!

DONNA ANNA: Come furia disperata ti saprò perseguitar, come furia disperata, disperata ti saprò perseguitar.

DON GIOVANNI: Questa furia disperata mi vuol far precipitar, questa furia disperata mi vuol far precipitar.

LEPORELLO: Che tumulto, oh ciel, che gridi! Sta a veder che il libertino mi farà precipitar, sta a veder che il libertino mi farà precipitar, sta a veder che il libertino mi farà precipitar, sta a veder che il libertino mi farà precipitar.

DONNA ANNA: I shall persecute you like a maddened fury, I shall persecute you like a maddened, maddened fury.

DON GIOVANNI: This desperate fury will be my undoing, this desperate fury will be my undoing.

LEPORELLO: What a racket, o heavens, what screams! I can see that the libertine will be my undoing, I can see that the libertine will be my undoing, I can see that the libertine will be my undoing, I can see that the libertine will be my undoing.

The Commendatore approaches, carrying a light in one hand, a sword in the other. Donna Anna flees into the palace, leaving Don Giovanni and the Commendatore to face one another.

COMMENDATORE: Lasciala, indegno, battiti meco!

DON GIOVANNI: Va, non mi degno di pugnar teco.

COMMENDATORE: Così pretendi da me fuggir?

DON GIOVANNI: Va, non mi degno, no!

LEPORELLO: (Potessi almeno di quà partir!)

COMMENDATORE: Così pretendi da me fuggir?

LEPORELLO: (Potessi almeno di quà partir!)

DON GIOVANNI: (Misero!)

COMMENDATORE: Battiti!

COMMENDATORE: Leave her be, wretch, and duel with me!

DON GIOVANNI: *Haughtily.* Go, I will not stoop to fight with you.

COMMENDATORE: Do you imagine you'll escape me thus?

DON GIOVANNI: Go, I will not stoop, no!

LEPORELLO: *Aside.* If at least I could get away from here!

COMMENDATORE: Do you imagine you'll escape me thus?

LEPORELLO: *Aside.* If at least I could get away from here!

DON GIOVANNI: *Aside.* Wretched man!

COMMENDATORE: Fight!

Act 1, Scene 1. Death of the Commendatore. Hans Hotter is the Don and Ludwig Weber the Commendatore in this Salzburg performance.

(Courtesy Teatro alla Scala, Milan, photo by Ezio Piccagliani)

Act 1, Scene 1. Leporello looks on in horror as the Commendatore dies.

Don Giovanni draws his sword.

DON GIOVANNI: Misero! Misero! attendi se vuoi morir!

DON GIOVANNI: Wretched man! Wretched man! Look out, if you wish to die!

He knocks the torch from the Commendatore's hand, and they duel. After several passes, Don Giovanni fatally wounds the Commendatore, who falls to the ground.

COMMENDATORE: Ah! soccorso!

COMMENDATORE Ah! help!

LEPORELLO: Qual misfatto! Qual eccesso! Entro il sen dallo spavento palpitar il cor mi sento! Io non sò che far, che dir, io non sò che far, che dir, entro il sen dallo spavento palpitar il cor mi sento, io no sò che far, che dir, io non sò che far, che dir!

LEPORELLO: What a tragedy! What a crime! I feel my heart pounding with fear in my breast! I don't know what to do, what to say, I don't know what to do, what to say, I feel my heart pounding with fear in my breast, I don't know what to do, what to say, I don't know what to do, what to say!

DON GIOVANNI: Ah! già cade il sciagurato, affannoso e agonizzante già dal seno palpitante veggo l'anima partir, veggo l'anima partir, già dal seno palpitante veggo l'anima partir.

DON GIOVANNI: Ah! already the villain is fallen, gasping and breathing his last, already I see his soul parting from his heaving breast, I see his soul parting, I see his soul parting from his heaving breast.

COMMENDATORE: —son tradito! l'assassino m'ha ferito, e dal seno palpitante sento l'anima partir, sento l'anima partir.

COMMENDATORE: —I am betrayed! the assassin has run me through, and I feel my soul parting from my heaving breast, I feel my soul parting.

Meanwhile, the palace windows are lighted up; servants run to and fro in great agitation. Some servants go to the street and return with Don Ottavio, who enters the palace in the background. Don Giovanni replaces his sword at his side.

DON GIOVANNI: Leporello, ove sei?

DON GIOVANNI: Leporello, where are you?

LEPORELLO: Son quì, per mia disgrazia; e voi?

LEPORELLO: I'm here, by my bad luck; and you?

DON GIOVANNI: Son quì.

DON GIOVANNI: I am here.

LEPORELLO: Chi è morto, voi o il vecchio?

LEPORELLO: Who's dead, you or the old man?

DON GIOVANNI: Che domanda da bestia! il vecchio.

DON GIOVANNI: What a stupid question! the old man.

LEPORELLO: Bravo! due imprese leggiadre! Sforzar la figlia, ed ammazzar il padre!

LEPORELLO: Hurray, two charming undertakings! Forcing the daughter and murdering the father.

DON GIOVANNI: L'ha voluto, suo danno.

DON GIOVANNI: He asked for it, it's his loss.

LEPORELLO: Ma Donn'Anna, cosa ha voluto?

LEPORELLO: But Donna Anna, what did she ask for?

Don Giovanni lashes out at Leporello.

DON GIOVANNI: Taci, non mi seccar! Vien meco, se no vuoi qualche cosa ancor tu.

DON GIOVANNI: Be quiet, don't anger me! Come with me, if you don't want something too.

LEPORELLO: Non vo' nulla, Signor, non parlo più.

LEPORELLO: I don't want anything, Sir, I won't say another word.

Don Giovanni and Leporello exit together. Donna Anna and Don Ottavio emerge from the palace, accompanied by servants who light the scene with torches.

DONNA ANNA: Ah! Del padre in periglio in soccorso voliam!

DONNA ANNA: Ah! Let us fly to the relief of my father in his danger!

Don Ottavio draws his sword.

DON OTTAVIO: Tutto il mio sangue verserò, se bisogna: ma dov'è il scellerato?

DON OTTAVIO: If need be, I shall shed all my blood: but where is the villain?

DONNA ANNA: In questo loco. | DONNA ANNA: Right here.

Donna Anna sees the Commendatore's body. She does not yet recognize it, and kneels to examine it.

DONNA ANNA: Ma qual mai s'offre, oh Dei, spettacolo funesto agli occhi miei!

DONNA ANNA: But oh Gods, what distressing sight presents itself to my eyes!

She embraces the body.

Padre, padre mio! mio caro padre!

Father, my father! my dear father!

DON OTTAVIO: Signore!

DON OTTAVIO: Sir!

DONNA ANNA: Ah, l'assassino mel trucidò. Quel sangue—quella piaga—quel volto—tinto e coperto del color di morte.

DONNA ANNA: Ah, the assassin has slain him. That blood—that wound—that face—stained and covered with the hue of death.

Don Ottavio tries to raise her, but she refuses.

Ei non respira più! Fredde le membra!

He breathes no more! His limbs are icy!

*She gets up and nearly swoons.
Don Ottavio helps her to a seat.*

Padre mio! caro padre! padre amato! io manco! io moro!

My father! dear father! beloved father! I falter! I shall die!

Don Ottavio assists her and addresses the servants.

DON OTTAVIO: Ah! soccorrete, amici, il mio tesoro! Cercatemi, recatemi qualche odor, qualche spirto! ah non tardate! Donn'Anna!

DON OTTAVIO: Ah! friends, help my loved one! Find for me, bring to me some smelling salts, some spirits! ah do not delay! Donna Anna!

A servant runs into the palace and returns with some smelling salts, which are offered to Donna Anna.

sposa! amica! il duolo estremo la meschinella uccide! Ahi! già rinviene! datele nuovi ajuti.

bride! friend! her extreme grief is killing the poor creature! Ah! she is reviving! give her more help.

DONNA ANNA: Padre mio!

DONNA ANNA: *Weakly.* My father!

Don Ottavio addresses the servants again.

DON OTTAVIO: Celate, allontanate agli occhi suoi quell'oggetto d'orrore!

DON OTTAVIO: Hurry, remove that object of horror from her sight!

Servants carry the Commendatore's body into the palace.

Anima mia, consolati! fa core!

My soul, console yourself! take heart!

Donna Anna leaps to her feet and turns wildly from Don Ottavio.

DONNA ANNA: Fuggi, crudele, fuggi! lascia che mora anch'io! Ora ch'è morto, o Dio! chi a me la vita diè.

DONNA ANNA: Get away, cruel one, get away! let me die too! Now he is dead, o God, he who gave life to me

DON OTTAVIO: Senti, cor mio, deh senti, guardami un solo istante, ti parla il caro amante, che vive sol per te.

DON OTTAVIO: Listen, my heart, come listen, attend me only a moment, your dear lover, who lives only for you, speaks to you.

Donna Anna, relenting, reaches out to Don Ottavio.

DONNA ANNA: Tu sei! Perdon, mio bene, l'affanno mio, le pene . . .

DONNA ANNA: It is you! Forgive me, my love—my suffering, my sorrows . . .

She looks at the place where the Commendatore lay.

ah! il padre mio dov'è?

ah! where is my father?

DON OTTAVIO: Il padre? Lascia, o cara, la rimembranza amara! hai sposo e padre in me.

DON OTTAVIO: Your father? Let the bitter memory be, o dearest! You have a husband and a father in me.

DONNA ANNA: Ah! il padre, il padre mio dov'è?

DONNA ANNA: Ah! my father, where is my father?

DON OTTAVIO: Lascia, o cara, la rimembranza amara! hai sposo e padre, hai sposo e padre in me.

DON OTTAVIO: Let the bitter memory be, o dearest! you have a husband and a father, you have a husband and a father in me.

Donna Anna turns proudly and faces Don Ottavio.

DONNA ANNA: Ah! vendicar, se il puoi, giura quel sangue ognor!

DON OTTAVIO: Lo giuro, lo giuro, lo giuro agli occhi tuoi, lo giuro al nostro amor!

DONNA ANNA AND DON OTTAVIO: Che giuramento, oh Dei! che barbaro momento! tra cento affetti e cento vammi ondeggiando il cor, tra cento affetti e cento vammi ondeggiando il cor.

DONNA ANNA: Vendicar quel sangue, giura!

DON OTTAVIO: Lo giuro agli occhi tuoi, al nostro amor!

DONNA ANNA AND DON OTTAVIO: Che giuramento, o Dei! che barbaro momento! Tra cento affetti e cento vammi ondeggiando il cor, tra cento affetti e cento vammi ondeggiando il cor,—

DONNA ANNA: —vammi ondeggiando, ondeggiando il cor, vammi ondeggiando, ondeggiando il cor, vammi ondeggiando il cor—

DON OTTAVIO: —vammi ondeggiando il cor, vammi ondeggiando il cor, vammi ondeggiando il cor, vammi ondeggiando il cor, vammi ondeggiando il cor, vammi ondeggiando il cor—

DONNA ANNA: Ah! swear ever to avenge that blood, if you are able!

DON OTTAVIO: I swear it, I swear it, I swear it by your eyes, I swear it by our love!

DONNA ANNA AND DON OTTAVIO: What an oath, oh Gods! what a cruel moment! My heart is wavering midst a hundred, hundred sorrows, my heart is wavering midst a hundred, hundred sorrows.

DONNA ANNA: Swear to avenge that blood!

DON OTTAVIO: I swear it by your eyes, by our love!

DONNA ANNA AND DON OTTAVIO: What an oath, oh Gods! what a cruel moment! My heart is wavering midst a hundred, hundred sorrows, my heart is wavering midst a hundred, hundred sorrows,—

DONNA ANNA: —my heart is wavering, wavering, my heart is wavering, wavering, my heart is wavering,—

DON OTTAVIO: —my heart is wavering, my heart is wavering, my heart is wavering, my heart is wavering, my heart is wavering, my heart is wavering—

DONNA ANNA AND DON OTTAVIO: —vammi ondeggiando il cor, vammi ondeggiando il cor, vammi ondeggiando il cor, vammi ondeggiando il cor, vammi ondeggiando il cor, ondeggiando il cor.

DONNA ANNA AND DON OTTAVIO: —my heart is wavering, my heart is wavering, my heart is wavering, my heart is wavering, my heart is wavering, my heart is wavering.

Together they slowly enter the palace.

Scene Two

A morning or two later, on a street in Seville. Don Giovanni and Leporello enter, conversing.

DON GIOVANNI: Orsù, spicciati presto—cosa vuoi?

DON GIOVANNI: Come, speak up quickly—what do you want?

LEPORELLO: L'affar, di cui si tratta, è importante!

LEPORELLO: The matter in question is important!

DON GIOVANNI: Lo credo.

DON GIOVANNI: I believe it.

LEPORELLO: È importantissimo!

LEPORELLO: It is very, *very* important!

DON GIOVANNI: Meglio, ancora, finiscila!

DON GIOVANNI: All the better then, come out with it!

LEPORELLO: Giurate di non andar in collera!

LEPORELLO: Promise you won't get angry!

DON GIOVANNI: Lo giuro sul mio onore, purchè non parli del Commendatore.

DON GIOVANNI: On my honor I promise, just don't speak about the Commendatore.

LEPORELLO: Siamo soli?

LEPORELLO: Are we alone?

DON GIOVANNI: Lo vedo!

DON GIOVANNI: Yes indeed!

LEPORELLO: Nessun ci sente?

LEPORELLO: Nobody is listening to us?

DON GIOVANNI: Via!

DON GIOVANNI: Come!

LEPORELLO: Vi posso dire tutto liberamente?

DON GIOVANNI: Sì!

Leporello begins confidentially and ends almost shouting.

LEPORELLO: Dunque quand'è così—Caro Signor padrone, la vita che menate è da briccone!

DON GIOVANNI: Temerario, in tal guisa?

LEPORELLO: E il giuramento?

DON GIOVANNI: Non sò di giuramenti; taci, o ch'io—

LEPORELLO: Non parlo più, non fiato, o padron mio!

DON GIOVANNI: Così saremo amici, or odi un poco! sai tu perchè son qui?

LEPORELLO: Non ne sò nulla! ma essendo l'alba chiara, non sarebbe qualche nuova conquista? io lo devo saper, per porla in lista!

DON GIOVANNI: Va là, che sei il grand'uom! Sappi ch'io sono innamorato d'una bella dama, e son certo che m'ama; la vidi, le parlai, meco al casino questa notte verrà: Zitto! mi pare sentir odor di femmina!

LEPORELLO: I can speak to you in complete freedom?

DON GIOVANNI: Yes!

LEPORELLO: Now then, if it is so—my dear master, you're leading a rogue's life!

DON GIOVANNI: Foolhardy one! Do you speak to me in this manner?

LEPORELLO: And your promise?

DON GIOVANNI: I know of no promises; be quiet, or I—

LEPORELLO: I won't speak any more, I won't breathe, o my master!

DON GIOVANNI: That way we shall be friends, now listen a bit! do you know why I am here?

LEPORELLO: No, I know nothing about it! but since it's clearly daybreak, mightn't it be some new conquest? I ought to know, in order to put it on the list!

DON GIOVANNI: Go on, what a fine specimen you are! Know that I am in love with a beautiful lady, and I am certain she loves me; I saw her, I spoke to her, she will come with me to the casino tonight: Hush! I seem to smell femininity!

LEPORELLO: (Cospetto, che odorato perfetto!)

LEPORELLO: *Aside.* Lord, what a perfect sense of smell!

DON GIOVANNI: All'aria, mi par bella.

DON GIOVANNI: At first glance, she seems pretty.

LEPORELLO: (E che occhio! dico!)

LEPORELLO: *Aside.* And what an eye! I must say!

DON GIOVANNI: Ritiriamoci un poco, e scopriamo terren.

DON GIOVANNI: Let's withdraw here a little and look over the terrain.

LEPORELLO: (Già prese foco!)

LEPORELLO: *Aside.* Already he's caught fire!

*Don Giovanni and Leporello step into a doorway
as Donna Elvira enters.*

DONNA ELVIRA: Ah! chi mi dice mai, quel barbaro dov'è? che per mio scorno amai, che mi mancò di fè? che mi mancò di fè?

DONNA ELVIRA: Ah! who will ever tell me where the cruel man is? he whom I loved to my disgrace, who broke faith with me? who broke faith with me?

*Meanwhile, Leporello brushes and tidies Don Giovanni,
helping him to primp.*

Ah! se ritrovo l'empio, e a me non torna ancor, vo' farne orrendo scempio, gli vo' cavar il cor, gli vo' cavar il cor!

Ah! if I find the wicked man again, and he still does not come back to me, I will devise a dreadful torture for him, I will tear out his heart, I will tear out his heart!

Don Giovanni prods Leporello.

DON GIOVANNI: Udisti? qualche bella, dal vago abbandonata?

DON GIOVANNI: *To Leporello.* Did you hear? Some pretty lady, abandoned by her lover?

DONNA ELVIRA: Vo' farne orrendo scempio, gli vo' cavar il cor!

DONNA ELVIRA: I will devise a dreadful torture for him, I will tear out his heart!

DON GIOVANNI: Poverina! Poverina!

DONNA ELVIRA: Gli vo' cavar il cor; sì, gli vo' cavar il cor!

DON GIOVANNI: Cerchiam di consolare il suo tormento.

LEPORELLO: (Così ne consolò mille e otto cento.)

DONNA ELVIRA: Ah! chi mi dice mai, quel barbaro dov'è?

DON GIOVANNI: *With exaggerated pity.* Poor little thing! Poor little thing!

DONNA ELVIRA: I will tear out his heart; yes, I will tear out his heart!

DON GIOVANNI: *To Leporello.* Let's try to console her sorrow.

LEPORELLO: *Aside.* That's how he's consoled eighteen hundred of them.

DONNA ELVIRA: Ah! who will ever tell me where the cruel man is?

*Leporello unsuccessfully tries to see
Donna Elvira's face.*

che per mio scorno amai, che mi mancò di fè? che mi mancò di fè? Ah, se ritrovo l'empio, e a me non torna ancor, vo farne orrendo scempio, gli vo' cavar il cor!

he whom I loved to my disgrace, who broke faith with me? who broke faith with me? Ah, if I find the wicked man again, and he still does not come back to me, I will devise a dreadful torture for him, I will tear out his heart!

DON GIOVANNI: Poverina! Poverina!

DONNA ELVIRA: Gli vo' cavar il cor, sì, gli vo cavar il cor!

DON GIOVANNI: Cerchiam di consolare il suo tormento.

LEPORELLO: Così ne consolò mille e otto cento.

DONNA ELVIRA: Gli vo' cavare il cor, gli vo' cavare il cor, gli

DON GIOVANNI: *To Leporello.* Poor little thing! Poor little thing!

DONNA ELVIRA: I will tear out his heart, yes, I will tear out his heart!

DON GIOVANNI: *To Leporello.* Let's try to console her sorrow.

LEPORELLO: *Aside.* That's how he's consoled eighteen hundred of them.

DONNA ELVIRA: I will tear out his heart, I will tear out his

vo' cavar il cor, cavar il cor!

heart, I will tear out his heart, tear out his heart!

Don Giovanni grows more and more interested. He tries to attract Donna Elvira's attention, but failing to do so, finally approaches her with a sweeping bow.

DON GIOVANNI: Signorina! Signorina!

DONNA ELVIRA: Chi è là?

DON GIOVANNI: Signorina! Signorina!

DONNA ELVIRA: Who is there?

Don Giovanni is startled.

DON GIOVANNI: Stelle! che vedo!

LEPORELLO: O bella! Donna Elvira!

DONNA ELVIRA: Don Giovanni! sei qui? mostro! fellon! nido d'inganni!

LEPORELLO: Che titoli cruscanti! manco male che lo conosce bene.

DON GIOVANNI: Via, cara Donna Elvira, calmate questa collera! sentite, lasciatemi parlar!

DONNA ELVIRA: Cosa puoi dire, dopo azion si nera? In casa mia entri furtivamente, a forza d'arte, di giuramenti, e lusinghe arrivi a sedurre il cor mio; m'innamori, o crudele! mi dichiari tua sposa, e poi, mancando della terra e del ciel al santo dritto, con enorme delitto dopo tre dì da Burgos t'allontani, m'abbandoni, mi fuggi, e lasci in

DON GIOVANNI: *To himself.* Ye Gods! whom do I see!

LEPORELLO: *To himself.* O lovely! Donna Elvira!

DONNA ELVIRA: *Furiously.* Don Giovanni! are you here? monster! criminal! bundle of deceit!

LEPORELLO: *Aside.* What refined titles! she obviously knows him well.

DON GIOVANNI: Come now, dear Donna Elvira, calm this rage! Listen, let me speak!

DONNA ELVIRA: What can you say after such a black deed? You entered my house furtively, you managed to seduce my heart with the strength of your artfulness, with promises and flatteries; you won my love, o cruel man! you declared me your wife, and then, breaking the sacred law of heaven and earth, in an enormous misdeed, you left

preda al rimorso ed al pianto per pena forse che t'amai cotanto.

LEPORELLO: (Pare un libro stampato!)

DON GIOVANNI: Oh in quanto a questo ebbi le mie ragioni! è vero?

LEPORELLO: È vero! e che ragioni forti!

DONNA ELVIRA: E quali sono, se non la tua perfidia, la leggerezza tua? Ma il giusto cielo volle ch'io ti trovassi, per far le sue, le mie vendette.

DON GIOVANNI: Eh via, siate più ragionevole: (mi pone a cimento, costei) se non credete al labbro mio, credete a questo galantuomo.

LEPORELLO: (Salvo il vero.)

DON GIOVANNI: Via, dille un poco.

LEPORELLO: (E cosa devo dirle?)

DON GIOVANNI: Sì, sì, dille pur tutto.

*Leporello addresses Donna Elvira
as Don Giovanni slyly slips away.*

DONNA ELVIRA: Ebben, fa presto!

Burgos after three days, you abandoned me, you ran away from me, and perhaps as punishment for loving you so much, you left me the prey to remorse and weeping.

LEPORELLO: *Aside.* Just like a printed book!

DON GIOVANNI: Oh, as for this I had my good reasons! *To Leporello.* Isn't that so?

LEPORELLO: That's so! and what powerful reasons!

DONNA ELVIRA: And what are such reasons, if not your deceitfulness and inconstancy? But a just heaven willed that I would find you, in order to accomplish its own revenge and mine.

DON GIOVANNI: Oh come now, be more reasonable: (she puts me to the test, this one) if you don't believe it from my lips, believe this gentleman.

LEPORELLO: *Aside.* Except for the truth.

DON GIOVANNI: *To Leporello.* Go on, tell her a little.

LEPORELLO: *To Don Giovanni.* And what should I tell her?

DON GIOVANNI: Yes, yes, tell her everything.

DONNA ELVIRA: *To Leporello.* Well, be quick!

LEPORELLO: Madama, vera-mente, in questo mondo con-ciossiacosa quando fosse che il quadro non è tondo!

LEPORELLO: Madam, truly seeing that however it might be in this world, a square is not round!

DONNA ELVIRA: Sciagurato! Così del mio dolor gioco ti prendi?

DONNA ELVIRA: Villain! Are you making fun of my sor-row in this way?

She turns to find Don Giovanni gone.

Ah voi! stelle! l'iniquo fuggì! misera me! dove? in qual parte?

Ah you! ye gods! the scoundrel has escaped! unhappy me! where? where did he go?

LEPORELLO: Eh, lasciate che vada; egli non merta che di lui ci pensiate.

LEPORELLO: Oh, let him go; he isn't worth thinking about.

DONNA ELVIRA: Il scellerato m'ingannò, mi tradì!

DONNA ELVIRA: The villain de-ceived me, he betrayed me!

She sadly turns to a bench and sits down.

LEPORELLO: Eh, consolatevi! non siete voi, non foste, e non sarete nè la prima, nè l'ulti-ma;

LEPORELLO: Oh, console your-self! you are not, you were not, and you will not be the first one or the last one;

Leporello produces a long quarto or scroll, which he opens so that it extends from his hands to the floor. He shows this to Donna Elvira.

guardate, questo non picciol libro è tutto pieno dei nomi di sue belle; ogni villa, ogni borgo, ogni paese, è testimon di sue donnesche imprese.

look, this not-so-small book is completely filled with the names of his beauties; every home, every village, every town has witnessed his enter-prises with womankind.

Madamina: il catalogo è questo delle belle che amò il padron mio; un catalogo egli è, che ho fatto io; osservate, leggete con me! osservate, leggete con me! In Italia sei

Dear lady: this is a catalogue of the beauties my master has loved; it is a catalogue which I have made; look at it, read it with me! look at it, read it with me! In Italy, six hundred and

(Courtesy San Francisco Opera Company, photo by Carolyn Mason Jones)

Act 1, Scene 2. Don Giovanni and Leporello admire Elvira as she wonders where the Don has fled ("Ah, chi mi dice mai"). In this San Francisco production Elisabeth Schwarzkopf is Donna Elvira, Giorgio Tozzi is Don Giovanni and Geraint Evans is Leporello.

(Courtesy Bolshoi Theater, Moscow)

Act 1, Scene 2. Leporello unfurls the catalogue of Don Giovanni's conquests for Elvira's edification. N. F. Shchegol'kov is Leporello.

Act 1, Scene 3. Don Giovanni makes the acquaintance of Zerlina, much to the chagrin of Masetto. Giorgio Tozzi is the Don, Jolanda Meneguzzer is Zerlina and Joshua Hecht is Masetto.

Ƨ.Ƨ.Ƨ.73

cento e quaranta; in Almagna due cento e trent'una, cento in Francia, in Turchia novant'una; ma in Ispagna, ma in Ispagna son già mille e tre! mille e tre! mille e tre!

V'han fra queste contadine, cameriere, cittadine, v'han contesse, baronesse, marchesane, principesse, e v'han donne d'ogni grado, d'ogni forma, d'ogni età, d'ogni forma, d'ogni età. In Italia sei cento e quaranta, In Almagna due cento e trent'una, cento in Francia, in Turchia novant'una, ma, ma, ma in Ispagna! ma in Ispagna son già mille e tre, mille e tre, mille e tre!

V'han fra queste contadine, cameriere, cittadine, v'han contesse, baronesse, marchesane, principesse, e v'han donne d'ogni grado, d'ogni forma, d'ogni età! d'ogni forma, d'ogni età! d'ogni forma, d'ogni età!

Nella bionda egli ha l'usanza di lodar la gentilezza, nella bruna la costanza, nella bianca la dolcezza. Vuol d'inverno la grassotta, vuol d'estate la magrotta. È la grande maestosa, è la grande maes-

forty; In Germany, two hundred and thirty-one, one hundred in France, ninety-one in Turkey; but in Spain, but in Spain there are already a thousand and three! a thousand and three! a thousand and three!

Among these there are countrywomen, chambermaids, citywomen, there are countesses, baronesses, marchionesses, princesses, and there are women of every rank, of every shape, of every age, of every shape, of every age. In Italy, six hundred and forty, In Germany, two hundred and thirty-one, one hundred in France, ninety-one in Turkey, but, but, but in Spain! but in Spain there are already a thousand and three, a thousand and three, a thousand and three!

Among these there are countrywomen, chambermaids, citywomen, there are countesses, baronesses, marchionesses, princesses, and there are women of every rank, of every shape, of every age! of every shape, of every age! of every shape, of every age!

With blondes it is his custom to praise their gentleness, with brunettes their constancy, with white-haired ones their sweetness. In winter he wants plumpness, in summer he wants leanness. The tall woman

tosa; la piccina, la piccina, la piccina, la piccina, la piccina, la piccina, la piccina, la piccina, la piccina è ognor vezzosa, è ognor vezzosa, è ognor vezzosa; delle vecchie fa conquista, pel piacer di porle in lista. Sua passion predominante è la giovin principiante; non si picca se sia ricca, se sia brutta, se sia bella, se sia ricca, brutta, se sia bella, purchè porti la gonnella, voi sapete quel che fa, voi sapete quel che fa, purchè porti la gonnella, voi sapete quel che fa, voi sapete, voi sapete quel che fa, quel che fa, quel che fa, voi sapete quel che fa.

is stately, the tall woman is stately; the little tiny girl, the little tiny girl, the little tiny girl, the little tiny girl, the little tiny girl, the little tiny girl, the little tiny girl, the little tiny girl, the little tiny girl is always charming, is always charming, is always charming; he makes conquests among old women for the pleasure of adding them to the list. His outstanding passion is the youthful beginner; he doesn't care if she's rich, if she's ugly, if she's beautiful, if she's rich, ugly, if she's beautiful, provided she wears a skirt, *you* know what he does, *you* know what he does, provided she wears a skirt, *you* know what he does, *you* know, *you* know what he does, what he does, what he does, *you* know what he does.

Leporello bows himself hurriedly off the stage.

DONNA ELVIRA: In questa forma dunque mi tradì il scellerato! è questo il premio che quel barbaro rende all'amor mio! Ah, vendicar vogl'io l'ingannato mio cor! pria ch'ei mi fugga, si ricorra, si vada; io sento in petto sol vendetta parlar, rabbia e dispetto!

In this manner, then, the villain betrayed me! this is the reward which that cruel man offers for my love! Ah, I want to avenge my deceived heart! before he flies from me, let me after him, let me go; in my breast I only hear revenge speaking, rage and spite!

Exit Donna Elvira.

Scene Three

This scene is supposed to take place in the countryside, near Don Giovanni's castle. Actually, it is often presented in the same setting as Scene Two, with little or no pause in the action. Zerlina and Masetto enter, surrounded by peasant youths and maidens who dance around them.

ZERLINA: Giovinette, che fate all'amore, che fate all'amore, non lasciate che passi l'età, che passi l'età! che passi l'età! Se nel seno vi bulica il core, vi bulica il core, il rimedio vedetelo quà! che piacer, che piacer che sarà!

ZERLINA: *To the girls.* Young maids who play at love, who play at love, don't let your youth pass by, your youth pass by! your youth pass by! If your heart leaps, if your heart leaps in your breast, you see the cure for it right here! what fun, what fun it will be!

GIRLS: Ah! che piacer, che piacer che sarà, lalarelala, lalarelala!

GIRLS: Ah! what fun, what fun it will be, lalarelala, lalarelala!

MASETTO: Giovinetti, leggieri di testa, leggieri di testa, non andate girando di quà e là e là e quà e là; poco dura de'matti la festa, de'matti la festa, ma per me cominciato non ha, cominciato non ha!

MASETTO: *To the boys.* Young lads, be carefree, be carefree, don't go moping about hither and yon, and yon and hither and yon; the fools' holiday, the fools' holiday will just last a short while, but for me it hasn't begun, it hasn't begun!

BOYS: Che piacer, che piacer che sarà! Che piacer, che piacer che sarà! lalarelala, lalarelala!

BOYS: What fun, what fun it will be! What fun, what fun it will be! lalarelala, lalarelala!

Both groups move toward center stage; Zerlina and Masetto come forward as the others continue to dance around them.

ZERLINA AND MASETTO: Vieni, vieni {carino, carina,} godiamo, e cantiamo, e balliamo, e suoniamo, vieni, vieni {carino, carina,} godiamo, che piacer, che piacer che sarà. Ah! che piacer, che piacer che sarà!

CHORUS: Ah! che piacer, che piacer che sarà! Lalarelala, relala, relala, lalarelala, relala, relala!

Meanwhile Don Giovanni and Leporello have appeared and are watching.

DON GIOVANNI: (Manco male, è partita.) Oh guarda, guarda che bella gioventù! che belle donne!

LEPORELLO: (Fra tante, per mia fè, vi sarà qualche cosa anche per me.)

Leporello advances toward the girls as Don Giovanni accosts Zerlina and Masetto.

DON GIOVANNI: Cari amici, buon giorno! seguitate a stare allegramente, seguitate a suonar, o buona gente! C'è qualche sposalizio?

Zerlina curtsies to the Don.

ZERLINA: Sì, Signore, e la sposa son io.

DON GIOVANNI: Me ne consolo —lo sposo?

ZERLINA AND MASETTO: Come, come dear, let's be merry, and let's sing, and let's dance, and let's rejoice, come, come dear, let's be merry, what fun, what fun it will be. Ah! what fun, what fun it will be!

CHORUS: Ah! what fun, what fun it will be! Lalarelala, relala, relala, lalarelala, relala, relala!

DON GIOVANNI: *Aside.* Good enough, she's gone. *To Leporello.* Oh look, look what attractive young people! what pretty girls!

LEPORELLO: *To himself.* By my faith, among so many, there will be something for me too.

DON GIOVANNI: Good day, dear friends! go on being merry, go on rejoicing, o good people! Is there a wedding?

ZERLINA: Yes, Sir, and I am the bride.

DON GIOVANNI: I'm glad of it— and the bridegroom?

Masetto comes forward with an awkward bow.

MASETTO: Io, per servirla.

DON GIOVANNI: Oh, bravo! per servirmi; questo è vero parlar da galantuomo.

LEPORELLO: (Basta, che sia marito!)

ZERLINA: Oh, il mio Masetto è un uom d'ottimo core.

DON GIOVANNI: Oh, anch'io, vedete! voglio che siamo amici; il vostro nome?

ZERLINA: Zerlina.

DON GIOVANNI: E il tuo?

MASETTO: Masetto.

MASETTO: I, at your service.

DON GIOVANNI: Oh, good! at my service; this is spoken like a gallant.

LEPORELLO: *Aside.* It's enough that he be a husband!

ZERLINA: Oh, my Masetto is a man of the best heart.

DON GIOVANNI: Oh, I too, do you see! I want us to be friends. *To Zerlina.* Your name?

ZERLINA: Zerlina.

DON GIOVANNI: *To Masetto.* And yours?

MASETTO: Masetto.

Don Giovanni slips one arm around Zerlina's waist and the other around Masetto.

DON GIOVANNI: O caro il mio Masetto! cara la mia Zerlina! v'esibisco la mia protezione: Leporello! cosa fai lì, birbone?

DON GIOVANNI: O my dear Masetto! my dear Zerlina! I offer you my protection: Leporello! what are you doing over there, rascal?

Leporello answers from among the peasant girls.

LEPORELLO: Anch'io, caro padrone, esibisco la mia protezione.

DON GIOVANNI: Presto va con costor; nel mio palazzo conducili sul fatto: ordina ch'abbiano cioccolate, caffè, vini, presciutti; cerca divertir tutti, mostra loro il giardino, la galleria, le camere; in effetto fa che resti contento il mio Masetto, hai capito?

LEPORELLO: I too, dear master, am offering my protection.

DON GIOVANNI: Go quickly with these people; take them to my palace immediately: order chocolate, coffee, wines, hams for them; try to amuse everyone, show them the garden, the gallery, the rooms; in short, see to it that Masetto is happy, do you understand?

At the last phrase he gives Leporello an insinuating dig in the side.

LEPORELLO: Ho capito; andiam.

LEPORELLO: I understand. *To the peasants.* Let's go.

MASETTO: Signore!

MASETTO: Sir!

DON GIOVANNI: Cosa c'è?

DON GIOVANNI: What is it?

He holds back Zerlina as the other peasants leave.

MASETTO: La Zerlina senza me non può star.

MASETTO: Zerlina can't stay without me.

LEPORELLO: In vostro loco ci sarà sua Eccellenza, e saprà bene fare le vostri parti.

LEPORELLO: *To Masetto.* His Excellency will be here in your place, and he can well take your part.

DON GIOVANNI: Oh, la Zerlina è in man d'un Cavalier; va pur, fra poco ella meco verrà.

DON GIOVANNI: Oh, Zerlina is is in the hands of a nobleman; you go now, she'll come with me in a little while.

ZERLINA: Va! non temere! nelle mani son io d'un Cavaliere.

ZERLINA: Go on! don't be afraid! I'm in the hands of a nobleman.

MASETTO: E per questo?

MASETTO: And so?

ZERLINA: E per questo non c'è da dubitar.

ZERLINA: And so there's nothing to worry about.

Masetto tries to pull Zerlina with him.

MASETTO: Ed io, cospetto—

MASETTO: And I, confound it—

Don Giovanni separates them cleverly.

DON GIOVANNI: Olà, finiam le dispute! Se subito senza altro replicar non te ne vai, Masetto, guarda ben, ti pentirai!

DON GIOVANNI: Well, let's put an end to the argument. If you don't leave immediately without another word, Masetto, look out, you'll be sorry!

Don Giovanni taps his sword significantly, and Masetto, somewhat abashed, begins to back away.

MASETTO: Ho capito, Signor, sì! Signor, sì! Chino il capo e me ne vo, giacchè piace a voi così, altre repliche non fo, no, no, no, no, no, no, non fo. Cavalier voi siete già, dubitar non posso affè, me lo dice la bontà che volete aver per me, aver per me, aver per me.

MASETTO: I understand, yes, Sir! yes, Sir! I'll bow my head and go away, since this is your pleasure, I have no further answers, no, no, no, no, no, no, I have not. You are indeed a nobleman, in faith, I cannot doubt it, the kindness which you have for me, have for me, have for me, tells me so.

He turns to Zerlina.

Bricconaccia, malandrina, fosti ognor la mia ruina, fosti ognor la mia ruina!

Little minx, evil girl, you were always my ruin, you were always my ruin!

He turns to Leporello who is waiting to take him away.

Vengo, vengo!
Resta, resta!

È una cosa molto onesta!

Faccia il nostro Cavaliere Cavaliera ancora te, Cavaliera ancora te. Bricconaccia, malandrina! fosti ognor la mia ruina, fosti ognor la mia ruina!
Vengo, vengo!

Resta, resta! È una cosa molto onesta! faccia il nostro Cavaliere Cavaliera ancora te, Cavaliera ancora te, faccia il nostro Cavaliere Cavaliera ancora te, faccia il nostro Cavaliere Cavaliera ancora te, Cavaliera ancora te, Cavaliera ancora te!

I'm coming, I'm coming!
To Zerlina: Stay here, stay here!
To himself. It's a very fine situation!
To Zerlina, with bitterness. Let our gentleman make a lady even of you, a lady even of you. Little minx, evil girl! you were always my ruin, you were always my ruin!
To Leporello. I'm coming, I'm coming!
To Zerlina. Stay here, stay here! It's a very fine situation! Let our gentleman make a lady even of you, a lady even of you, let our gentleman make a lady even of you, let our gentleman make a lady even of you, a lady even of you, a lady even of you!

Leporello finally succeeds in leading Masetto away.

DON GIOVANNI: Al fin siam liberati, Zerlinetta gentil, da quel scioccone, che ne dite, mio ben? sò far pulito?

DON GIOVANNI: At last we're free of that stupid oaf, pretty little Zerlina, what do you say to that, my dear? do I know how to get what I want?

He tries to put his arm around Zerlina,
but she shrinks back.

ZERLINA: Signore, è mio marito!

ZERLINA: Sir, he's my fiancé!

DON GIOVANNI: Chi? colui? vi par che un onest'uomo, un nobil Cavalier, qual io mi vanto, possa soffrir che quel visetto d'oro, quel viso inzuccherato da un bifolcaccio vil sia strapazzato?

DON GIOVANNI: Who? He? do you think that an honest man, a noble gentleman such as I am proud of being, can suffer that little precious face, that sweet face, to be insulted by a low boor?

ZERLINA: Ma Signor, io gli diedi parola di sposarlo.

ZERLINA: But Sir, I gave him my word to marry him.

DON GIOVANNI: Tal parola non vale un zero: voi non siete fatta per esser paesana, un altra sorte vi procuran quegli occhi bricconcelli, quei labbretti sì belli, quelle dituccia candide e odorose; parmi toccar giuncata, e fiutar rose.

DON GIOVANNI: Such a word is not worth anything: you are not destined to be a peasant, those roguish little eyes will win you another lot, those lovely little lips, those white and fragrant little fingers; it's like touching reeds and smelling roses.

ZERLINA: Ah, non vorrei—

ZERLINA: Ah, I wouldn't—

DON GIOVANNI: Che non vorréste?

DON GIOVANNI: What wouldn't you?

ZERLINA: Alfine ingannata restar. Io sò che raro colle donne voi altri cavalieri siete onesti e sinceri.

ZERLINA: Be betrayed in the end. I know how seldom it is that you noblemen are honest and sincere with women.

DON GIOVANNI: Eh, un'impostura della gente plebea! la

DON GIOVANNI: Oh, that's a slander among the common

nobiltà ha dipinta negli occhi l'onestà. Orsù, non perdiam tempo; in questo istante io vi voglio sposar.

ZERLINA: Voi?

Don Giovanni waves a hand in the direction of his castle.

DON GIOVANNI: Certo, io. Quel casinetto è mio, soli saremo. E là, giojello mio, ci sposeremo. Là ci darem la mano, là mi dirai di sì; vedi, non è lontano, partiam, ben mio, da qui.

ZERLINA: Vorrei, e non vorrei, mi trema un poco il cor, felice, è ver, sarei ma può burlarmi ancor, ma può burlarmi ancor!

DON GIOVANNI: Vieni, mio bel diletto!

ZERLINA: Mi fa pietà Masetto!

DON GIOVANNI: Io cangierò tua sorte!

ZERLINA: Presto non son più forte, non son più forte, non son più forte!

Meanwhile, Donna Elvira appears on the sidelines and watches these goings-on.

DON GIOVANNI: Vieni, vieni! Là ci darem la mano—

ZERLINA: Vorrei, e non vorrei—

people! the aristocracy has honesty painted in its eyes. Now then, let's not lose any time; I want to marry you this instant.

ZERLINA: You?

DON GIOVANNI: Certainly, I. That little house is mine, we shall be alone. And there, my jewel, we shall wed one another. There we shall join our hands, there you shall say yes to me; you see, it isn't far away, let's go, my dear.

ZERLINA: I would, and I would not, my heart is trembling a little, I would be happy, it's true, but you may yet be making fun of me, but you may yet be making fun of me!

DON GIOVANNI: Come, my lovely delight!

ZERLINA: I feel sorry for Masetto!

DON GIOVANNI: I'll change your lot!

ZERLINA: Soon I'll no longer resist, I'll no longer resist, I'll no longer resist!

DON GIOVANNI: Come, come! There we shall join hands—

ZERLINA: I would, and I would not—

DON GIOVANNI: Là mi dirai di sì—

ZERLINA: Mi trema un poco il cor—

DON GIOVANNI: Partiam, ben mio, da qui—

ZERLINA: Ma può burlarmi ancor—

DON GIOVANNI: Vieni, mio bel diletto—

ZERLINA: Mi fa pietà Masetto—

She coyly ducks under the Don's arm to the other side.

DON GIOVANNI: Io cangierò tua sorte—

ZERLINA: Presto non son più forte, non son più forte, non son più forte!

DON GIOVANNI: Andiam! Andiam!

Zerlina flings herself at the Don.

ZERLINA: Andiam!

ZERLINA AND DON GIOVANNI: Andiam, andiam, mio bene, a ristorar le pene d'un innocente amor! Andiam, andiam, mio bene, a ristorar le pene d'un innocente amor!

DON GIOVANNI: Andiam!

ZERLINA: Andiam! Andiam!

DON GIOVANNI: Andiam!

ZERLINA AND DON GIOVANNI: Andiam, mio bene, andiam, le pene a ristorar d'un innocente amor!

DON GIOVANNI: There you shall say yes to me—

ZERLINA: My heart is trembling a little—

DON GIOVANNI: Let's go, my dear, from here—

ZERLINA: You may yet be making fun of me—

DON GIOVANNI: Come, my lovely delight—

ZERLINA: I feel sorry for Masetto—

DON GIOVANNI: I'll change your lot—

ZERLINA: Soon I'll no longer resist, I'll no longer resist, I'll no longer resist!

DON GIOVANNI: Let us go! Let us go!

ZERLINA: Let us go!

ZERLINA AND DON GIOVANNI: Let us go, let us go, my dear, to relieve the pangs of an innocent love! Let us go, let us go, my dear, to relieve the pangs of an innocent love!

DON GIOVANNI: Let us go!

ZERLINA: Let us go! Let us go!

DON GIOVANNI: Let us go!

ZERLINA AND DON GIOVANNI: Let us go, my dear, let us go to relieve the pangs of an innocent love!

Donna Elvira, who has been moving nearer and nearer to the pair during all this, catches up with them and stops them, just as they are about to leave with their arms around one another.

DONNA ELVIRA: Fermati, scellerato! il ciel mi fece udir le perfidie; io sono a tempo di salvar questa misera innocente dal tuo barbaro artiglio!

ZERLINA: Meschina! cosa sento!

DON GIOVANNI: (Amor, consiglio!)
Idol mio, non vedete ch'io voglio divertirmi?

DONNA ELVIRA: Divertirti? È vero! divertirti! io sò, crudele, come tu ti diverti.

ZERLINA: Ma, Signor Cavaliere, è ver quel ch'ella dice?

DON GIOVANNI: La povera infelice è di me innamorata, e per pietà deggio fingere amore; ch'io son per mia disgrazia uom di buon core.

DONNA ELVIRA: Ah! fuggi il traditor! Non lo lasciar più dir; il labbro è mentitor, fallace il ciglio! Dai miei tormenti impara a creder a quel cor; e nasca il tuo timor dal mio periglio, ah fuggi, fuggi! Ah, fuggi il traditor! non lo

DONNA ELVIRA: Stop, villain! heaven made me overhear your lies; I am in time to save this unhappy innocent girl from your cruel clutches!

ZERLINA: Poor me! what do I hear!

DON GIOVANNI: *To himself.* Cupid, help me!
Aside to Donna Elvira. My idol, don't you see that I want to amuse myself?

DONNA ELVIRA: Amuse yourself? That's true! amuse yourself! Cruel man, I know how you amuse yourself.

ZERLINA: *To Don Giovanni.* But Sir Nobleman, is what she says true?

DON GIOVANNI: *To Zerlina.* The poor unhappy thing is in love with me, and out of pity I must pretend to love her; it's my undoing that I'm a kindhearted man.

DONNA ELVIRA: Ah! fly from the betrayer! Do not let him say any more; his lips are lying, his brow is deceitful! Learn from my suffering to believe my heart; and may my danger give birth to your fear, ah fly, fly! Ah, fly from the

lasciar più dir; il labbro è mentitor, fallace il ciglio, il labbro è mentitor, fallace il ciglio, sì, fallace il ciglio!

betrayer! Do not let him say any more; his lips are lying, his brow is deceitful, his lips are lying, his brow is deceitful, yes, his brow is deceitful!

Donna Elvira takes Zerlina by the hand and they exit together. Donna Anna, dressed in deep mourning, enters with Don Ottavio.

DON GIOVANNI: Mi par ch'oggi il demonio si diverta d'opporsi a miei piacevoli progressi; vanno mal tutti quanti.

DON GIOVANNI: I think today the devil is amusing himself by opposing the progress of my pleasure; everything is going wrong.

DON OTTAVIO: Ah ch'ora, idolo mio, son vani i pianti, di vendetta si parli! Oh, Don Giovanni!

DON OTTAVIO: Ah, my idol, now tears are in vain, one must speak of revenge! Oh, Don Giovanni!

DON GIOVANNI: (Mancava questo, in ver!)

DON GIOVANNI: *To himself.* Just what I needed, in truth!

DONNA ANNA: Signore, a tempo vi ritroviam: avete core? avete anima generosa?

DONNA ANNA: *To Don Giovanni.* Sir, we meet you at the right time: have you a heart? have you a noble spirit?

DON GIOVANNI: (Sta a vedere che il diavolo le ha detto qualche cosa.)
Che domanda! perchè?

DON GIOVANNI: *To himself.* I can see that the devil has told her something.
To Donna Anna. What a question! why?

DONNA ANNA: Bisogno abbiamo della vostra amicizia.

DONNA ANNA: We have need of your friendship.

DON GIOVANNI: (Mi torna il fiato in corpo.)
Comandate; i congiunti, i parenti, questa man, questo ferro, i beni, il sangue spenderò per servirvi: ma voi, bella Donn'Anna, perchè così piangete? Il crudele chi

DON GIOVANNI: *To himself.* I can breathe again.
To Donna Anna. Command it: my friends, my relatives, this hand, this sword, my wealth, my life—I would sacrifice them all to serve you: but you, beautiful Donna Anna, why

Act 1, Scene 3. Don Giovanni invites Zerlina to his *casinetto* ("Là ci darem la mano").

Act 1, Scene 3. Don Giovanni offers his aid to Donna Anna in her distress. Left to right: Charles K. L. Davis as Ottavio, Leontyne Price as Donna Anna and Cesare Siepi as the Don.

(Courtesy Bolshoi Theater, Moscow)

Act 1, Scene 3. Don Ottavio and Donna Anna are puzzled as Don Giovanni and Donna Elvira exchange recriminations ("Non ti fidar, o misera").

fu che osò la calma turbar del viver vostro?

are you weeping like this? What cruel person dared trouble your tranquil life?

Donna Elvira returns.

DONNA ELVIRA: Ah, ti ritrovo ancor, perfido mostro? Non ti fidar, o misera, di quel ribaldo cor! me già tradì quel barbaro, te vuol tradir ancor.

DONNA ELVIRA: Ah, do I meet you again, lying monster? *To Donna Anna.* o unhappy woman, do not place your trust in that evil heart! that cruel man has already betrayed me, he wants to betray you, too.

DONNA ANNA AND DON OTTAVIO: Cieli! che aspetto nobile! che dolce maestà! il suo dolor, le lagrime m'empiono di pietà, m'empiono di pietà!

DONNA ANNA AND DON OTTAVIO: Heavens! what a noble aspect! what sweet dignity! her sorrow, her tears fill me with pity, fill me with pity!

Don Giovanni attempts to pull Donna Elvira away, but she refuses to leave. Presently he takes her hand and draws her beside him.

DON GIOVANNI: La povera ragazza è pazza, amici miei! lasciatemi con lei, è pazza, amici miei, forse si calmerà, forse si calmerà!

DON GIOVANNI: *In a stage whisper.* The poor girl is mad, my friends! leave me with her, she's mad, my friends, perhaps she'll pull herself together, perhaps she'll pull herself together!

DONNA ELVIRA: Ah! non credete al perfido!

DONNA ELVIRA: Ah! don't believe the liar!

DON GIOVANNI: È pazza, non badate!

DON GIOVANNI: She's mad, don't pay any attention!

DONNA ELVIRA: Restate, oh Dei, restate!

DONNA ELVIRA: Stay here, ye Gods, stay here!

DONNA ANNA AND DON OTTAVIO: A chi si crederà?—

DONNA ANNA AND DON OTTAVIO: *Aside.* Whom should one believe?

DON GIOVANNI: È pazza!

DON GIOVANNI: She's mad!

DONNA ANNA AND DON OTTAVIO: A chi si crederà?

DONNA ELVIRA: Restate!

DONNA ANNA AND DON OTTAVIO: A chi si crederà? si crederà?

DONNA ELVIRA: Ah non credete al perfido! restate!

DONNA ANNA, DON OTTAVIO AND DON GIOVANNI: Certo moto d'ignoto tormento—

DONNA ELVIRA: Sdegno, rabbia, dispetto, pavento—

DONNA ANNA, DON OTTAVIO AND DON GIOVANNI: —dentro l'alma girar mi sento—

DONNA ELVIRA: —dentro l'alma girar mi sento—

DONNA ANNA: —che mi dice per quella infelice cento cose, che intender, che intender non sa, no, no!

DONNA ELVIRA: —che mi dice di quel traditore cento cose che intender non sa, no—

DON GIOVANNI: —che mi dice per quella infelice cento cose, che intender non sa, no, no!

DON OTTAVIO: —che mi dice per quella infelice cento cose, che intender non sa, no, no!

DONNA ANNA AND DON OTTAVIO: *Aside.* Whom should one believe?

DONNA ELVIRA: Stay here!

DONNA ANNA AND DON OTTAVIO: Whom should one believe? should one believe?

DONNA ELVIRA: Ah don't believe the liar! stay here!

DONNA ANNA, DON OTTAVIO AND DON GIOVANNI: I feel an impulse of unknown anguish—

DONNA ELVIRA: Anger, fury, spite, fear—

DONNA ANNA, DON OTTAVIO AND DON GIOVANNI:—turning within my mind—

DONNA ELVIRA: —turning within my mind—

DONNA ANNA: —something that tells me a hundred things in favor of that unhappy girl, which it cannot speak, speak, no, no!

DONNA ELVIRA: —something that tells me a hundred things about that betrayer, which it cannot speak, no—

DON GIOVANNI: —something that tells me a hundred things in favor of that unhappy girl, which it cannot speak, no, no!

DON OTTAVIO: —something that tells me a hundred things in favor of that unhappy girl, which it cannot speak, no, no!

DONNA ELVIRA: —che mi dice di quel traditore, di quel traditore cento cose, che intender non sa, che mi dice, mi dice di quel traditore cento cose che intender non sa!

DON GIOVANNI: —cento cose che intender non sa, cento cose che intender non sa!

DONNA ANNA AND DON OTTAVIO: —che intender non sa, che intender non sa!

DON OTTAVIO: Io di quà non vado via, se non sò com'è l'affar!

DONNA ANNA: Non ha l'aria di pazzia il suo tratto, il suo parlar.

DON GIOVANNI: Se men vado, si potria qualche cosa sospettar.

DONNA ELVIRA: —something that tells me a hundred things about that betrayer, about that betrayer, which it cannot speak, something that tells me, tells me a hundred things about that betrayer, which it cannot speak!

DON GIOVANNI: —a hundred things which it cannot speak, a hundred things which it cannot speak!

DONNA ANNA AND DON OTTAVIO: —which it cannot speak, which it cannot speak!

DON OTTAVIO: *Aside.* I shall not leave here if I don't know how this matter goes!

DONNA ANNA: *Aside.* She does not have the appearance of madness in her bearing, in her speech.

DON GIOVANNI: *Aside.* If I go away, somebody may suspect something.

Donna Elvira angrily turns to Don Giovanni.

DONNA ELVIRA: Da quel ceffo si dovria la ner'alma giudicar.

DON OTTAVIO: Dunque quella—?

DON GIOVANNI: È pazzarella!

DONNA ANNA: Dunque quegli—?

DONNA ELVIRA: È un traditore—

DONNA ELVIRA: One ought to recognize your black soul by your ugly face.

DON OTTAVIO: *To Don Giovanni.* Then she—?

DON GIOVANNI: She's a little crazy!

DONNA ANNA: *To Donna Elvira.* Then he—?

DONNA ELVIRA: He's a betrayer—

DON GIOVANNI: Infelice!

DONNA ELVIRA: —mentitore, mentitore, mentitore!

DONNA ANNA AND DON OTTAVIO: Incomincio a dubitar.

DON GIOVANNI: Zitta, zitta, che la gente si raduna a noi d'intorno. Siate un poco più prudente, vi farete criticar.

DONNA ELVIRA: Non sperarlo, o scellerato, ho perduta la prudenza, le tue colpe ed il mio stato voglio a tutti palesar, voglio a tutti palesar!

DON GIOVANNI: Zitta, zitta, che la gente si raduna a noi d'intorno, siate un poco più prudente, vi farete criticar, siate un poco più prudente!

Donna Anna and Don Ottavio look at Don Giovanni curiously.

DONNA ANNA AND DON OTTAVIO: Quegli accenti sì sommessi, quel cangiarsi di colore, son indizi troppo espressi—

DONNA ELVIRA: Non sperarlo, o scellerato! ho perduta la prudenza! le tue colpe ed il mio stato voglio a tutti palesar, ho perduta la prudenza!

DON GIOVANNI: Unhappy girl!

DONNA ELVIRA: *To Don Giovanni.* —liar, liar, liar!

DONNA ANNA AND DON OTTAVIO: I am beginning to have doubts.

DON GIOVANNI: *Aside to Donna Elvira.* Hush, hush, for a crowd is gathering around us. Be a little more prudent, you'll make yourself ridiculous.

DONNA ELVIRA: *To Don Giovanni.* Don't hope it, o villain, I have lost my prudence, I want to show everyone your guilt and my condition, I want to show everyone!

DON GIOVANNI: *To Donna Elvira.* Hush, hush, for a crowd is gathering around us, be a little more prudent, you'll make yourself ridiculous, be a little more prudent!

DONNA ANNA AND DON OTTAVIO: Those very subdued tones, that change of coloring are expressive enough signs—

DONNA ELVIRA: Don't hope it, o villain! I have lost my prudence! I want to show everyone your guilt and my condition, I have lost my prudence!

DONNA ANNA AND DON OTTA-
VIO: —che mi fan determin-
ar—

DON GIOVANNI: Zitto, zitto!—
che la gente—

DONNA ELVIRA: Non sperarlo!

DON GIOVANNI: —si raduna a
noi d'intorno!

DONNA ELVIRA: —ho perduta
la prudenza, non sperarlo, o
scellerato! le tue colpe ed il
mio stato voglio a tutti palesar!

DONNA ANNA AND DON OTTA-
VIO: —che mi fan deter-
minar, che mi fan determin-
ar!

DON GIOVANNI: —zitto, zitto!
che la gente, siate un poco
più prudente! vi farete, vi
farete criticar!

DONNA ANNA AND DON OTTA-
VIO: —to make me resolve—

DON GIOVANNI: Hush, hush!
For a crowd—

DONNA ELVIRA: Don't hope it!

DON GIOVANNI: —is gathering
around us!

DONNA ELVIRA: —I have lost
my prudence, don't hope it, o
villain! I want to show everyone your guilt and my condition!

DONNA ANNA AND DON OTTA-
VIO: —to make me resolve, to
make me resolve!

DON GIOVANNI: —hush, hush!
for a crowd, be a little more
prudent! you'll make yourself,
you'll make yourself ridiculous!

*Don Giovanni finally manages to draw Donna Elvira
away from the scene, and then returns to the others.*

DON GIOVANNI: Povera sven-
turata! i passi suoi voglio se-
guir; non voglio che faccia
un precipizio: Perdonate,
bellissima Donn'Anna! se
servirvi poss'io, in mia casa
v'aspetto. Amici, addio!

DON GIOVANNI: Poor wretched
girl! I will follow her; I
don't want her to do anything
rash: Pardon me, most beautiful Donna Anna! if I can serve
you, I shall await you in my
house. Friends, goodbye!

*He leaves hastily, pretending to follow Donna Elvira.
Donna Anna becomes very upset.*

DONNA ANNA: Don Ottavio!
son morta!

DONNA ANNA: Don Ottavio! I
am dead!

DON OTTAVIO: Cosa è stato?

DONNA ANNA: Per pietà, soccorretemi!

DON OTTAVIO: Mio bene, fate coraggio!

Donna Anna makes a sweeping gesture in the direction of Don Giovanni's exit.

DONNA ANNA: O Dei! O Dei! Quegli è il carnefice del padre mio!

DON OTTAVIO: Che dite?

DONNA ANNA: Non dubitate più; gli ultimi accenti che l'empio proferì, tutta la voce, richiamar nel cor mio di quell'indegno, che nel mio appartamento—

DON OTTAVIO: Oh ciel! possibile, che sotto il sacro manto d'amicizia—ma come fu, narratemi lo strano avvenimento.

DONNA ANNA: Era già alquanto avanzata la notte, quando nelle mie stanze, ove soletta mi trovai per sventura, entrar io vidi in un mantello avvolto un uom che al primo istante avea preso per voi; ma riconobbi poi, che un'inganno era il mio!

DON OTTAVIO: Stelle! seguite!

DONNA ANNA: Tacito a me s'appressa, e mi vuole abbracciar; scogliermi cerco, ei

DON OTTAVIO: What is the matter?

DONNA ANNA: For pity's sake, help me!

DON OTTAVIO: Have courage, my dear!

DONNA ANNA: Ye Gods! Ye Gods! That man is my father's murderer!

DON OTTAVIO: What are you saying?

DONNA ANNA: Do not doubt it any longer; the last words which that wicked man spoke, his whole voice, made me think of that wretch within my rooms—

DON OTTAVIO: Oh heavens! is it possible that under the sacred cloak of friendship—but how did it happen, tell me about those strange events.

DONNA ANNA: It was already quite late at night, I was alone in my rooms, to my misfortune, when I saw someone enter, wrapped in a cloak, whom I at first took to be you; but then I perceived my mistake!

DON OTTAVIO: O God! go on!

DONNA ANNA: Stealthily he approached me and would embrace me; I tried to free

più mi stringe, io grido! non
viene alcun; con una mano
cerca d'impedire la voce, e
coll'altra m'afferra stretta
così, che gìa mi credo vinta.

DON OTTAVIO: Perfido! e alfin?

DONNA ANNA: Alfine il duol,
l'orrore dell'infame attentato
accrebbe sì la lena mia, che a
forza di svincolarmi, torcer-
mi, e piegarmi da lui mi
sciolsi!

DON OTTAVIO: Ohimè! respiro.

DONNA ANNA: Allora rinforzo i
stridi miei, chiamo soccorso,
fugge il fellon, arditamente il
seguo fin nella strada per
fermarlo, e sono assalitrice
d'assalita; il padre v'accorre,
vuol conoscerlo, e l'indegno,
che del povero vecchio era
più forte, compie il misfatto
suo, compie il misfatto suo,
col dargli morte.

Or sai chi l'onore rapire a me
volse, che fu il traditore, che
il padre, che il padre, mi
tolse. Vendetta ti chieggio,
la chiede il tuo cor, la chiede
il tuo cor. Rammenta la piaga del misero seno, rimira
di sangue coperto, coperto il

myself, he held me more tightly; I shouted! no one came;
with one hand he tried to
stifle my cries, and with the
other he caught hold of me so
tightly that I thought myself
surely overcome.

DON OTTAVIO: *Excitedly.* Villain! and finally?

DONNA ANNA: Finally, the
pain, the horror of the attempted outrage gave me
enough breath that I had
strength to struggle, twist,
and I wrenched myself free
from him!

DON OTTAVIO: *Relieved.* Oh! I
can breathe again.

DONNA ANNA: Then I renewed
my cries, I shouted for help,
the criminal fled, boldly I followed him down to the street
to stop him, and I became the
assailer of the assailant; my
father came running, de-
manded his identity, and the
criminal who was stronger
than the poor old man,
crowned his misdeeds,
crowned his misdeeds by killing him.
Now you know who tried to
rob me of my honor, who the
traitor was that stole my
father, my father, from me. I
demand revenge of you, your
heart demands it, your heart
demands it. Remember the
wounds in that poor breast,

terreno, se l'ira in te langue d'un giusto furor, d'un giusto furor! Or sai chi l'onore rapire a me volse, chi fu il traditore, che il padre, che il padre mi tolse, vendetta ti chieggio, la chiede il tuo cor, la chiede il tuo cor! Rammenta la piaga, rimira di sangue! Vendetta ti chieggio, la chiede il tuo cor, la chiede il tuo cor, vendetta ti chieggio, la chiede il tuo cor, vendetta ti chieggio, la chiede il tuo cor, la chiede il tuo cor, la chiede il tuo cor, la chiede il tuo cor, la chiede il tuo cor, vendetta ti chieggio, la chiede il tuo cor!

recall the ground, covered, covered with blood, should the fury of a just anger, of a just anger wane in you! Now you know who tried to rob me of my honor, who the traitor was that stole my father, my father from me, I demand revenge of you, your heart demands it, your heart demands it! Remember the wounds, recall the blood! I demand revenge of you, your heart demands it, your heart demands it, I demand revenge of you, your heart demands it, I demand revenge of you, your heart demands it, your heart demands it, your heart demands it, your heart demands it, your heart demands it, I demand revenge of you, your heart demands it!

Donna Anna leaves, and Don Ottavio remains alone on the stage.

DON OTTAVIO: Come mai creder deggio di sì nero delitto capace un cavaliere! Ah, di scoprire il vero ogni mezzo si cerchi; io sento in petto e di sposo e d'amico il dover che mi parla; disingannar la voglio, o vendicarla!

Dalla sua pace, la mia dipende, quel che a lei piace, vita mi rende, quel che le incresce, morte mi dà, morte, morte mi dà. S'ella sospira, sospiro anch'io, è mia quel-

DON OTTAVIO: How can I ever believe a nobleman to be capable of such a black crime! Ah, every means must be sought to discover the truth; In my heart I hear speaking to me the duty of both a husband and a friend; I will undeceive her, or avenge her!
My peace depends on hers, that which pleases her is life to me, that which grieves her is death to me, is death, death to me. If she sighs, I sigh also, her wrath is mine, her tears

l'ira, quel pianto è mio; e non ho bene s'ella non l'ha, e non ho bene s'ella non l'ha, e non ho bene s'ella non l'ha!

Dalla sua pace, la mia dipende, quel ch'a lei piace, vita mi rende, quel che le incresce, morte mi dà, morte, morte mi dà; dalla sua pace, la mia dipende, quel che a lei piace, vita mi rende, quel che le incresce, morte mi dà, morte, morte mi dà, morte mi dà, quel che le incresce, morte mi dà!

are mine; and I have no pleasure if she has none, and I have no pleasure if she has none, and I have no pleasure if she has none!

My peace depends on hers, that which pleases her is life to me, that which grieves her is death to me, is death, death to me; my peace depends on hers, that which pleases her is life to me, that which grieves her is death to me, is death, death to me, is death to me, that which grieves her is death to me!

Exit Don Ottavio.

In the score, the following action takes place without a pause or change of scene. In production, however, there is sometimes a break, and this scene is set in Don Giovanni's castle, an introduction, as it were, to the "Party Scene" (Scene Five) which ends Act One. When the action is continuous, Don Giovanni and Leporello re-enter from opposite sides; the Don is in fine fettle, his servant is grumbling.

LEPORELLO: Io deggio ad ogni patto per sempre abbandonar questo bel matto! eccolo qui; guardate, con qual indifferenza se ne viene!

DON GIOVANNI: Oh, Leporello mio! va tutto bene?

LEPORELLO: Don Giovannino mio, va tutto male!

DON GIOVANNI: Come va tutto male?

LEPORELLO: I ought to leave this madman forever, on any condition! there he is; look how nonchalantly he comes along!

DON GIOVANNI: *Cheerfully.* Oh, my Leporello! is everything going all right?

LEPORELLO: *Angrily.* My little Don Giovanni, everything is going all wrong!

DON GIOVANNI: How is everything going wrong?

LEPORELLO: Vado a casa, come m'ordinaste, con tutta quella gente.

DON GIOVANNI: Bravo!

LEPORELLO: A forza di chiacchere, di vezzi e di bugie, ch'ho imparato sì bene a star con voi, cerco d'intrattenerli.

DON GIOVANNI: Bravo!

LEPORELLO: Dico mille cose a Masetto per placarlo, per trargli dal pensier la gelosia—

DON GIOVANNI: Bravo! in coscienza mia!

LEPORELLO: Faccio che bevano, e gli uomini e le donne son già mezzi ubbriacchi: altri canta, altri scherza, altri seguita a ber; in sul più bello, chi credete che capiti?

DON GIOVANNI: Zerlina!

LEPORELLO: Bravo! e con lei chi viene?

DON GIOVANNI: Donna Elvira!

LEPORELLO: Bravo! e disse di voi—

DON GIOVANNI: Tutto quel mal che in bocca le venia!

LEPORELLO: Bravo! in coscienza mia!

DON GIOVANNI: E tu, cosa facesti?

LEPORELLO: I went to the house with all those people, as you ordered me to.

DON GIOVANNI: Splendid!

LEPORELLO: I tried to entertain them with chit-chat, flatteries, and lies, all of which I have learned so well from being with you.

DON GIOVANNI: Splendid!

LEPORELLO: I told Masetto thousands of things to calm him, to distract him from his jealous thoughts—

DON GIOVANNI: Splendid! by my faith!

LEPORELLO: I made them drink, and soon the men and women were half-drunk; some sang, some joked, some went on drinking; on top of it all, who do you think came along?

DON GIOVANNI: *Carelessly.* Zerlina!

LEPORELLO: Splendid! and who came with her?

DON GIOVANNI: *Carelessly.* Donna Elvira!

LEPORELLO: Splendid! and she said of you—

DON GIOVANNI: *Cheerfully.* Everything nasty that came into her mouth!

LEPORELLO: Splendid! by my faith!

DON GIOVANNI: And you, what did you do?

LEPORELLO: Tacqui.

DON GIOVANNI: Ed ella?

LEPORELLO: Seguì a gridar.

DON GIOVANNI: E tu?

LEPORELLO: Quando mi parve che già fosse sfogata, dolcemente fuor dell'orto la trassi, e con bell'arte, chiusa la porta a chiave io mi cavai, e sulla via soletta la lasciai.

DON GIOVANNI: Bravo! bravo! arcibravo! l'affar non può andar meglio; incominciasti, io saprò terminar. Troppo mi premono queste contadinotte; le voglio divertir finchè vien notte.

Finch'han dal vino calda la testa, una gran festa fa preparar! Se trovi in piazza qualche ragazza, teco ancor quella cerca menar, teco ancor quella cerca menar, cerca menar, cerca menar. Senza alcun ordine la danza sia, chi'l menuetto, chi la follia, chi l'alemana farai ballar, chi'l menuetto farai ballar, chi la follia farai ballar, chi l'alemana farai ballar!

Ed io frattanto dall'altro canto con questa e quella vo' amoreggiar, vo' amoreggiar,

LEPORELLO: I kept still.

DON GIOVANNI: And she?

LEPORELLO: She went right on screaming.

DON GIOVANNI: And you?

LEPORELLO: When I thought she had run dry, I gently led her out of the garden, and with fine skill locked the gate and took off, and left her alone in the street.

DON GIOVANNI: Splendid! Splendid! Absolutely splendid! the thing couldn't have gone better; you began it, I can end it. These country girls are very dear to me; I will amuse them until nightfall.

Have a grand party prepared so that their heads will be hot with the wine! If you find some girl in the square, try to bring her with you too, try to bring her with you too, try to bring her, try to bring her. Let there be dancing without any order, have some dance the minuet, some the follia,* some the allemande,† have some dance the minuet, have some dance the follia, have some dance the allemande!

And meanwhile, on the other hand, I'll make love, I'll make love, I'll make love to this one

---

* Follia: a dance of Portuguese origin.
† Allemande: name of various dances of German origin.

vo' amoreggiar. Ah, la mia lista doman mattina d'una decina devi aumentar, ah, la mia lista d'una decina devi aumentar. Se trovi in piazza qualche ragazza, teco ancor quella cerca menar. Ah, la mia lista doman mattina d'una decina devi aumentar! Senza alcun ordine la danza sia, chi'l menuetto, chi la follia, chi l'alemana farai ballar. Ah, la mia lista doman mattina d'una decina devi aumentar, d'una decina devi aumentar, d'una decina devi aumentar, devi aumentar, devi aumentar, devi, devi aumentar!

and that one. Ah, tomorrow morning my list should be increased by half a score, ah, my list should be increased by half a score. If you find some girl in the square, try to bring her with you too. Ah, tomorrow morning my list should be increased by half a score! Let there be dancing without any order, have some dance the minuet, some the follia, some the allemande. Ah, tomorrow morning my list should be increased by half a score, should be increased by half a score, should be increased by half a score, should be increased, should be increased, should, should be increased!

Don Giovanni usually laughs boisterously at the end of this aria. When the scene takes place in the Don's castle, it is often the custom, at the end of the song, for the Don to shatter a champagne glass he has been holding.

Scene Four

Evening of the same day, in the garden outside Don Giovanni's castle. A balcony of the castle overlooks arbors and shrubbery. Masetto enters, striding huffily; he tries to shake off Zerlina, who follows him, tugging at his sleeve or his hand, and doing her best to gain his attention.

ZERLINA: Masetto, senti un po'! Masetto, dico!

ZERLINA: Masetto, listen a bit! Masetto, I say!

MASETTO: Non mi toccar!

ZERLINA: Perchè?

MASETTO: Perchè mi chiedi? perfida! il tatto sopportar dovrei d'una man infedele?

ZERLINA: Ah no, taci, crudele, io non merto da te tal trattamento.

MASETTO: Come? ed hai l'ardimento di scusarti? star sola con un uom: abbandonarmi il dì delle mie nozze! porre in fronte a un villano d'onore questa marca d'infamia! Ah, se non fosse, se non fosse lo scandalo, vorrei—

MASETTO: Don't touch me!

ZERLINA: Why?

MASETTO: You ask me why? faithless girl! am I supposed to put up with the touch of an unfaithful hand?

ZERLINA: Ah no, cruel fellow, be quiet, I don't deserve such treatment from you.

MASETTO: What? and you have the insolence to make excuses? to remain alone with a man: to desert me on my wedding day! to put this mark of shame on the forehead of an honorable villager! Ah, if there wouldn't be, if there wouldn't be a scandal, I'd like to—

Zerlina ducks out of Masetto's reach.

ZERLINA: Ma se colpa io non ho, ma se da lui ingannata rimasi, e poi che temi? tranquillati, mia vita: non mi toccò la punta delle dita: non me lo credi? Ingrato! vien qui: sfogati, ammazzami, fa tutto di me quel che ti piace; ma poi, Masetto mio, ma poi fa pace.

Batti, batti, o bel Masetto, la tua povera Zerlina: starò qui come agnellina le tue botte ad aspettar. Batti, batti la tua Zerlina; starò qui, starò qui le tue botte ad aspettar.

ZERLINA: But if I'm blameless, even if I was misled by him, then what are you afraid of? calm yourself, my life: he didn't touch my fingertips: don't you believe me? Thankless fellow! come here: give vent to your anger, murder me, do anything you like to me; but then, my Masetto, but then make peace.

O handsome Masetto, beat, beat your poor Zerlina: I'll stand here like a little lamb and wait for your blows. Beat, beat your Zerlina; I'll stand here, I'll stand here and wait for your blows.

Masetto looks at Zerlina crossly.

Lascierò straziarmi il crine, lascierò cavarmi gli occhi, e le care tue manine lieta poi saprò baciar, saprò baciar, baciar, saprò, saprò baciar.

I'll let you tear my hair, I'll let you gouge out my eyes, and then I shall kiss your dear hands happily, I shall kiss them, kiss them, I shall, I shall kiss them.

Masetto visibly begins to give in.

Batti, batti, o bel Masetto, la tua povera Zerlina: starò qui come agnellina le tue botte ad aspettar. O bel Masetto! Batti, batti! Starò qui, starò qui le tue botte ad aspettar. Ah, lo vedo, non hai core, ah, non hai core, ah, lo vedo, non hai core. Pace, pace, o vita mia! pace, pace, o vita mia! in contento ed allegria notte e dì vogliam passar, notte e dì vogliam passar, notte e dì vogliam passar, notte e dì vogliam passar. Pace, pace, o vita mia! Pace, pace, o vita mia! in contento ed allegria notte e dì vogliam passar, sì, sì, sì, sì, sì, sì, notte e dì vogliam passar, sì, sì, sì, sì, sì, sì, notte e dì vogliam passar, vogliam, vogliam passar, vogliam, vogliam passar.

O handsome Masetto, beat, beat your poor Zerlina: I'll stand here like a little lamb and wait for your blows. O handsome Masetto! Beat me, beat me! I'll stand here, I'll stand here and wait for your blows. Ah, I see, you haven't the heart, ah, you haven't the heart, ah, I see, you haven't the heart. Peace, peace, oh my life! peace, peace, oh my life! we'll spend our days and nights in contentment and happiness, we'll spend our days and nights, we'll spend our days and nights, we'll spend our days and nights. Peace, peace, oh my life! Peace, peace, oh my life! We'll spend our days and nights in contentment and happiness, yes, yes, yes, yes, yes, yes, we'll spend our days and nights, yes, yes, yes, yes, yes, yes, we'll spend our days and nights, we'll, we'll spend them, we'll, we'll spend them.

Masetto relents and they fly into one another's arms.

MASETTO: Guarda un po', come seppe questa strega sedurmi! siamo pure i deboli di testa!

MASETTO: Just see how that witch was able to win me over! Ah, but we men are a weak-headed lot!

Don Giovanni's voice comes from off-stage.

DON GIOVANNI: Sia preparato tutto a una gran festa.

DON GIOVANNI: Let everything be made ready for a grand ball.

Zerlina draws nearer to Masetto.

ZERLINA: Ah, Masetto, Masetto, odi la voce del Monsù Cavaliero!

ZERLINA: Ah, Masetto, Masetto, do you hear the voice of his Lordship the Cavalier!

MASETTO: Ebben, che c'è?

MASETTO: Well, what of it?

ZERLINA: Verrà!

ZERLINA: He's coming!

MASETTO: Lascia che venga.

MASETTO: Let him come.

ZERLINA: Ah, se vi fosse un buco da fuggir!

ZERLINA: Ah, if there were a hiding place to run to!

MASETTO: Di cosa temi, perchè diventi pallida? Ah, capisco! capisco, bricconcella: Hai timor ch'io comprenda com'è tra voi passata la faccenda.

MASETTO: What are you afraid of, why are you turning pale? Ah, I understand! I understand, little minx: you're afraid I might see what has been going on between you.

He indicates some shrubbery to one side.

Presto, presto, pria ch'ei venga, pormi vo' da qualche lato; c'è una nicchia—qui celato, cheto, cheto mi vo' star.

Quick, quick, before he comes, I'll step off to the side; there's a corner—here I'll stay hidden, quietly, quietly.

ZERLINA: Senti, senti! dove vai? ah, non t'asconder, o Masetto! se ti trova, poveretto! tu non sai quel che può far, poveretto! tu non sai quel che può far.

ZERLINA: Listen, listen! where are you going? Ah, don't hide yourself, oh Masetto! if he finds you, poor you! you don't know what he might do, poor you! you don't know what he might do.

Zerlina tries to hold Masetto back, but he is insistent.

MASETTO: Faccia, dica quel che vuole.

MASETTO: Let him do and say whatever he wants.

ZERLINA: (Ah, non giovan le parole!)

ZERLINA: *To herself.* Ah, words aren't of any use!

MASETTO: Parla forte e qui t'arresta!

MASETTO: Speak loudly and stay right here!

ZERLINA: Che capriccio ha nella testa, che capriccio ha nella testa!

ZERLINA: What mischief has he got in his head, what mischief has he got in his head!

MASETTO: Parla forte e qui t'arresta. Capirò se m'è fedele, e in qual modo andò l'affar! Capirò se m'è fedele, se m'è fedele, e in qual modo andò l'affar, in qual modo andò l'affar.

MASETTO: Speak loudly, and stay right here. I'll find out if she's faithful to me, and how the affair went! I'll find out if she's faithful to me, if she's faithful to me, and how the affair went, how the affair went.

He hides in some shrubbery to one side.

ZERLINA: Quell'ingrato, quel crudele, oggi vuol precipitar; quell'ingrato, quel crudele, oggi vuol precipitar, quell'ingrato, quel crudele, oggi vuol precipitar.

ZERLINA: That thankless fellow, that cruel man wants to be rash today; that thankless fellow, that cruel man wants to be rash today, that thankless fellow, that cruel man wants to be rash today.

Peasants and villagers begin to come on stage. Don Giovanni, in full finery, enters with his servants.

DON GIOVANNI: Sù! svegliatevi da bravi! Sù! coraggio, o buona gente! vogliam stare allegramente, vogliam ridere e scherzar.

Alla stanza della danza conducete tutti quanti, ed a tutti

DON GIOVANNI: *To the crowd.* Come! rouse yourselves like good folk! Come! be of good heart, o good people! we will be happy, we will laugh and joke.
To the servants. Take everyone to the ballroom and have

in abbondanza, gran rinfreschi fate dar! gran rinfreschi fate dar!

them all given many refreshments in abundance, have them given many refreshments!

SERVANTS: Sù, svegliatevi da bravi! Sù, coraggio, o buona gente! vogliam stare allegramente, vogliam ridere e scherzar, vogliam stare allegramente, vogliam ridere e scherzar, vogliam ridere e scherzar, vogliam ridere e scherzar, vogliam ridere e scherzar.

SERVANTS: Come, rouse yourselves like good folk! Come, be of good heart, o good people! We will be happy, we will laugh and joke, we will be happy, we will laugh and joke, we will laugh and joke, we will laugh and joke, we will laugh and joke.

The servants lead the peasants and villagers into the castle, and Don Giovanni begins to look about for Zerlina. She, seeing that the Don is looking for her, tries to hide.

ZERLINA: Tra quest' arbori celata, si può dar che non mi veda.

ZERLINA: If I'm hidden among those trees, maybe he won't see me.

Don Giovanni sees her and tries to hold her.

DON GIOVANNI: Zerlinetta, mia garbata, t'ho già visto, t'ho già visto, non scappar.

DON GIOVANNI: Little Zerlina, my pleasure, I've already seen you, I've already seen you, don't break away.

Zerlina tries to wrench loose.

ZERLINA: Ah, lasciatemi andar via!

ZERLINA: Ah, let me go away!

DON GIOVANNI: No, no, resta, gioja mia!

DON GIOVANNI: No, no, stay, my joy!

ZERLINA: Se pietade avete in core—

ZERLINA: If you have pity in your heart—

DON GIOVANNI: Sì, ben mio, son tutto amore; vieni un poco in questo loco!

DON GIOVANNI: Yes, my dear, I am all love; come into this place a while!

He tries to pull Zerlina into the shrubbery with him.

fortunata io ti vo' far!

I want to make you rich!

ZERLINA: Ah! s'ei vede il sposo mio, sò ben io quel che può far, sò ben io, sò ben io, sò quel che può far, sò ben io, sò ben io, sò quel che può far!

ZERLINA: Ah! if he sees my husband, I well know what he might do, I well know, I well know, I know what he might do, I well know, I well know, I know what he might do!

DON GIOVANNI: —vieni un poco in questo loco, fortunata io ti vo' far! fortunata io ti vo' far! fortunata io ti vo' far!

DON GIOVANNI:—come into this place a while, I want to make you rich! I want to make you rich! I want to make you rich!

Don Giovanni drags Zerlina into the shrubbery and stops in amazement as he sees Masetto.

DON GIOVANNI: Masetto?!

DON GIOVANNI: Masetto?!

MASETTO: Sì, Masetto!

MASETTO: Yes, Masetto!

Momentarily taken aback, the Don quickly regains his poise.

DON GIOVANNI: E chiuso là, perchè? La bella tua Zerlina non può, la poverina, più star senza di te, non può più star senza di te.

DON GIOVANNI: And why hidden there? Your pretty Zerlina, the poor thing, couldn't stand it any more without you, she couldn't stand it any more without you.

MASETTO: Capisco, sì, Signore.

MASETTO: *With heavy sarcasm.* I understand, yes, Sir.

DON GIOVANNI: Adesso fate core, fate core.

DON GIOVANNI: Now take heart, take heart.

He offers an arm to each of them.

I suonatori udite, venite omai con me!

Listen to the musicians, now come with me!

ZERLINA: Sì, sì, facciamo core—

ZERLINA: Yes, yes, let's take heart—

ZERLINA AND MASETTO: Sì, sì, facciamo core, ed a ballar

ZERLINA AND MASETTO: Yes, yes, let's take heart, and all

(Courtesy San Francisco Opera Company, photo by Carolyn Mason Jones)

Act 1, Scene 3. "That man is my father's murderer!" Donna Anna recognizes Don Giovanni as her assailant. Victoria de los Angeles is Donna Anna.

Act 1, Scene 3. The "Champagne Aria." The Don orders Leporello to prepare a magnificent party ("Fin ch'han dal vino").

Act 1, Scene 4. Zerlina asks Masetto's forgiveness for her apparent flirtation with Don Giovanni ("Batti, batti, o bel Masetto").

(Courtesy San Francisco Opera Company, photo by Carolyn Mason Jones)

Act 1, Scene 4. As they approach Don Giovanni's palace, the maskers consider the danger involved in their proceedings. Left to right: Elisabeth Schwarzkopf as Donna Elvira, Richard Lewis as Don Ottavio and Victoria de los Angeles as Donna Anna.

(Courtesy Sadler's Wells Opera, photo by Angus McBean)

Act 1, Scene 5. The dominoes enter Don Giovanni's palace and find his party in full swing.

(Courtesy Teatro alla Scala, Milan, photo by Ezio Piccagliani)

Act 1, Scene 5. Confronted by his enemies, Don Giovanni accuses Leporello of attempting to molest Zerlina.

cogli altri andiamo tutti tre,
andiamo, andiamo tutti tre,
andiamo, andiamo tutti tre,
andiamo tutti tre, andiamo
tutti tre!

DON GIOVANNI: Venite, omai,
venite omai con me, venite,
venite omai con me, venite,
venite omai con me, venite
omai con me, venite omai
con me!

three go dance with the others,
let's go, let's all three go, let's
go, let's all three go, let's all
three go, let's all three go!

DON GIOVANNI: Now come,
now come with me, come,
now come with me, come,
now come with me, now come
with me, now come with me!

*These three enter the castle together as Don Ottavio,
Donna Anna, and Donna Elvira approach, dressed in
cloaks and dominoes.*

DONNA ELVIRA: Bisogna aver
coraggio, o cari amici miei!
e i suoi misfatti rei scoprir,
scoprir potremo allor.

DON OTTAVIO: L'amica dice
bene! coraggio aver con-
viene; discaccia, o vita mia,
l'affanno ed il timor!

DONNA ANNA: Il passo è peri-
glioso, può nascer qualche
imbroglio. Io temo pel caro
sposo, pel caro sposo, e per
noi temo ancor! temo pel
caro sposo, pel caro sposo, e
per noi temo ancor!

DONNA ELVIRA: We must have
courage, o my dear friends!
and then we can expose, expose his base misdeeds.

DON OTTAVIO: Our friend
speaks truly! it's necessary to
have courage; dispel, o my
life, your uneasiness and your
fear!

DONNA ANNA: It is a dangerous
way, some complication may
arise. I am afraid for my dear
fiancé, for my dear fiancé, and
I am afraid for us as well! I am
afraid for my dear fiancé, for
my dear fiancé, and I am
afraid for us as well!

*Leporello opens the door, leans over the balcony, and
sees the masked trio. The famous minuet can be heard
from inside.*

LEPORELLO: Signor, guardate
un poco che maschere gal-
anti!

LEPORELLO: *Calling.* Sir, look
a bit, what elegant masqueraders!

Don Giovanni comes to the balcony to see.

DON GIOVANNI: Falle passar avanti, di' che ci fanno onor!

DON GIOVANNI: Have them come near, request them to honor us.

DON OTTAVIO, DONNA ANNA AND DONNA ELVIRA: Al volto ed alla voce si scopre il traditore!

DON OTTAVIO, DONNA ANNA AND DONNA ELVIRA: We recognize the betrayer by his face and by his voice!

LEPORELLO: Zì! zì! Signore maschere! Zì! zì!

LEPORELLO: St! st! Masked gentlefolk! st! st!

DONNA ANNA AND DONNA ELVIRA: Via rispondete.

DONNA ANNA AND DONNA ELVIRA: *To Don Ottavio.* Come, answer.

LEPORELLO: Zì! zì! Signore maschere!

LEPORELLO: St! st! Masked gentlefolk!

DON OTTAVIO: Cosa chiedete?

DON OTTAVIO: *To Leporello.* What do you ask?

LEPORELLO: Al ballo, se vi piace, v'invita il mio Signor.

LEPORELLO: If it please you, my Lord invites you to the ball.

DON OTTAVIO: Grazie di tanto onore!
Andiam, compagne belle!

DON OTTAVIO: *To Leporello.* Thank you for such an honor! *To his ladies.* Let us go, lovely companions!

LEPORELLO: L'amico anche su quelle prova farà d'amor!

LEPORELLO: *To himself.* My friend will try to make love to those ladies too!

*The trio remove their dominoes
and prepare to enter the castle.*

DONNA ANNA AND DON OTTAVIO: Protegga il giusto cielo il zelo del mio cor!

DONNA ANNA AND DON OTTAVIO: May the just heaven protect the fervor of my heart!

DONNA ELVIRA: Vendichi il giusto cielo il mio tradito amor—

DONNA ELVIRA: May the just heaven avenge my betrayed love—

DONNA ANNA: —protegga il giusto cielo il zelo del mio cor, protegga il giusto cielo il zelo del mio cor, protegga il giusto cielo il zelo del mio cor!

DON OTTAVIO: —protegga il giusto cielo il zelo del mio cor, il zelo, il zelo del mio cor! protegga il giusto cielo il zelo del mio cor, il zelo, il zelo del mio cor, protegga il giusto cielo il zelo del mio cor!

DONNA ELVIRA: —vendichi il giusto cielo il mio tradito amor, il mio tradito, tradito amor! Vendichi il giusto cielo il mio tradito amor, il mio, il mio tradito amor, vendichi, vendichi il giusto cielo il mio tradito, tradito amor, tradito amor!

DONNA ANNA: —may the just heaven protect the fervor of my heart, may the just heaven protect the fervor of my heart, may the just heaven protect the fervor of my heart!

DON OTTAVIO: —may the just heaven protect the fervor of my heart, the fervor, the fervor of my heart, may the just heaven protect the fervor of my heart, the fervor, the fervor of my heart, may the just heaven protect the fervor of my heart!

DONNA ELVIRA:—may the just heaven avenge my betrayed love, my betrayed, betrayed love! May the just heaven avenge my betrayed love, my my betrayed love, may the just heaven avenge, avenge my betrayed, betrayed love, betrayed love!

*They resume their dominoes
and solemnly enter the castle.*

Scene Five

The brilliantly lighted and decorated ballroom of Don Giovanni's castle. Three separate orchestras on the stage provide three different kinds of dance music. The dancing is in progress; Don Giovanni escorts various girls, and Leporello busies himself among other guests.

DON GIOVANNI: Riposate, vezzose ragazze!

DON GIOVANNI: Rest, charming girls!

LEPORELLO: Rinfrescatevi, bei giovinetti!

DON GIOVANNI AND LEPORELLO: Tornerete a far presto le pazze, tornerete a scherzar e ballar, a scherzar e ballar!

LEPORELLO: Ehi, caffè! Cioccolatte!

MASETTO: Ah, Zerlina! giudizio!

DON GIOVANNI: Sorbetti!

LEPORELLO: Confetti!

MASETTO: Ah, Zerlina, giudizio!

ZERLINA AND MASETTO: Troppo dolce comincia la scena, in amaro potria terminar, sì, in amaro potria terminar!

DON GIOVANNI: Sei pur vaga, brillante Zerlina!

ZERLINA: Sua bontà!

MASETTO: La briccona fa festa!

LEPORELLO: Sei pur cara, Giannotta, Sandrina!

MASETTO: Tocca pur, che ti cada la testa.

LEPORELLO: Refresh yourselves, handsome youths!

DON GIOVANNI AND LEPORELLO: You'll soon be wildly celebrating again, joking and dancing, joking and dancing.

LEPORELLO: *To servants.* Hey, coffee! chocolate!

MASETTO: *Worriedly.* Ah, Zerlina! be sensible!

DON GIOVANNI: Ices!

LEPORELLO: Sweets!

MASETTO: Ah, Zerlina, be sensible!

ZERLINA AND MASETTO: *Both to themselves.* This scene is beginning too sweetly, it could end bitterly, yes, it could end bitterly!

DON GIOVANNI: *Insinuatingly.* You're so delightful, sparkling Zerlina!

ZERLINA: You are kind!

MASETTO: *Aside, furiously.* The minx is having fun!

LEPORELLO: *Mimicking Don Giovanni to other girls.* You're so sweet, Giannotta, Sandrina!

MASETTO: *To himself.* Touch her, and I'll take your head off.

Zerlina gives an anxious side-glance at Masetto.

ZERLINA: Quel Masetto mi par stralunato, brutto, brutto si fa quest'affar!

ZERLINA: I think that Masetto is in a frenzy, this affair is going nastily, nastily!

DON GIOVANNI AND LEPOR-
ELLO: Quel Masetto mi par
stralunato—

ZERLINA: Quel Masetto mi par
stralunato!

MASETTO: La briccona fa festa!

DON GIOVANNI AND LEPORELLO: Qui bisogna cervello
adoprar.

ZERLINA: Brutto, brutto si fa
quest'affar!

MASETTO: Tocca pur, che ti
cada la testa!

ZERLINA, LEPORELLO AND DON
GIOVANNI: Quel Masetto mi
par stralunato—

ZERLINA: —brutto, brutto si
fa quest'affar, si fa quest'affar.

DON GIOVANNI AND LEPOR-
ELLO: —qui bisogna cervello
adoprar, cervello adoprar!

MASETTO: Tocca, tocca!

ZERLINA: —quel Masetto mi
par stralunato, brutto, brutto
si fa quest'affar, si fa quest'affar, brutto, brutto si fa
quest'affar!

DON GIOVANNI AND LEPOR-
ELLO: —quel Masetto mi par
stralunato, qui bisogna cervello adoprar, cervello adoprar, qui bisogna cervello
adoprar!

MASETTO: Ah, briccona! ah,
briccona! mi vuoi disperar!
ah briccona! mi vuoi disperar!

DON GIOVANNI AND LEPOR-
ELLO: I think that Masetto is
in a frenzy—

ZERLINA: I think that Masetto is in a frenzy!

MASETTO: The minx is having
fun!

DON GIOVANNI AND LEPOR-
ELLO: Here one needs to use
one's brains.

ZERLINA: This affair is going
nastily, nastily!

MASETTO: Touch her, and I'll
take your head off!

ZERLINA, LEPORELLO AND DON
GIOVANNI: I think that Masetto is in a frenzy—

ZERLINA: This affair is going,
this affair is going nastily,
nastily.

DON GIOVANNI AND LEPOR-
ELLO: —here one needs to use
one's brains, to use one's brains!

MASETTO: Touch her, touch her!

ZERLINA: —I think that Masetto is in a frenzy, this
affair is going nastily, nastily,
this affair is going, this affair
is going nastily, nastily!

DON GIOVANNI AND LEPOR-
ELLO: —I think that Masetto
is in a frenzy, here one needs
to use one's brains, to use one's
brains, here one needs to use
one's brains!

MASETTO: Ah, minx! ah, minx!
You drive me to despair! ah
minx! you drive me to despair!

*Don Ottavio, Donna Anna and
Donna Elvira enter, masked.*

LEPORELLO: Venite pur
avanti, vezzose mascherette!

LEPORELLO: *To the newcomers.*
Now come forward, charming
masqueraders!

Don Giovanni greets the masked trio.

DON GIOVANNI: È aperto a
tutti quanti, viva la libertà.

DON GIOVANNI: Everyone is
free to come in, long live freedom.

DONNA ANNA, DONNA ELVIRA
AND DON OTTAVIO: Siam grati
a tanti segni di generosità, di
generosità;

DONNA ANNA, DONNA ELVIRA
AND DON OTTAVIO: We are
grateful for so many signs of
generosity, of generosity;

DON GIOVANNI: È aperto a
tutti—

DON GIOVANNI: Everyone is
free to come in—

DONNA ANNA, DONNA ELVIRA
AND DON OTTAVIO: —siam
grati a tanti segni di generosità!

DONNA ANNA, DONNA ELVIRA
AND DON OTTAVIO: —we are
grateful for so many signs of
generosity!

DON GIOVANNI: —a tutti
quanti, viva, viva la libertà!

DON GIOVANNI: —everyone,
long live, long live freedom!

LEPORELLO: Viva la libertà!
la libertà!

LEPORELLO: Long live freedom! freedom!

DONNA ANNA, DONNA ELVIRA,
DON OTTAVIO AND DON GIO-
VANNI: Viva la libertà, la li-
bertà—

DONNA ANNA, DONNA ELVIRA,
DON OTTAVIO AND DON GIO-
VANNI: Long live freedom,
freedom—

LEPORELLO: Viva la libertà—

LEPORELLO: Long live freedom—

DONNA ANNA, DONNA ELVIRA,
DON OTTAVIO AND DON GIO-
VANNI: Viva la libertà—

DONNA ANNA, DONNA ELVIRA,
DON OTTAVIO AND DON GIO-
VANNI: Long live freedom—

DONNA ANNA, DONNA ELVIRA,
DON OTTAVIO, DON GIOVANNI
AND LEPORELLO: —la libertà,
viva, viva la libertà, viva,

DONNA ANNA, DONNA ELVIRA,
DON OTTAVIO, DON GIOVANNI
AND LEPORELLO: —freedom,
long live, long live freedom,

viva la libertà, la libertà, la libertà!

long live, long live freedom, freedom, freedom!

DON GIOVANNI: Ricominciate il suono! tu accoppia i ballerini! Meco tu dei ballare; Zerlina, vien pur quà!*

DON GIOVANNI: *To the stage orchestras.* Start playing again! *To Leporello.* You pair off the dancers! *To Zerlina.* You must dance with me; come here now, Zerlina!*

Don Giovanni and Zerlina dance.

LEPORELLO: Da bravi via ballate!

LEPORELLO: *To other guests.* Dance on like good folk!

DONNA ELVIRA: Quella è la contadina.

DONNA ELVIRA: *To Donna Anna.* That one is the country girl.

DONNA ANNA: Io moro!

DONNA ANNA: *To Don Ottavio.* I am dying!

DON OTTAVIO: Simulate.

DON OTTAVIO: *To Donna Anna.* Dissemble.

DON GIOVANNI AND LEPORELLO: Va bene, in verità!

DON GIOVANNI AND LEPORELLO: In truth, it goes well!

MASETTO: Va bene, va bene, va bene in verità!

MASETTO: *With heavy sarcasm.* In truth, it goes well, it goes well, it goes well!

DON GIOVANNI: A bada tien Masetto.

DON GIOVANNI: *To Leporello.* Keep Masetto at bay.

Leporello approaches Masetto with deep mock concern.

LEPORELLO: Non balli, poveretto, poveretto!

LEPORELLO: You poor man, you poor man, you're not dancing!

DON GIOVANNI: Il tuo compagno io sono, Zerlina, Zerlina, vien pur quà!

DON GIOVANNI: *To Zerlina.* I'm your partner, Zerlina, Zerlina, now come here!

LEPORELLO: Vien quà, Maset-

LEPORELLO: *To Masetto.* Come

* "Meco . . . quà!" According to Schirmer's score and Jahn's biography, this line is present in early copies of the voice-parts, though neither in the original score nor libretto. The line has been omitted from later scores, and is not sung in present-day performances.

to caro, caro! facciam quel ch'altri fa.

MASETTO: No, no, ballar non voglio!

LEPORELLO: Eh, balla, amico mio!

MASETTO: No!

Leporello tries to force Masetto to dance.

LEPORELLO: Sì! caro Masetto!

DONNA ANNA: Resister non poss'io!

LEPORELLO: Balla!

MASETTO: No, no, non voglio!

DONNA ELVIRA AND DON OTTAVIO: Fingete, per pietà!

LEPORELLO: Balla!
MASETTO: No, no, non voglio!

here, dear, dear Masetto! Let's do what the others are doing.

MASETTO: *Angrily.* No, no, I don't want to dance!

LEPORELLO: Ah, dance, my friend!

MASETTO: No!

LEPORELLO: Yes! dear Masetto!

DONNA ANNA: *To Don Ottavio and Donna Elvira.* I cannot endure it!

LEPORELLO: *To Masetto.* Dance!

MASETTO: No, no, I don't want to!

DONNA ELVIRA AND DON OTTAVIO: *To Donna Anna.* Pretend, for pity's sake!

LEPORELLO: Dance!
MASETTO: No, no, I don't want to!

Don Giovanni, dancing with Zerlina, has slyly maneuvered her toward a door on one side; now he tries to pull her through it.

LEPORELLO: Eh, balla, amico mio! facciam quel ch'altri fa.

LEPORELLO: Ah, dance, my friend! let's do what the others are doing.

Awkwardly, Leporello forces an extremely unwilling Masetto to dance with him.

DON GIOVANNI: Vieni con me, mia vita! vieni, vieni!

MASETTO: Lasciami! Ah no! Zerlina!

DON GIOVANNI: *To Zerlina.* Come with me, my life! come, come!

MASETTO: Let me go! Ah no! Zerlina!

ZERLINA: O numi! son tradita!

ZERLINA: Ye gods! I'm betrayed!

Don Giovanni pulls Zerlina with him off to the side.

LEPORELLO: Qui nasce una ruina.

LEPORELLO: A disaster is hatching here.

He hurriedly follows the Don and Zerlina.

DONNA ANNA, DONNA ELVIRA AND DON OTTAVIO: L'iniquo da se stesso nel laccio se ne va!

DONNA ANNA, DONNA ELVIRA AND DON OTTAVIO: The wicked man is throwing himself into the trap!

Zerlina screams from off-stage, causing a great commotion. The musicians stop playing, etc.

ZERLINA: Gente, aiuto! aiuto! gente!

ZERLINA: Somebody, help! help! somebody!

Donna Anna, Donna Elvira and Don Ottavio start toward the sound of Zerlina's screams.

DONNA ANNA, DONNA ELVIRA AND DON OTTAVIO: Soccorriamo l'innocente, soccorriamo l'innocente!

DONNA ANNA, DONNA ELVIRA AND DON OTTAVIO: Let us help the innocent girl, let us help the innocent girl!

MASETTO: Ah, Zerlina, ah, Zerlina!

MASETTO: Ah, Zerlina, ah, Zerlina!

ZERLINA: Scellerato!

ZERLINA: *From off-stage.* Villain!

DONNA ANNA, DONNA ELVIRA AND DON OTTAVIO: Ora grida da quel lato, da quel lato!

DONNA ANNA, DONNA ELVIRA AND DON OTTAVIO: Now she is calling from that side, from that side!

ZERLINA: Scellerato!

ZERLINA: Villain!

DONNA ANNA, DONNA ELVIRA AND DON OTTAVIO: Ah, gittiamo giù la porta, giù la porta!

DONNA ANNA, DONNA ELVIRA AND DON OTTAVIO: Ah, let us knock the door down, the door down!

ZERLINA: Soccorretemi! Ah soccorretemi! son morta!

ZERLINA: Help me! Ah help me! I am dead!

DONNA ANNA, DONNA ELVIRA, DON OTTAVIO AND MASETTO: Siam qui noi per tua difesa, siam qui noi per tua difesa, per tua difesa, per tua difesa!

DONNA ANNA, DONNA ELVIRA, DON OTTAVIO AND MASETTO: We are here in your defense, we are here in your defense, in your defense, in your defense!

Just as they manage to batter down the door, Don Giovanni re-enters, holding Leporello at arm's length, and pretending with simulated fury that the servant is the culprit.

DON GIOVANNI: Ecco il birbo che t'ha offesa! ma da me la pena avrà, la pena avrà! Mori, iniquo!

DON GIOVANNI: Here's the rogue who has offended you! but he'll get his punishment, he'll get his punishment from me! Die, wretch!

Don Giovanni touches the sword at his side, and Leporello falls to his knees.

LEPORELLO: Ah, cosa fate!

LEPORELLO: Ah, what are you doing!

DON GIOVANNI: Mori, dico!
LEPORELLO: Ah, cosa fate!

DON GIOVANNI: Die, I say!
LEPORELLO: Ah, what are you doing!

DON GIOVANNI: Mori, dico!

DON GIOVANNI: Die, I say!

LEPORELLO: Ah, cosa fate!

LEPORELLO: Ah, what are you doing!

Don Ottavio produces a pistol and points it at Don Giovanni.

DON OTTAVIO: Nol sperate! nol sperate!

DON OTTAVIO: Don't try that! don't try that!

Donna Anna, Donna Elvira and Don Ottavio remove their dominoes.

DONNA ANNA AND DON OTTAVIO: L'empio crede con tal frode, con tal frode, con tal frode di nasconder l'empietà, l'empietà!

DONNA ELVIRA: L'empio crede con tal frode, con tal frode di nasconder l'empietà, l'empietà!

DONNA ANNA AND DON OTTAVIO: With such fraud, with such fraud, with such fraud the wicked man thinks he will disguise his wickedness, his wickedness!

DONNA ELVIRA: With such fraud, with such fraud the wicked man thinks he will disguise his wickedness, his wickedness!

*Don Giovanni releases Leporello
and starts back in surprise.*

DON GIOVANNI: Donna Elvira!

DON GIOVANNI: Donna Elvira!

DONNA ELVIRA: Sì, malvagio!

DONNA ELVIRA: Yes, evil one!

DON GIOVANNI: Don Ottavio?!

DON GIOVANNI: Don Ottavio?!

DON OTTAVIO: Sì, Signore!

DON OTTAVIO: Yes, sir!

DON GIOVANNI: Ah credete—

DON GIOVANNI: Ah believe—

DONNA ANNA: Traditore—

DONNA ANNA: Betrayer—

DONNA ANNA, DONNA ELVIRA, ZERLINA, DON OTTAVIO AND MASETTO: Traditore, traditore!

DONNA ANNA, DONNA ELVIRA, ZERLINA, DON OTTAVIO AND MASETTO: Betrayer, betrayer!

ZERLINA: Tutto, tutto già si sa—

ZERLINA: We already know everything, everything—

MASETTO: Tutto, tutto già si sa—

MASETTO: We already know everything, everything—

DONNA ANNA, DONNA ELVIRA AND DON OTTAVIO: Tutto, tutto già si sa—

DONNA ANNA, DONNA ELVIRA AND DON OTTAVIO: We already know everything, everything—

ZERLINA: —tutto, tutto già si sa—

ZERLINA: —we already know everything, everything—

MASETTO: —tutto, tutto già si sa—

MASETTO: —we already know everything, everything—

DONNA ANNA, DONNA ELVIRA AND DON OTTAVIO: —tutto, tutto già si sa—

DONNA ANNA, DONNA ELVIRA AND DON OTTAVIO: —we already know everything, everything—

ZERLINA: —tutto, tutto già si sa, già si sa, tutto, tutto, tutto, tutto già si sa, tutto, tutto, tutto!

ZERLINA: —we already know, we already know everything, everything, we already know everything, everything, everything, everything, everything, everything, everything!

DONNA ANNA AND DONNA ELVIRA: —tutto, tutto già si sa, tutto, tutto, tutto, tutto già si sa, tutto, tutto, tutto!

DONNA ANNA AND DONNA ELVIRA: —we already know everything, everything, we already know everything, everything, everything, everything, everything, everything, everything!

DON OTTAVIO: —tutto, tutto già si sa, tutto, tutto già si sa, tutto, tutto, tutto!

DON OTTAVIO: —we already know everything, everything, we already know everything, everything, everything, everything, everything!

MASETTO: —tutto, tutto già si sa, tutto, tutto già si sa, tutto, tutto, tutto!

MASETTO: —we already know everything, everything, we already know everything, everything, everything, everything, everything!

Don Ottavio, Masetto and several of the men guests begin closing in on Don Giovanni, who stands quite coolly, hand on sword, and looks at them.

DONNA ANNA, DONNA ELVIRA, ZERLINA, DON OTTAVIO AND MASETTO: Trema, trema, scellerato!—

DONNA ANNA, DONNA ELVIRA, ZERLINA, DON OTTAVIO AND MASETTO: Tremble, tremble, villain!

DON GIOVANNI: È confusa la mia testa.

DON GIOVANNI: My mind is confused.

LEPORELLO: È confusa la sua testa.

LEPORELLO: His mind is confused.

DONNA ANNA, DONNA ELVIRA, ZERLINA, DON OTTAVIO AND MASETTO: —trema, trema, scellerato!

DONNA ANNA, DONNA ELVIRA, ZERLINA, DON OTTAVIO AND MASETTO: —tremble, tremble, villain!

DON GIOVANNI: Non sò più quel ch'io mi faccia, e un orribile tempesta minacciando, o Dio, mi va!

LEPORELLO: Non sa più quel ch'ei si faccia, e un orribile tempesta minacciando, o Dio, lo va!

DONNA ANNA, DONNA ELVIRA, ZERLINA, DON OTTAVIO AND MASETTO: —saprà tosto il mondo intero il misfatto orrendo e nero, la tua fiera crudeltà, la tua fiera crudeltà!

DON GIOVANNI: È confusa la mia testa, non sò più quel ch'io mi faccia, e un orribile tempesta minacciando, o Dio, mi va.

LEPORELLO: È confusa la sua testa, non sa più quel ch'ei si faccia, e un orribile tempesta minacciando, o Dio, lo va.

DONNA ANNA, DONNA ELVIRA, ZERLINA, DON OTTAVIO AND MASETTO: Trema! trema!

DONNA ANNA AND ZERLINA: Trema, trema, scellerato!

DONNA ELVIRA, DON OTTAVIO AND MASETTO: Trema, trema, trema, trema, o scellerato!

DON GIOVANNI: È confusa la mia testa, non sò più quel ch'io mi faccia—

LEPORELLO: È confusa la sua testa, non sa più quel ch'ei si faccia—

DON GIOVANNI: I no longer know what to do with myself, and a horrible storm is threatening me, oh God!

LEPORELLO: He no longer knows what to do with himself, and a horrible storm is threatening him, oh God!

DONNA ANNA, DONNA ELVIRA, ZERLINA, DON OTTAVIO AND MASETTO: —soon the whole world will know your black and dreadful crime, your cruelty, your cruelty!

DON GIOVANNI: My mind is confused, I no longer know what to do with myself, and a horrible storm is threatening me, oh God!

LEPORELLO: His mind is confused, he no longer knows what to do with himself, and a horrible storm is threatening him, oh God!

DONNA ANNA, DONNA ELVIRA, ZERLINA, DON OTTAVIO AND MASETTO: Tremble! tremble!

DONNA ANNA AND ZERLINA: Tremble, tremble, villain!

DONNA ELVIRA, DON OTTAVIO AND MASETTO: Tremble, tremble, tremble, tremble, o villain!

DON GIOVANNI: My mind is confused, I no longer know what to do with myself—

LEPORELLO: His mind is confused, he no longer knows what to do with himself—

DONNA ANNA, DONNA ELVIRA, ZERLINA, DON OTTAVIO AND MASETTO: Odi il tuon della vendetta!

DONNA ANNA, DONNA ELVIRA, ZERLINA, DON OTTAVIO AND MASETTO: Hear the thunder of revenge!

DON GIOVANNI: —e un orribile tempesta minacciando, o Dio, mi va!

DON GIOVANNI: —and a horrible storm is threatening me, oh God!

LEPORELLO: —e un orribile tempesta minacciando, o Dio, lo va!

LEPORELLO: —and a horrible storm is threatening him, oh God!

Leporello ducks behind Don Giovanni who now brandishes his sword and tries to clear a path for himself through the crowd.

DONNA ANNA, DONNA ELVIRA, ZERLINA, DON OTTAVIO AND MASETTO: Odi il tuon della vendetta, che ti fischia intorno, intorno, sul tuo capo in questo giorno il suo fulmine cadrà, il suo fulmine cadrà!

DONNA ANNA, DONNA ELVIRA, ZERLINA, DON OTTAVIO AND MASETTO: Hear the thunder of revenge clattering around and around you, on this day its bolt will fall, its bolt will fall on your head.

DON GIOVANNI: È confusa la mia testa—

DON GIOVANNI: My mind is confused—

LEPORELLO: È confusa la sua testa—

LEPORELLO: His mind is confused—

DONNA ANNA, DONNA ELVIRA, ZERLINA, DON OTTAVIO AND MASETTO: —trema!

DONNA ANNA, DONNA ELVIRA, ZERLINA, DON OTTAVIO AND MASETTO: —tremble!

DON GIOVANNI: —non sò più quel ch'io mi faccia, e un orribile tempesta minacciando, o Dio, mi va!

DON GIOVANNI: —I no longer know what to do with myself, and a horrible storm is threatening me, oh God!

LEPORELLO: —non sa più quel ch'ei si faccia, e un orribile tempesta minacciando, o Dio, lo va!

LEPORELLO: —he no longer knows what to do with himself, and a horrible storm is threatening him, oh God!

DONNA ANNA, DONNA ELVIRA, ZERLINA, DON OTTAVIO AND MASETTO: —trema!

DONNA ANNA, DONNA ELVIRA, ZERLINA, DON OTTAVIO AND MASETTO: —tremble!

DONNA ANNA: —trema, trema, scellerato!

ZERLINA: —trema, trema, o scellerato!

DONNA ELVIRA, DON OTTAVIO AND MASETTO: —trema, trema, trema, trema, o scellerato!

DON GIOVANNI: È confusa la mia testa, non sò più quel ch'io mi faccia—

LEPORELLO: È confusa la sua testa, non sa più quel ch'ei si faccia—

DONNA ANNA, DONNA ELVIRA, ZERLINA, DON OTTAVIO AND MASETTO: Odi il tuon della vendetta!

DON GIOVANNI: —e un orribile tempesta minacciando, o Dio, mi va!

LEPORELLO: —e un orribile tempesta minacciando, o Dio, lo va!

DONNA ANNA, DONNA ELVIRA, ZERLINA, DON OTTAVIO AND MASETTO: Odi il tuon della vendetta, che ti fischia intorno, intorno, sul tuo capo in questo giorno il suo fulmine cadrà, sì, cadrà, il suo fulmine cadrà!

DON GIOVANNI: Ma non manca in me coraggio—

LEPORELLO: Ma non manca in lui coraggio—

DONNA ANNA, DONNA ELVIRA, ZERLINA, DON OTTAVIO AND MASETTO: Odi il tuon!

DONNA ANNA: —tremble, tremble, villain!

ZERLINA: —tremble, temble, o villain!

DONNA ELVIRA, DON OTTAVIO AND MASETTO: tremble, tremble, tremble, tremble, o villain!

DON GIOVANNI: My mind is confused, I no longer know what to do with myself—

LEPORELLO: His mind is confused, he no longer knows what to do with himself—

DONNA ANNA, DONNA ELVIRA, ZERLINA, DON OTTAVIO AND MASETTO: Hear the thunder of revenge!

DON GIOVANNI: —and a horrible storm is threatening me, oh God!

LEPORELLO: —and a horrible storm is threatening him, oh God!

DONNA ANNA, DONNA ELVIRA, ZERLINA, DON OTTAVIO AND MASETTO: Hear the thunder of revenge clattering around and around you, on this day its bolt will fall, yes, will fall, its bolt will fall on your head!

DON GIOVANNI: But I do not lack courage—

LEPORELLO: But he does not lack courage—

DONNA ANNA, DONNA ELVIRA, ZERLINA, DON OTTAVIO AND MASETTO: Hear the thunder!

DON GIOVANNI: —non mi perdo, o mi confondo.

DON GIOVANNI: —I'll not lose heart or go to pieces.

LEPORELLO: —non si perde, o si confonde.

LEPORELLO: —he'll not lose heart or go to pieces.

DONNA ANNA, DONNA ELVIRA, ZERLINA, DON OTTAVIO AND MASETTO: Odi il tuon!

DONNA ANNA, DONNA ELVIRA, ZERLINA, DON OTTAVIO AND MASETTO: Hear the thunder!

DON GIOVANNI: Se cadesse ancora il mondo, cadesse ancora il mondo, nulla mai temer, temer mi fa, se cadesse ancora il mondo, se cadesse ancora il mondo, nulla mai temer, temer mi fa, nulla mai temer mi fa, nulla mai temer mi fa, nulla mai temer mi fa!

DON GIOVANNI: Even if the world should fall apart, even if the world should fall apart, nothing will ever make me be afraid, be afraid, even if the world should fall apart, even if the world should fall apart, nothing will ever make me be afraid, be afraid, nothing will ever make me be afraid, nothing will ever make me be afraid, nothing will ever make me be afraid!

DONNA ANNA, DONNA ELVIRA AND ZERLINA: Sul tuo capo in questo giorno il suo fulmine cadrà, il suo fulmine cadrà, sul tuo capo in questo giorno il suo fulmine cadrà, il suo fulmine cadrà, il suo fulmine cadrà, il suo fulmine cadrà, il suo fulmine cadra!

DONNA ANNA, DONNA ELVIRA AND ZERLINA: On this day its bolt will fall on your head, its bolt will fall, on this day its bolt will fall on your head, its bolt will fall, its bolt will fall, its bolt will fall, its bolt will fall!

DON OTTAVIO AND MASETTO: Sul tuo capo in questo giorno il suo fulmine cadrà, sul tuo capo in questo giorno il suo fulmine cadrà, il suo fulmine cadrà, il suo fulmine cadrà, il suo fulmine cadrà!

DON OTTAVIO AND MASETTO: On this day its bolt will fall on your head, on this day its bolt will fall on your head, its bolt will fall, its bolt will fall, its bolt will fall!

Don Giovanni seizes Leporello, and pushing the servant before himself, forces his way through the crowd which surrounds him and escapes.

End of Act One

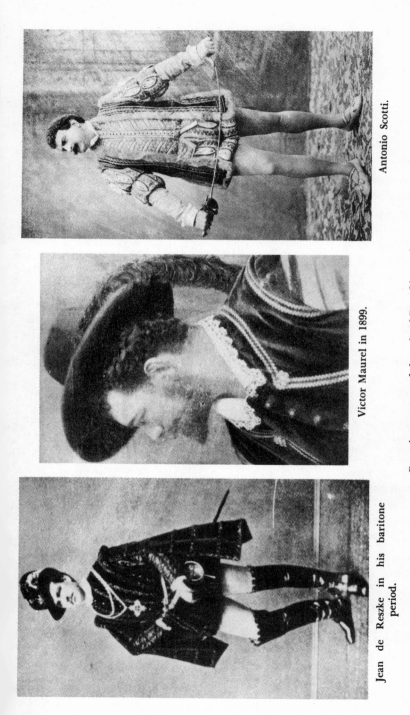

Jean de Reszke in his baritone period.

Victor Maurel in 1899.

Antonio Scotti.

Great interpreters of the role of Don Giovanni.

Ezio Pinza.

Cesare Siepi.

(Courtesy London Records)

Great interpreters of the role of Don Giovanni.

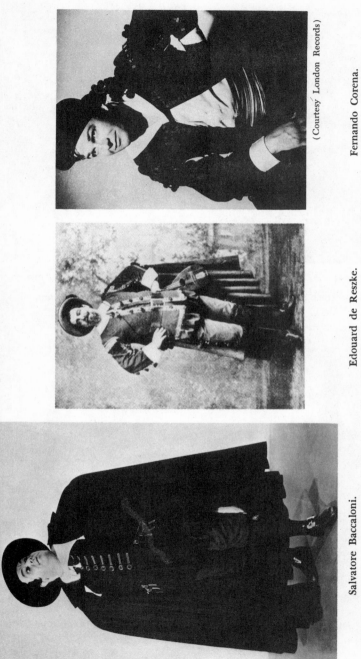

Fernando Corena.

Edouard de Reszke.

Salvatore Baccaloni.

Three great basses in the role of Leporello.

Eleanor Steber as Donna Anna.　　　　Rosa Ponselle as Donna Anna.

Great singers of the past and present in roles from *Don Giovanni*.

(Courtesy London Records)

Lisa Della Casa as Donna Elvira.　　　Birgit Nilsson as Donna Anna.

Leopold Simoneau.

Jan Peerce.

Great contemporary tenors in the role of Don Ottavio.

Cesare Valletti.

Nicolaï Gedda.

Tito Schipa as Don Ottavio.

John McCormack as Don Ottavio (his favorite role).

Great singers of the past especially associated with roles from *Don Giovanni*.

Adelina Patti, a great Zerlina.

Marcella Sembrich as Zerlina.

Act Two

ACT TWO

Scene One

Evening in a square by the house of Donna Elvira.
Don Giovanni and Leporello appear, arguing.

DON GIOVANNI: Eh via, buffone, eh via buffone, non mi seccar.

LEPORELLO: No, no, padrone, no, no, padrone! non vo' restar!

DON GIOVANNI: Sentimi, amico—

LEPORELLO: Vo' andar, vi dico!

DON GIOVANNI: Ma che ti ho fatto, che vuoi lasciarmi?

LEPORELLO: O niente affatto, quasi ammazzarmi.

DON GIOVANNI: Va che sei matto, va che sei matto, matto, matto, fu per burlar.

LEPORELLO: Ed io non burlo, ed io non burlo, burlo, burlo, ma voglio andar!

DON GIOVANNI: Eh via, buffone, sentimi, amico: va che sei matto, va che sei matto, va che sei matto, va che sei matto, matto, matto, matto!

DON GIOVANNI: Oh, come now, clown, oh, come now, clown, don't bother me.

LEPORELLO: No, no, master, no, no, master! I don't want to stay!

DON GIOVANNI: Listen to me, friend—

LEPORELLO: I want to go, I tell you!

DON GIOVANNI: What have I done to you, that you want to leave me?

LEPORELLO: Oh nothing at all, you almost murdered me.

DON GIOVANNI: Don't be crazy, don't be crazy, crazy, crazy, it was in fun.

LEPORELLO: And I'm not joking, and I'm not joking, joking, joking, but I want to go!

DON GIOVANNI: Oh, come now, clown, listen to me, friend: don't be crazy, don't be crazy, don't be crazy, don't be crazy, crazy, crazy, crazy!

Va che sei matto, va che sei matto, va che sei matto, va che sei matto, matto, matto, matto! Eh via, buffone, buffone, non mi seccar, va che sei matto, va che sei matto, fu per burlar, fu per burlar, fu per burlar, fu per burlar!

Don't be crazy, don't be crazy, don't be crazy, don't be crazy, crazy, crazy, crazy! Oh, come now, clown, clown, don't bother me, don't be crazy, don't be crazy, it was in fun, it was in fun, it was in fun, it was in fun!

LEPORELLO: No, no, padrone! vo' andar, vi dico, no, no, no, no, no, no, no, no, no, no, no, no, non vo' restar, no, non vo' restar, sì, sì, sì, sì, sì, sì, sì, sì, sì, sì, sì, sì, sì, sì, sì, voglio andar, sì, sì, voglio andar! no, no, padrone, no, no, padrone, non vo' restar! ed io non burlo, ed io non burlo, ma voglio andar, ma voglio andar, ma voglio andar, ma voglio andar!

LEPORELLO: No, no, master! I want to go, I tell you, no, no, no, no, no, no, no, no, no, no, no, no, no, no, no, no, no, I don't want to stay, yes, yes, yes, yes, yes, yes, yes, yes, yes, yes, yes, yes, yes, yes, yes, I want to go, yes, yes, I want to go! no, no, master, no, no, master, I don't want to stay! and I'm not joking, and I'm not joking, but I want to go, but I want to go, but I want to go, but I want to go!

Half-heartedly, Leporello tries to sneak away. Don Giovanni pulls him back and tosses him a purse of money.

DON GIOVANNI: Leporello!

LEPORELLO: Signore!

DON GIOVANNI: Vien qui, facciamo pace, prendi!

LEPORELLO: Cosa?

DON GIOVANNI: Quattro doppie.

DON GIOVANNI: Leporello!

LEPORELLO: Sir!

DON GIOVANNI: Come here, let's make peace, take this!

LEPORELLO: What?

DON GIOVANNI: Four doubloons.

Leporello eagerly counts his money.

LEPORELLO: Oh, sentite, per questa volta la cerimonia accetto; ma non vi ci avvezzate; non credete di sedurre i

LEPORELLO: Oh, listen, for this time I'll accept your compliments; but don't accustom yourself to it; don't think of

miei pari come le donne, a forza di danari.

DON GIOVANNI: Non parliam più di ciò! ti basta l'animo di far quel ch'io ti dico?

LEPORELLO: Purchè lasciam le donne.

DON GIOVANNI: Lasciar le donne? pazzo! lasciar le donne! Sai ch'elle per me son necessarie più del pan che mangio, più dell'aria che spiro!

LEPORELLO: E avete core d'ingannarle poi tutte?

DON GIOVANNI: È tutto amore; chi a una sola è fedele, verso l'altre è crudele; io che in me sento sì esteso sentimento, vo' bene a tutte quante; le donne poichè calcolar non sanno, il mio buon natural chiamano inganno.

LEPORELLO: Non ho veduto mai naturale più vasto, e più benigno! Orsù, cosa vorreste?

DON GIOVANNI: Odi! vedesti tu la cameriera di Donn'Elvira?

LEPORELLO: Io, no.

DON GIOVANNI: Non hai veduto qualche cosa di bello, caro il mio Leporello; ora io con lei

buying someone like *me* in the same way as women, with your money.

DON GIOVANNI: Let's not talk about it any more. Have you enough spirit to do what I tell you?

LEPORELLO: Provided that we leave women alone.

DON GIOVANNI: Leave women alone? madman! leave women alone! You know that they're more necessary to me than the bread I eat, more than the air I breathe!

LEPORELLO: And you have the heart then to deceive them all?

DON GIOVANNI: It's all love; whoever is faithful only to one is cruel to the others; I, who feel such ample sentiment in myself, love all of them; and since women don't comprehend these things, they call my natural goodness deceit.

LEPORELLO: Never have I seen a nature more ample and more kind! Now then, what would you like?

DON GIOVANNI: Listen! have you seen Donna Elvira's chambermaid?

LEPORELLO: Not I.

DON GIOVANNI: Then you have not seen a thing of beauty, my dear Leporello; I now want to

vo' tentar la mia sorte, ed ho pensato, giacchè siam verso sera, per aguzzarle meglio l'appetito, di presentarmi a lei col tuo vestito.

LEPORELLO: E perchè non potreste presentarvi col vostro?

DON GIOVANNI: Han poco credito con gente di tal rango, gli abiti signorili. Sbrigati, via!

LEPORELLO: Signor, per più ragioni—

DON GIOVANNI: Finiscila! Non soffro opposizione!

try my luck with her, and since it's toward evening, I have thought that I will better arouse her desire by presenting myself to her in your clothes.

LEPORELLO: And why couldn't you present yourself in yours?

DON GIOVANNI: Noble garments have little prestige with people of such station. Come on, hurry!

LEPORELLO: Sir, for many reasons—

DON GIOVANNI: *Impatiently.* Have done with it! I won't stand any opposition!

Leporello gives up in disgust and exchanges hat and cloak with his master. The scene darkens as evening advances. Don Giovanni and Leporello stand in the shadows of Donna Elvira's house as Donna Elvira steps out onto a balcony.

DONNA ELVIRA: Ah, taci, ingiusto core! Non palpitarmi in seno! è un empio, è un traditore, è colpa aver pietà, è colpa aver pietà.

LEPORELLO: Zitto! di Donna Elvira, Signor, la voce io sento!

DON GIOVANNI: Cogliere io vo' il momento, tu fermati un po' là! tu fermati un po' là!

DONNA ELVIRA: Ah, be still, unreasonable heart! Do not pound in my breast! he is a wicked man, he is a betrayer, it is wrong to have pity, it is wrong to have pity.

LEPORELLO: *Whispering to Don Giovanni.* Hush! Sir, I hear Donna Elvira's voice!

DON GIOVANNI: *Whispering to Leporello.* I want to make use of this moment, you stand there a while! you stand there a while!

Don Giovanni pushes Leporello under the balcony, just within Donna Elvira's view, gets behind him, and manipulates his arms in the fashion of a serenader.

Elvira, idolo mio! Elvira, idolo mio!

Elvira, my idol! Elvira, my idol!

Donna Elvira looks down, sees Leporello, and believes him to be Don Giovanni.

DONNA ELVIRA: Non è costui, l'ingrato?

DON GIOVANNI: Sì, vita mia, son' io, e chiedo carità!

DONNA ELVIRA: Numi, che strano effetto mi si risveglia in petto, mi si risveglia in petto!

LEPORELLO: State a veder la pazza, che ancor gli crederà, gli crederà, gli crederà.

DONNA ELVIRA: Isn't it he, the ingrate?

DON GIOVANNI: Yes, my life, it's I, and I plead for your mercy!

DONNA ELVIRA: Gods, what a strange sensation is awakening in my breast, is awakening in my breast!

LEPORELLO: *Aside.* You'll see that the madwoman is going to believe him, believe him, believe him again.

Don Giovanni nudges Leporello into more excited motions.

DON GIOVANNI: Discendi, o gioia bella, o gioia bella! vedrai che tu sei quella, che adora l'alma mia, pentito io sono già!

DONNA ELVIRA: No, non ti credo, o barbaro!

DON GIOVANNI: Ah, credimi! ah, credimi! ah, credimi! o m'uccido!

DONNA ELVIRA: No, non ti credo, o barbaro! no, non ti credo, o barbaro! non ti credo!

DON GIOVANNI: Come down, o beautiful joy, o beautiful joy! You will see that you're the one whom my soul adores, oh yes, I am repentant!

DONNA ELVIRA: No, I do not believe you, o cruel man!

DON GIOVANNI: Ah, believe me! ah, believe me! ah, believe me! or I'll kill myself!

DONNA ELVIRA: No, I do not believe you, o cruel man! no, I do not believe you, o cruel man! I do not believe you!

LEPORELLO: Se seguitate, io rido!

DON GIOVANNI: —o m'uccido!

LEPORELLO: Se seguitate, io rido!

DON GIOVANNI: —ah, m'uccido!

LEPORELLO: —se seguitate, io rido, rido, rido, rido, rido, rido, rido, rido, rido, rido!

DON GIOVANNI: —idolo mio, vien quà!

DONNA ELVIRA: Dei, che cimento è questo! non sò s'io vado, o resto? ah, proteggete voi la mia credulità, credulità! Dei, che cimento è questo, Dei, che cimento è questo, non sò s'io vado, non sò s'io resto! Dei, che cimento è questo, non sò s'io vado o resto! ah, proteggete voi la mia credulità, credulità, la mia credulità, la mia credulità!

DON GIOVANNI: Spero che cada presto! che bel colpetto è questo? più fertile talento del mio, no, non si dà, più fertile talento, no, del mio, no, non si dà! Spero che cada presto! che bel colpetto è questo, che bel colpetto, spero che cada presto, che bel colpetto è questo! più fertile talento del mio, no, non si dà, più fertile

LEPORELLO: *Softly.* If you keep it up, I'll laugh!

DON GIOVANNI: —or I'll kill myself!

LEPORELLO: If you keep it up, I'll laugh!

DON GIOVANNI: —ah, I'll kill myself!

LEPORELLO: —if you keep it up, I'll laugh, laugh, laugh, laugh, laugh, laugh, laugh, laugh, laugh, laugh!

DON GIOVANNI: —my idol, come here!

DONNA ELVIRA: Gods, what a trial this is! I don't know whether to go or to stay? ah, protect ye my trust, trust! Gods, what a trial this is, Gods, what a trial this is, I don't know whether to go, I don't know whether to stay! Gods, what a trial this is, I don't know whether to go or to stay! ah, protect ye my trust, trust, my trust, my trust!

DON GIOVANNI: I hope she will break down soon! what a pretty little trick this is? there is no talent more versatile than mine, no, there is no talent more versatile, no, than mine, no! I hope she will break down soon! what a pretty little trick this is, what a pretty little trick, I hope she will break down soon, what a

talento, no, del mio, no, non si dà, no, non si dà, no, non si dà!

pretty little trick this is! there is no talent more versatile than mine, no, there is no talent more versatile than mine, no, no, no, there is not, no, there is not!

LEPORELLO: Già quel mendace labbro torna a sedur costei, deh proteggete, oh Dei! la sua credulità, credulità! Già quel mendace labbro torna a sedur costei, già quel mendace labbro torna a sedur costei, deh proteggete, oh Dei, la sua credulità, credulità, credulità, credulità!

LEPORELLO: Already those lying lips begin to seduce her again, come, protect, oh Gods! her trust, trust! already those lying lips begin to seduce her again, already those lying lips begin to seduce her again, come protect, oh Gods, her trust, trust, trust, trust!

Donna Elvira leaves the balcony and re-enters the house.

DON GIOVANNI: Amico, che ti par?

DON GIOVANNI: Friend, what do you think?

LEPORELLO: Mi par che abbiate un'anima di bronzo.

LEPORELLO: I think you have a lot of nerve.

DON GIOVANNI: Va la, che sei'l gran gonzo! Ascolta bene: quando costei qui viene, tu corri ad abbracciarla, falle quattro carezze, fingi la voce mia; poi con bell'arte cerca teco condurla in altra parte.

DON GIOVANNI: Go on, you're a big blockhead! listen closely: when she comes here, you run to embrace her, give her a couple of caresses, imitate my voice; then, with nice artfulness, try to lead her elsewhere.

LEPORELLO: Ma, Signore—

LEPORELLO: But Sir—

DON GIOVANNI: Non più repliche.

DON GIOVANNI: Don't talk back.

LEPORELLO: E se poi mi conosce?

LEPORELLO: And then if she recognizes me?

DON GIOVANNI: Non ti conoscerà, se tu non vuoi; zitto: ell'apre, ehi, giudizio!

DON GIOVANNI: She won't recognize you if you don't want her to; hush, she's unlocking the door, careful!

Don Giovanni takes cover and watches. Donna Elvira
comes out of the house and meets Leporello, who goes
to her, keeping his face averted.

DONNA ELVIRA: Eccomi a voi.

DON GIOVANNI: (Veggiamo che farà.)

LEPORELLO: (Che imbroglio!)

DONNA ELVIRA: Dunque creder potrò che i pianti miei abbian vinto quel cor? dunque pentito, l'amato Don Giovanni, al suo dovere, e all'amor mio ritorna?

DONNA ELVIRA: *To Leporello.* I've come to you.

DON GIOVANNI: *To himself.* Let's see what she will do.

LEPORELLO: *To himself.* What a mess!

DONNA ELVIRA: Can I believe that my tears have conquered that heart? so repentant, my beloved Don Giovanni returns to his obligation and to my love?

Leporello manages a muffled approximation
of Don Giovanni's voice.

LEPORELLO: Sì, carina!

DONNA ELVIRA: Crudele! se sapeste quante lagrime e quanti sospir voi mi costate!

LEPORELLO: Io, vita mia?

DONNA ELVIRA: Voi.

LEPORELLO: Poverina! quanto mi dispiace!

DONNA ELVIRA: Mi fuggirete più?

LEPORELLO: No, muso bello!

DONNA ELVIRA: Sarete sempre mio?

LEPORELLO: Sempre!

LEPORELLO: Yes, dear!

DONNA ELVIRA: Cruel man! if you knew how many tears and how many sighs you cost me!

LEPORELLO: I, my life?

DONNA ELVIRA: You.

LEPORELLO: Poor little girl! how sorry I am!

DONNA ELVIRA: Will you run away from me again?

LEPORELLO: No, pretty little face!

DONNA ELVIRA: Will you always be mine?

LEPORELLO: *Most amorously.* Always!

DONNA ELVIRA: Carissimo!

DONNA ELVIRA: Dearest!

LEPORELLO: Carissima! (La burla mi dà gusto.)

LEPORELLO: Dearest!
To himself. This joke suits me.

DONNA ELVIRA: Mio tesoro!

DONNA ELVIRA: My treasure!

LEPORELLO: Mia Venere!

LEPORELLO: My Venus!

Donna Elvira flings her arms about Leporello.

DONNA ELVIRA: Son per voi tutta foco.

DONNA ELVIRA: I'm all aflame for you.

LEPORELLO: Io tutto cenere.

LEPORELLO: I'm all ashes.

DON GIOVANNI: (Il birbo si riscalda.)

DON GIOVANNI: *To himself.* The rascal is becoming passionate.

DONNA ELVIRA: E non m'ingannerete?

DONNA ELVIRA: And you won't deceive me?

LEPORELLO: No, sicuro.

LEPORELLO: Certainly not.

DONNA ELVIRA: Giuratemi.

DONNA ELVIRA: Swear it to me.

LEPORELLO: Lo giuro a questa mano, che bacio con trasporto, e a quei bei lumi.

LEPORELLO: I swear it by this hand, which I kiss with rapture, and by those beautiful eyes.

Don Giovanni leaps out in front of them and pretends to be a robber assaulting them.

DON GIOVANNI: Ih, eh, ah, ah; sei morto!

DON GIOVANNI: Hee, heh, hah, hah; you're dead!

DONNA ELVIRA AND LEPORELLO: O Numi!

DONNA ELVIRA AND LEPORELLO: O Gods!

Donna Elvira and Leporello flee hastily. Don Giovanni recovers the mandolin which Leporello had pretended to use earlier.

DON GIOVANNI: Ih, eh, ih, eh, ah, ah! Par che la sorte mi secondi; veggiamo. Le finestre son queste; ora cantiamo.

DON GIOVANNI: Hee, heh, hee, heh, hah, hah! It seems luck is with me; let's see. These are the windows; now let's sing.

*He strums the mandolin beneath the balcony
and sings a serenade.*

Deh vieni alla finestra, o mio tesoro, deh vieni a consolar il pianto mio. Se neghi a me di dar qualche ristoro, davanti agli occhi tuoi morir vogl'io! Tu ch'hai la bocca dolce, più che il miele, tu che il zucchero porti in mezzo al core! Non esser, gioia mia, con me crudele! lasciati almen veder, mio bell'amore!

Come, come to the window, oh my treasure, come, come to console my tears. If you refuse to give me some relief, I will die before your eyes! You have a mouth sweeter than honey, you who bring sweetness to the depths of my heart! Do not be cruel with me, my joy! At least let yourself be seen, my beautiful love!

*As Don Giovanni finishes his serenade, Masetto
appears, carrying weapons. With him are peasants and
village men, also armed with guns and clubs.*

DON GIOVANNI: V'è gente alla finestra; sarà dessa! Zi, zi!

DON GIOVANNI: There's somebody at the window; it must be she! Psst, psst!

MASETTO: Non ci stanchiamo; il cor mi dice che trovarlo dobbiam.

MASETTO: *To his companions.* Let's not give up; my heart tells me that we shall find him.

DON GIOVANNI: (Qualcuno parla!)

DON GIOVANNI: *To himself.* Someone is speaking!

MASETTO: Fermatevi; mi pare che alcuno qui si muova.

MASETTO: Stand still; I think someone is moving around here.

*Don Giovanni wraps Leporello's cloak about himself
and pulls his servant's hat over his face.*

DON GIOVANNI: (Se non fallo, è Masetto!)

DON GIOVANNI: *To himself.* If I'm not mistaken, it's Masetto!

MASETTO: Chi va là? non risponde; animo, schioppo al muso! Chi va là?

MASETTO: Who goes there? He doesn't answer; courage, guns up! Who goes there?

Act 2, Scene 1. Don Giovanni, with mandolin, serenades Donna Elvira's maid. John Brownlee as Don Giovanni.

Act 2, Scene 1. Donna Elvira, on her balcony, as Leporello serenades her below, believes that Don Giovanni may really love her. Elisabeth Schwarzkopf is Donna Elvira.

Act 2, Scene 1. Don Giovanni, disguised as Leporello, tells Masetto he will help him find and kill the Don. Giorgio Tozzi is Don Giovanni, Joshua Hecht is Masetto.

DON GIOVANNI: (Non è solo; ci vuol giudizio.)

DON GIOVANNI: *To himself.* He's not alone; this needs prudence.

Don Giovanni feigns Leporello's voice.

Amici! (Non mi voglio scoprir.) Sei tu, Masetto?

Friends! (I don't want to be found out.) Is it you, Masetto?

MASETTO: Appunto quello: e tu?

MASETTO: *With surprise.* Just so: and you?

DON GIOVANNI: Non mi conosci? il servo son io di Don Giovanni.

DON GIOVANNI: Don't you know me? I'm Don Giovanni's servant.

MASETTO: Leporello! servo di quell'indegno cavaliere!

MASETTO: Leporello! servant of that unworthy nobleman!

DON GIOVANNI: Certo, di quel briccone!

DON GIOVANNI: Certainly, of that rogue!

MASETTO: Di quell'uom senza onore: ah, dimmi un poco, dove possiam trovarlo; lo cerco con costor per trucidarlo.

MASETTO: Of that man without honor: ah, tell me a bit where we can find him; I'm looking for him with these men in order to kill him.

DON GIOVANNI: (Bagatelle!) Bravissimo, Masetto! anch'io con voi m'unisco, per fargliela a quel birbo di padrone; or senti un po' qual è la mia intenzione. Metà di voi quà vadano, e gli altri vadan là! e pian pianin lo cerchino, lontan non sia di quà, no! lontan, lontan non sia di quà! Se un uom e una ragazza passeggian per la piazza, se sotto a una finestra fare all'amor sentite, ferite, pur, ferite, ferite, pur, ferite, il mio padron sarà! In testa egli ha un cappello con candidi pennacchi, addosso un gran

DON GIOVANNI: *Aside.* Rubbish! *Aloud.* Very good, Masetto! I'll join you, too, in order to do in that rogue of a master; now listen a bit to what my plan is. Half of you go that way, and the others go there! and look for him quietly, quietly, he may not be far from here, no! he may not be far, far from here! If a man and a maid are walking through the square, if you hear someone making love under a window, strike, then, strike, strike, then, strike, it will be my master! He has a hat with white plumes on his

mantello, e spada al fianco egli ha, e spada al fianco egli ha, e spada al fianco egli ha, e spada al fianco egli ha, e spada al fianco egli ha. Se un uom e una ragazza passeggian per la piazza, se sotto a una finestra fare all'amor sentite, ferite, ferite, ferite, pur ferite, ferite, pur ferite, ferite! Metà di voi quà vadano, e gli altri vadan là. E pian pianin lo cerchino, lontan non sia di quà, no, lontan, lontan non sia di quà.

head, a big cloak around him, and he has a sword at his side, and he has a sword at his side, and he has a sword at his side, and he has a sword at his side, and he has a sword at his side. If a man and a maid are walking through the square, if you hear someone making love under a window, strike, strike, strike, then strike, strike, then strike, strike! Half of you go that way, and the others go there. And look for him quietly, quietly, he may not be far from here, no, he may not be far, far from here.

He waves the men off in all directions.

Andate, fate presto, andate, fate presto, fate presto, fate presto, fate presto, fate presto.

Go, be quick, go, be quick, be quick, be quick, be quick, be quick.

He turns to Masetto.

Tu sol verrai con me, tu sol verrai con me, verrai con me, verrai con me.

You alone will come with me, you alone will come with me, will come with me, will come with me.

He pretends great friendship for Masetto.

Noi far dobbiam il resto, e già vedrai cos'è, cos'è, cos'è, noi far dobbiam il resto, e già vedrai cos'è, cos'è, cos'è, e già vedrai cos'è, cos'è, cos'è, e già vedrai cos'è, e già vedrai cos'è, e già vedrai cos'è, e già vedrai cos'è!

We must do what's left, and you'll soon see what it is, what it is, what it is, we must do what's left, and you'll soon see what it is, what it is, what it is, and you'll soon see what it is, what it is, what it is, and you'll soon see what it is, and you'll soon see what it is, and you'll soon see what it is, and you'll soon see what it is!

*The peasants scatter in all directions. Don Giovanni
maneuvers Masetto into the shadows.*

Zitto, lascia ch'io senta!
Ottimamente! Dunque dob-
biam ucciderlo?

Hush, let me listen! Excellent!
Should we kill him, then?

MASETTO: Sicuro!

MASETTO: Surely!

DON GIOVANNI: E non ti baste-
ria rompergli l'ossa, fracassar-
gli le spalle?

DON GIOVANNI: And it won't
satisfy you to break his bones,
to fracture his back?

MASETTO: No, no, voglio ammazzarlo, vo' farlo in cento
brani.

MASETTO: *Angrily and with de-
termination.* No, no, I want to
kill him, I want to chop him
into a hundred pieces.

DON GIOVANNI: Hai buone
armi?

DON GIOVANNI: Have you got
good weapons?

MASETTO: Cospetto! ho pria
questo moschetto, e poi,
questa pistola.

MASETTO: Yes, by God! I've
got first this musket, and then
this pistol.

*Masetto proudly hands his weapons to the supposed
Leporello for inspection.*

DON GIOVANNI: E poi?

DON GIOVANNI: And then?

MASETTO: Non basta?

MASETTO: Isn't that enough?

*Don Giovanni knocks Masetto down with his own
weapons and beats him.*

DON GIOVANNI: Oh, basta, certo: or prendi, questa per la
pistola, questa per il moschetto!

DON GIOVANNI: Oh, it's
enough, certainly: now take
this for the pistol, this for the
musket!

MASETTO: Ahi, ahi! la testa
mia!

MASETTO: Oh, oh! my head!

DON GIOVANNI: Taci, o sei morto! Questa per ammazzarlo, questa per farlo in brani! Villano, mascalzon! ceffo da cani!

DON GIOVANNI: Be quiet, or you're dead! This is for killing him, this for chopping him into bits! Villain, scoundrel! Dirty dog!

Tossing the gun and pistol down beside Masetto, Don Giovanni beats a hasty retreat.

MASETTO: Ahi, ahi! la testa mia! ahi, ahi! le spalle, e il petto—

MASETTO: Oh, oh! my head! oh, oh! my shoulders and my chest—

Zerlina enters, carrying a light.

ZERLINA: Di sentire mi parve la voce di Masetto!

ZERLINA: I think I hear Masetto's voice!

MASETTO: O Dio, Zerlina, Zerlina mia, soccorso!

MASETTO: O God, Zerlina, my Zerlina, help!

ZERLINA: Cosa è stato?

ZERLINA: What's happened?

MASETTO: L'iniquo, il scellerato mi ruppe l'ossa e i nervi.

MASETTO: The wicked man, the villain broke my bones and sinews.

ZERLINA: Oh poveretta me! chi?

ZERLINA: Oh poor me! who?

MASETTO: Leporello! o qualche diavol che somiglia a lui!

MASETTO: Leporello! or some devil that looks like him!

Zerlina helps Masetto stagger to his feet.

ZERLINA: Crudel! non tel diss'io che con questa tua pazza gelosia ti ridurresti a qualche brutto passo? dove ti duole?

ZERLINA: Cruel man! didn't I tell you that your crazy jealousy would bring you to grief? where does it hurt you?

MASETTO: Qui.

MASETTO: *Whining.* Here.

ZERLINA: E poi?

ZERLINA: Where else?

MASETTO: Qui, ancora qui.

MASETTO: Here, here too.

ZERLINA: E poi non ti duol altro?

ZERLINA: And it doesn't hurt you anywhere else?

MASETTO: Duolmi un poco questo piè, questo braccio, e questo mano.

ZERLINA: Via, via, non è gran mal, se il resto è sano. Vientene meco a casa; purchè tu mi prometta d'essere men geloso, io, io ti guarirò, caro il mio sposo.
Vedrai, carino, se sei buonino, che bel rimedio ti voglio dar. È naturale, non dà disgusto, e lo speziale non lo sa far, no, non lo sa far, no, non lo sa far.

È un certo balsamo che porto addosso, dare tel posso, se il vuoi provar. Saper vorresti dove mi sta, dove, dove, dove mi sta?

Zerlina takes Masetto's hand and holds it to her heart.

Sentilo battere, toccami quà, sentilo battere, sentilo battere, toccami quà! sentilo battere, sentilo battere, sentilo battere, toccami quà, quà, quà! Sentilo battere, toccami quà, quà! toccami quà, quà! toccami quà, quà! toccami quà!

MASETTO: This foot hurts me a little, this arm, and this hand.

ZERLINA: Come, come, it's not very bad if the rest is all right. Come home with me; provided you promise me to be less jealous, I, I'll heal you, my dear husband.
You'll see, dearest, if you're very good, what a lovely medicine I'll give you. It's natural, it won't make you sick, and the apothecary doesn't know how to make it, no, he doesn't know how to make it, no, he doesn't know how to make it.
It's a certain balm that I carry with me, I can give it to you if you want to try it. Would you like to know where I keep it, where, where, where I keep it?

Feel it beating, touch me here, feel it beating, feel it beating, touch me here! feel it beating, feel it beating, feel it beating, touch me here, here, here! Feel it beating, touch me here, here! touch me here, here! touch me here, here! touch me here!

Exit Zerlina and Masetto, their arms about one another.

Scene Two

Later the same night, in a dark courtyard or garden outside the house of Donna Anna. Leporello enters, escorting Donna Elvira. He is still dressed in the Don's hat and cloak, and still tries to keep his face averted from Donna Elvira's direct sight.

LEPORELLO: Di molte faci il lume s'avvicina, o mio ben; stiamo qui ascosi, finchè da noi si scosta.

LEPORELLO: Lights are coming toward us from all around, o my dear; let's stay hidden here until they go away from us.

DONNA ELVIRA: Ma che temi, adorato mio sposo?

DONNA ELVIRA: But what are you afraid of, my adored husband?

LEPORELLO: Nulla, nulla, certi riguardi, io vo' veder se il lume è già lontano. (Ah, come da costei liberarmi?) Rimanti, anima bella.

LEPORELLO: Nothing, nothing, certain considerations, I want to see whether the lights are gone away yet. *To himself.* Ah, how to get rid of her? *Aloud.* Stay here, beautiful spirit.

DONNA ELVIRA: Ah! non lasciarmi! Sola, sola in buio loco palpitar il cor mi sento, e m'assale un tal spavento, che mi sembra di morir, che mi sembra di morir.

DONNA ELVIRA: Ah! don't leave me! Alone, alone in a dark place, I feel my heart pounding, and such fear overwhelms me that I think I'm dying, I think I'm dying.

Leporello fumbles about in the dark.

LEPORELLO: Più che cerco, men ritrovo questa porta, questa porta sciagurata;

LEPORELLO: The more I look, the less I find this door, this confounded door;

He gropes his way to the door and loses it again in the dark.

piano, piano, l'ho trovata, l'ho trovata! ecco il tempo di fuggir, ecco il tempo di fuggir, ecco il tempo, ecco il tempo, ecco il tempo di fuggir!

softly, softly, I've found it, I've found it! now's the time to get away, now's the time to get away, now's the time, now's the time, now's the time to get away!

Don Ottavio and Donna Anna enter.
She is still dressed in mourning.

DON OTTAVIO: Tergi il ciglio, o vita mia, e dà calma al tuo dolore! l'ombra omai del genitore pena avrà de' tuoi martir, de' tuoi martir.

DON OTTAVIO: Dry your eyes, o my life, and calm your sorrow! you will grieve your parent's shade with your torment, with your torment.

DONNA ANNA: Lascia almen alla mia pena questo piccolo ristoro; sol la morte, sol la morte, o mio tesoro, il mio pianto può finir, il mio pianto può finir.

DONNA ANNA: Leave at least this small relief to my suffering; only death, only death, o my treasure, can end my weeping, can end my weeping.

Meanwhile, Donna Elvira and
Leporello remain unnoticed.

DONNA ELVIRA: Ah, dov'è lo sposo mio?

DONNA ELVIRA: Ah, where is my husband?

LEPORELLO: Se mi trova, son perduto!

LEPORELLO: If I'm found, I'm lost!

DONNA ELVIRA: Una porta là vegg'io, cheta, cheta io vo' partir, cheta, cheta io vo' partir.

DONNA ELVIRA: I see a door over there, I want to depart quietly, quietly, I want to depart quietly, quietly.

LEPORELLO: Una porta là vegg'io, cheto, cheto io vo' partir, cheto, cheto, cheto, cheto, cheto cheto io vo' partir.

LEPORELLO: I see a door over there, I want to depart quietly, quietly, I want to depart quietly, quietly, quietly, quietly, quietly, quietly.

As Leporello tries to sneak through the door, he is
seized by Masetto and Zerlina, who enter.

ZERLINA AND MASETTO: Ferma, briccone, dove ten vai?

ZERLINA AND MASETTO: Stop, rogue, where are you going?

They push Leporello before Don Ottavio and Donna Anna. Leporello falls to his knees and buries his face in his (i.e. Don Giovanni's) cloak.

DONNA ANNA AND DON OTTAVIO: Ecco il fellone, com'era quà?

DONNA ANNA AND DON OTTAVIO: Here is the criminal, how came he here?

DONNA ANNA, ZERLINA, DON OTTAVIO AND MASETTO: Ah, mora il perfido! che m'ha tradito, che m'ha tradito!

DONNA ANNA, ZERLINA, DON OTTAVIO AND MASETTO: Ah, death to the wicked man! he that has betrayed me, he that has betrayed me!

Donna Elvira steps forth and reveals her presence to the others.

DONNA ELVIRA: O mio marito! pietà, pietà, pietà!

DONNA ELVIRA: O my husband! have pity, have pity, have pity!

DONNA ANNA: È Donna Elvira? è Donna Elvira quella ch'io vedo? appena il credo!

DONNA ANNA: Is it Donna Elvira? is it Donna Elvira that I see? I can hardly believe it!

ZERLINA: È Donna Elvira? è Donna Elvira quella ch'io vedo? appena il credo, appena il credo!

ZERLINA: Is it Donna Elvira? is it Donna Elvira that I see? I can hardly believe it, I can hardly believe it!

DON OTTAVIO: È Donna Elvira? Donna Elvira quella ch'io vedo? appena il credo!

DON OTTAVIO: Is it Donna Elvira? Donna Elvira that I see? I can hardly believe it!

MASETTO: È Donna Elvira quella ch'io vedo? appena il credo!

MASETTO: Is it Donna Elvira that I see? I can hardly believe it!

DONNA ANNA, ZERLINA, DON OTTAVIO AND MASETTO: No, no, no, no, morrà!

DONNA ANNA, ZERLINA, DON OTTAVIO AND MASETTO: No, no, no, no, he shall die!

DONNA ELVIRA: Pietà—

DONNA ELVIRA: Have pity—

DONNA ANNA, ZERLINA, DON OTTAVIO AND MASETTO: No!

DONNA ELVIRA: Pietà!

DONNA ANNA, ZERLINA, DON OTTAVIO AND MASETTO: No,—

DONNA ELVIRA: Pietà, pietà—

DONNA ANNA, ZERLINA, DON OTTAVIO AND MASETTO: No, no, no, no, morrà!

DONNA ANNA, ZERLINA, DON OTTAVIO AND MASETTO: No!

DONNA ELVIRA: Have pity!

DONNA ANNA, ZERLINA, DON OTTAVIO AND MASETTO: No,—

DONNA ELVIRA: Have pity, have pity—

DONNA ANNA, ZERLINA, DON OTTAVIO AND MASETTO: No, no, no, no, he shall die!

As they seize the supposed Don Giovanni, Leporello grovels before them and reveals his identity. All the others are appalled, especially Donna Elvira, who runs to Donna Anna, as if for comfort.

LEPORELLO: Perdon, perdono! Signori miei! quello io non sono, sbaglia costei, viver lasciatemi, per carità, viver lasciatemi per carità, per carità, per carità!

DONNA ANNA, DONNA ELVIRA, ZERLINA, DON OTTAVIO AND MASETTO: Dei! Leporello? Che inganno è questo! Leporello? Che inganno è questo!

DONNA ANNA, DONNA ELVIRA AND ZERLINA: Stupida resto!

DON OTTAVIO AND MASETTO: Stupido resto!

DONNA ANNA: Che mai sarà, che mai sarà, che mai sarà, che mai sarà!

DONNA ELVIRA, ZERLINA AND DON OTTAVIO: Che mai sarà, che mai sarà, che mai sarà, che mai sarà, che mai sarà!

LEPORELLO: Forgive me, forgive me! my lords and ladies! I'm not him, she's mistaken, let me live, for pity's sake, let me live, for pity's sake, for pity's sake, for pity's sake!

DONNA ANNA, DONNA ELVIRA, ZERLINA, DON OTTAVIO AND MASETTO: Gods! Leporello? what deceit is this! Leporello? what deceit is this!

DONNA ANNA, DONNA ELVIRA AND ZERLINA: I am stunned!

DON OTTAVIO AND MASETTO: I am stunned!

DONNA ANNA: Whatever can it mean, whatever can it mean, whatever can it mean, whatever can it mean!

DONNA ELVIRA, ZERLINA AND DON OTTAVIO: Whatever can it mean, whatever can it mean, whatever can it mean,

MASETTO: Che mai sarà, che mai sarà, che mai sarà, che mai sarà!

LEPORELLO: Mille torbidi pensieri mi s'aggiran per la testa.

DONNA ANNA, DONNA ELVIRA, ZERLINA, DON OTTAVIO AND MASETTO: Mille torbidi pensieri mi s'aggiran per la testa.

LEPORELLO: Mille torbidi pensieri mi s'aggiran per la testa; se mi salvo in tal tempesta è un prodigio in verità.

DONNA ANNA, DONNA ELVIRA, ZERLINA, DON OTTAVIO AND MASETTO: Che giornata, o stelle, è questa, o stelle, è questa!

LEPORELLO: È un prodigio in verità, se mi salvo in tal tempesta è un prodigio in verità, è un prodigio in verità, in verità, in verità, è un prodigio in verità!

DONNA ANNA, DONNA ELVIRA, ZERLINA, DON OTTAVIO AND MASETTO: Che impensata novità!

LEPORELLO: Mille torbidi pensieri mi s'aggiran per la testa! se mi salvo in tal tempesta è un prodigio in verità!

whatever can it mean, whatever can it mean!

MASETTO: Whatever can it mean, whatever can it mean, whatever can it mean, whatever can it mean!

LEPORELLO: A thousand confused thoughts are churning through my head.

DONNA ANNA, DONNA ELVIRA, ZERLINA, DON OTTAVIO AND MASETTO: A thousand confused thoughts are churning through my head.

LEPORELLO: A thousand confused thoughts are churning through my head; if I save myself in this storm, it will truly be a marvel.

DONNA ANNA, DONNA ELVIRA, ZERLINA, DON OTTAVIO AND MASETTO: What a day, o my stars, is this, o my stars, is this!

LEPORELLO: It will truly be a marvel if I save myself in this storm, it will truly be a marvel, it will truly, truly be a marvel, it will truly be a marvel!

DONNA ANNA, DONNA ELVIRA, ZERLINA, DON OTTAVIO AND MASETTO: What an unexpected development!

LEPORELLO: A thousand confused thoughts are churning through my head! if I save myself in this storm, it will truly be a marvel!

DONNA ANNA, DONNA ELVIRA, ZERLINA, DON OTTAVIO AND MASETTO: Che impensata, che impensata novità!

DONNA ANNA, DONNA ELVIRA, ZERLINA, DON OTTAVIO AND MASETTO: What an unexpected, what an unexpected development!

DONNA ELVIRA, DON OTTAVIO AND MASETTO: Che impensata novita!

DONNA ELVIRA, DON OTTAVIO AND MASETTO: What an unexpected development!

ZERLINA: Che impensata novità!

ZERLINA: What an unexpected development!

DONNA ANNA: —novità!

DONNA ANNA: —development!

LEPORELLO: È un prodigio in verità!

LEPORELLO: It will truly be a marvel!

DONNA ANNA AND DON OTTAVIO: Mille torbidi pensieri mi s'aggiran per la testa.

DONNA ANNA AND DON OTTAVIO: A thousand confused thoughts are churning through my head.

DONNA ELVIRA: Mille, mille torbidi pensieri mi s'aggiran per la testa.

DONNA ELVIRA: A thousand, thousand confused thoughts are churning through my head.

ZERLINA AND MASETTO: Mille torbidi pensieri mi s'aggiran per la testa.

ZERLINA AND MASETTO: A thousand confused thoughts are churning through my head.

LEPORELLO: Mille torbidi pensieri mi s'aggiran per la testa, se mi salvo in tal tempesta, è un prodigio in verità,—

LEPORELLO: A thousand confused thoughts are churning through my head, if I save myself in this storm, it will truly be a marvel,—

DONNA ANNA, DONNA ELVIRA, ZERLINA, DON OTTAVIO AND MASETTO: Che giornata, o stelle, è questa, o stelle, è questa!

DONNA ANNA, DONNA ELVIRA, ZERLINA, DON OTTAVIO AND MASETTO: What a day, o my stars, is this, o my stars, is this!

LEPORELLO: —è un prodigio in verità, se mi salvo in tal

LEPORELLO: —it will truly be a marvel, if I save myself in this

tempesta è un prodigio in verità, è un prodigio in verità! in verità, in verità, è un prodigio in verità!

DONNA ANNA, DONNA ELVIRA, ZERLINA, DON OTTAVIO AND MASETTO: Che impensata novità!

LEPORELLO: Mille torbidi pensieri mi s'aggiran per la testa! se mi salvo in tal tempesta, è un prodigio in verità!

DONNA ANNA, DONNA ELVIRA, ZERLINA, DON OTTAVIO AND MASETTO: Che impensata, che impensata novità,—

DONNA ELVIRA, DON OTTAVIO AND MASETTO: —che impensata novità, che impensata novità, novità,—

ZERLINA: —che impensata novità, che impensata novità, che impensata novità,—

DONNA ANNA: —novità, che impensata novità, che impensata novità,—

LEPORELLO: —è un prodigio in verità, è un prodigio in verità, in verità, è un prodigio in verità, è un prodigio in verità, è un prodigio,—

DONNA ANNA, DONNA ELVIRA, ZERLINA, DON OTTAVIO AND

storm, it will truly be a marvel, it will truly be a marvel! it will truly, truly, truly be a marvel!

DONNA ANNA, DONNA ELVIRA, ZERLINA, DON OTTAVIO AND MASETTO: What an unexpected development!

LEPORELLO: A thousand confused thoughts are churning through my head! if I save myself in this storm, it will truly be a marvel!

DONNA ANNA, DONNA ELVIRA, ZERLINA, DON OTTAVIO AND MASETTO: What an unexpected, what an unexpected development,—

DONNA ELVIRA, DON OTTAVIO AND MASETTO: —what an unexpected development, what an unexpected development, development,—

ZERLINA: —what an unexpected development, what an unexpected development, what an unexpected development,—

DONNA ANNA: —development, what an unexpected development, what an unexpected development,—

LEPORELLO: —it will truly be a marvel, it will truly, truly be a marvel, it will truly be a marvel, it will truly be a marvel, it will be a marvel,—

DONNA ANNA, DONNA ELVIRA, ZERLINA, DON OTTAVIO AND

MASETTO: —che impensata novità, che impensata novità, che impensata, che impensata novità,—

LEPORELLO: —è un prodigio in verità, è un prodigio in verità, è un prodigio in verità!

DONNA ANNA, DONNA ELVIRA, ZERLINA, DON OTTAVIO AND MASETTO: —che impensata novità, che impensata novità, che impensata novità!

LEPORELLO: Ah, pietà! Signori miei! ah, pietà, pietà, pietà, pietà di me, pietà! Dò ragioni a voi, a lei, a voi, a lei. Ma, ma il delitto, il delitto mio non è, mio non è. Il padron con prepotenza l'innocenza mi rubò, l'innocenza mi rubò.

Donna Elvira! compatite! compatite! Voi capite come andò, voi capite, voi capite, voi capite come andò!

Di Masetto non sò nulla, non sò nulla, nulla, nulla, nulla, nulla, vel dirà questa fanciulla, questa fanciulla. È un'oretta circumcirca, che con lei girando vo, che con lei girando vo.

MASETTO: —what an unexpected development, what an unexpected development, what an unexpected, what an unexpected development,—

LEPORELLO: —it will truly be a marvel, it will truly be a marvel, it will truly be a marvel!

DONNA ANNA, DONNA ELVIRA, ZERLINA, DON OTTAVIO AND MASETTO: —what an unexpected development, what an unexpected development, what an unexpected development!

LEPORELLO: Ah, have mercy! My lords and ladies! ah, have mercy, have mercy, have mercy, have mercy for me, have mercy! I'll explain to you, to her, to you, to her. But, but the fault, the fault isn't mine, isn't mine. My master haughtily robbed me of my innocence, robbed me of my innocence.

To Donna Elvira. Donna Elvira! have sympathy! have sympathy! You know how it went, how it went, you know, you know, you know how it went!

To Masetto. About Masetto I know nothing, I know nothing, nothing, nothing, nothing, nothing, this girl, this girl, will tell you so. It's more or less a short hour that I've been strolling with her, that I've been strolling with her.

A voi, Signore! non dico niente, certo timore—certo accidente—di fuori chiaro—di dentro oscuro—non c'è riparo—la porta, il muro—io me ne vo da quel lato, poi qui celato, l'affar si sa, oh, si sa! ma s'io sapeva, fuggia per quà, fuggia per quà, fuggia per quà, fuggia per quà.

To Don Ottavio. To you, Sir! I'll say nothing—a certain fear—certain events—light outside—dark inside—there wasn't any shelter—the door, the wall—I want to get away this way, then hidden here—the matter is plain, oh, it is plain! But if I had known, I'd have left this way, left this way, left this way, left this way.

As he sings, Leporello edges toward the garden door and escapes.

DONNA ELVIRA: Ferma, perfido, ferma!

MASETTO: Il birbo ha l'ali ai piedi!

ZERLINA: Con qual arte si sottrasse l'iniquo.

DON OTTAVIO: Amici miei, dopo eccessi sì enormi, dubitar non possiam che Don Giovanni non sia l'empio uccisore del padre di Donn'Anna; in questa casa poche ore fermatevi, un ricorso vo' far a chi si deve, e in poch'istanti vendicarvi prometto. Così vuole dover, pietade, affetto.
Il mio tesoro intanto andate, andate a consolar! e del bel ciglio il pianto cercate di asciugar, cercate, cercate, cercate di asciugar, cercate di asciugar. Ditele che i suoi

DONNA ELVIRA: Stop, deceiver, stop!

MASETTO: The rogue has wings on his feet!

ZERLINA: How artfully the wicked man got away.

DON OTTAVIO: My friends, after his enormous excesses, we cannot doubt that Don Giovanni is the wicked murderer of Donna Anna's father; wait a few hours in this house, I want to make an appeal to those whose business it is, and in a little while I promise you vengeance. Thus duty, pity and affection will it.
Meanwhile, go, go to console my treasure! and try to dry the tears from her lovely lashes, try, try, try to dry them, try to dry them. Tell her that I am going to avenge her

torti a vendicar io vado, a vendicar io vado; che sol di stragi e morti nunzio vogl'io tornar, nunzio vogl'io tornar, sì, nunzio vogl'io tornar! Il mio tesoro intanto andate, andate a consolar! e del bel ciglio il pianto cercate di a-sciugar, cercate, cercate, cer-cate di asciugar, cercate di asciugar. Ditele che i suoi torti a vendicar io vado, a vendicar io vado, che sol di stragi e mor-ti nunzio vogl'io tornar, nun-zio, nunzio vogl'io tornar, che sol di stragi e morti nun-zio vogl'io tornar, sì, nunzio vogl'io tornar!

wrongs, I am going to avenge her wrongs; that I will return only as news-bearer of destruc-tion and death, I will return as news-bearer, yes, I will return as news-bearer! Meanwhile, go, go to console my treasure! and try to dry the tears from her lovely lashes, try, try, try to dry them, try to dry them. Tell her that I am going to avenge her wrongs, I am going to avenge her wrongs, that I will return only as news-bearer of destruction and death, that I will return as news-bearer, news-bearer, that I will return only as news-bearer of des-truction and death, yes, I will return as news-bearer.

The aria " Il mio tesoro" originally marked the end of Scene 2, Act II. Mozart added the following scene and Donna Elvira's aria " Mi tradì" for the Vienna première of Don Giovanni. Because the scene itself is hardly ever performed, Donna Elvira generally sings her aria immediately after Don Ottavio makes his exit, above.

Scene Three

A sparsely furnished room with a window on one side. Zerlina, flourishing a razor, half chases, half drags Leporello onto the stage.

ZERLINA: Restati quà! Restati quà!

LEPORELLO: Per carità!

ZERLINA: Stay right there! Stay right there!

LEPORELLO: For pity's sake!

ZERLINA: Restati quà! Restati quà, quà, quà!

ZERLINA: Stay right there! Stay right there, right there, right there!

Leporello struggles.

LEPORELLO: Per carità, Zerlina!

LEPORELLO: For pity's sake, Zerlina!

ZERLINA: Eh! non c'è carità per pari tuoi.

ZERLINA: Eh! there is no pity for the likes of you.

LEPORELLO: Dunque cavarmi vuoi . . . ?

LEPORELLO: So you want to tear out . . . ?

ZERLINA: I cappelli, la testa, il core, e gli occhi.

ZERLINA: Your hair, your head, your heart, and your eyes.

LEPORELLO: Senti, carina mia!

LEPORELLO: *Pleadingly.* Listen, my little dear!

ZERLINA: Guai, se mi tocchi! Vedrai, schiuma de' birbi, qual premio n'ha chi le ragazze ingiuria.

ZERLINA: Look out if you touch me! You'll see, rascally scum, what reward there is for someone who wrongs girls.

LEPORELLO: (Liberatemi, o Dei, da questa furia!)

LEPORELLO: *Aside.* Deliver me, o Gods, from this fury!

Zerlina continues to harass Leporello.

ZERLINA: Masetto! Olà! Masetto! dove diavolo è ito? Servi! gente! nessun vien, nessun sente—

ZERLINA: Masetto! Hey there! Masetto! where the devil has he gone? Servants! people! nobody comes, nobody hears—

A peasant wanders in.

LEPORELLO: Fa piano, per pietà! non strascinarmi a coda di cavallo!

LEPORELLO: Be careful, for pity's sake! don't drag me along tied to a horse's tail!

ZERLINA: Vedrai, vedrai come finisce il ballo! Presto quà quella sedia!

ZERLINA: You'll see, you'll see how the party ends! Quick, that chair here!

LEPORELLO: Eccola!

LEPORELLO: Here it is!

ZERLINA: Siedi!

ZERLINA: Sit down!

LEPORELLO: Stanco non son!

ZERLINA: Siedi, o con queste mani ti strappo il cor, e poi lo getto a'cani.

LEPORELLO: I'm not tired!

ZERLINA: Sit down or with these hands I'll tear out your heart, and then I'll throw it to the dogs.

Leporello seats himself with a sigh.

LEPORELLO: Siedo, ma tu, di grazia, metti giù quel rasoio! mi vuoi forse sbarbar?

LEPORELLO: I'll sit, but would you kindly put down that razor! possibly you want to shave me?

ZERLINA: Si, mascalzone, io sbarbare ti vo' senza sapone.

ZERLINA: Yes, scoundrel, I'll shave you without soap.

LEPORELLO: Eterni Dei!

LEPORELLO: Almighty Gods!

ZERLINA: Dammi la man.

ZERLINA: Give me your hand.

Leporello nervously extends his hand.

LEPORELLO: La mano.

LEPORELLO: My hand.

ZERLINA: L'altra!

ZERLINA: The other one!

Leporello complies.

LEPORELLO: Ma che vuoi farmi?

LEPORELLO: But what will you do to me?

ZERLINA: Voglio far, voglio far quello che parmi.

ZERLINA: I'll do, I'll do what I please.

The peasant wanders over and helps Zerlina tie Leporello's hands.

LEPORELLO: Per queste tue manine, candide e tenerelle, per questa fresca pelle, abbi pietà di me, abbi pietà di me!

LEPORELLO: By these white and young little hands of yours, by that fresh complexion, have pity on me, have pity on me!

ZERLINA: Non v'è pietà, briccone, non v'è pietà, briccone, son una tigre irata, un'aspide, un leone, no, no, pietà non v'è, pietà non v'è, no, no,

ZERLINA: There is no pity for you, rascal, there is no pity for you, rascal, I'm a furious tigress, an asp, a lioness, no, no, there is no pity for you, there

pietà non v'è, no, no, pietà
non v'è!

LEPORELLO: Ah, di fuggir si
provi, ah, di fuggir si provi!

ZERLINA: Sei morto se ti movi,
sei morto se ti movi, se ti
movi, se ti movi!

LEPORELLO: Barbari, ingiusti
Dei!

ZERLINA: Barbaro traditore—

LEPORELLO: Barbari, ingiusti
Dei—

ZERLINA: —barbaro traditore,
del tuo padrone il core avessi
qui con te, del tuo padrone il
core avessi qui con te!

LEPORELLO: In mano di costei,
chi capitar mi fe', chi capitar
mi fe'? Deh non mi stringer
tanto! l'anima sen va!

ZERLINA: Sen vada, sen vada,
o resti, intanto non partirai
di quà!

LEPORELLO: Che strette, oh
Dei, che botte! è giorno ov-
ver è notte?

ZERLINA: Di gioia e di diletto
sento brillarmi il petto! di
gioia e di diletto sento brillarmi il petto! così, così cogl'uomini, così, così si fa, così,
così cogl'uomini, così, così si
fa!

is no pity for you, no, no,
there is no pity for you, there
is no pity for you!

LEPORELLO: Ah, let me try to
flee, ah, let me try to flee!

ZERLINA: You're dead if you
move, you're dead if you
move, if you move, if you move!

LEPORELLO: Cruel, unfair
Gods!

ZERLINA: Cruel betrayer—

LEPORELLO: Cruel, unfair
Gods—

ZERLINA: —cruel betrayer, if I
only had your master's heart
here with you, if I only had
your master's heart here with
you!

LEPORELLO: Who made me
fall into her hands, who made
me fall? Come, don't squeeze
me so hard! my breath is leaving me!

ZERLINA: Let it leave, let it
leave, or let it stay, meanwhile you won't get away
from here!

LEPORELLO: What squeezes,
oh Gods, what beatings! is it
day or is it night?

ZERLINA: I feel my breast
burning with joy and delight!
I feel my breast burning with
joy and delight! thus, thus
one acts with men, thus, thus,
thus, thus one acts with men,
thus, thus!

LEPORELLO: Che scosse di tremuoto, che buia oscurità, che
buia oscurità. Ah! di fuggir si
provi, ah! di fuggir si provi!

ZERLINA Sei morto, morto,
morto, morto, se ti movi, se ti
movi!

LEPORELLO: Deh, non mi
stringer tanto, l'anima mia
sen va!

ZERLINA: Sen vada, sen vada,
o resti, intanto non partirai
di quà, non partirai, non partirai, non partirai di quà!

LEPORELLO: Che strette, oh
Dei! che botte! è giorno ov-
ver è notte?

ZERLINA: Di gioia e di diletto
sento brillarmi il petto, di
gioia e di diletto sento brillarmi il petto! così, così cogl'uomini, così, così si fa, così,
così cogl'uomini, così, così si
fa, così, così, così si fa.—

LEPORELLO: Che scosse di tremuoto, che buia oscurità, che
buia oscurità! oh Dei, che
strette! oh Dei, che botte!

ZERLINA: —così, così, così si fa,
così, così, così, così, così così
si fa, così, così, così, così, così
si fa, così, così, così, così, così
si fa, così, così, così, si fa, così,

LEPORELLO: What earthquake
tremblings, what gloomy
darkness, what gloomy darkness. Ah! let me try to flee, ah!
let me try to flee!

ZERLINA: You're dead, dead,
dead, dead, if you move, if you
move!

LEPORELLO: Come, don't
squeeze me so hard, my breath
is leaving me!

ZERLINA: Let it leave, let it
leave, or let it stay, meanwhile you won't get away from
here, you won't get away, you
won't get away, you won't get
away from here!

LEPORELLO: What squeezes,
oh Gods! what beatings! is it
day or is it night?

ZERLINA: I feel my breast
burning with joy and delight,
I feel my breast burning with
joy and delight! thus, thus one
acts with men, thus, thus, thus,
thus one acts with men, thus,
thus, thus, thus one acts.—

LEPORELLO: What earthquake
tremblings, what gloomy
darkness, what gloomy darkness! oh Gods, what squeezes!
oh Gods, what beatings!

ZERLINA: thus, thus, thus one
acts, thus, thus, thus, thus,
thus, thus one acts, thus, thus,
thus, thus, thus one acts, thus,
thus, thus, thus, thus one acts,

così, così, così si fa, così, così, così si fa!

thus, thus, thus, one acts, thus, thus, thus, thus one acts, thus, thus, thus one acts!

LEPORELLO: È notte o giorno, è giorno o notte? che scosse di tremuoto, che buia oscurità, che buia oscurità, che buia, buia oscurità!

LEPORELLO: Is it night or day, is it day or night? what earthquake tremblings, what gloomy darkness, what gloomy darkness, what gloomy, gloomy darkness!

Zerlina leaves, and Leporello turns hopefully to the peasant.

Amico, per pietà un poco d'acqua fresca, o ch'io mi moro. Guarda un po' come stretto mi legò l'assassina.

Friend, for pity's sake, a little cold water, or else I'll die. Look a bit at how tightly the murderess tied me.

The peasant goes out.

Se potessi liberarmi coi denti? Oh venga il diavolo a disfar questi gruppi! io vo' vedere di rompere la corda —come è forte! paura della morte! E tu, Mercurio, protettor de' ladri, proteggi un galant'uom! coraggio— bravo! pria che costei ritorni, bisogna dar di sprone alle calcagna, e strascinar, se occorre, una montagna!

Could I free myself with my teeth? Oh, may the devil come untie these knots! I'll manage to break this rope—how strong it is! I'm scared of death! And you, Mercury, protector of thieves, protect a gallant! courage—hurray! before that woman returns, I'll have to give full speed to my heels, and if need be, drag along a mountain!

Wriggling violently, he manages to loosen his ropes, and jumps out the window, chair, ropes and all. Zerlina returns, accompanied by Donna Elvira, Masetto and some peasants.

ZERLINA: Andiam, andiam, Signora! vedrete in qual maniera ho concio il scellerato.

ZERLINA: *To Donna Elvira.* Come, come, my lady! you'll see how I have fixed the villain.

DONNA ELVIRA: Ah, sopra lui si sfoghi il mio furor.

ZERLINA: Stelle! in qual modo si salvò quel briccone?

DONNA ELVIRA: L'avrà sottratto l'empio suo padrone.

ZERLINA: Fu desso senza fallo: anche di questo informiam Don Ottavio: a lui si spetta far per noi tutti, o domandar vendetta!

DONNA ELVIRA: Ah, let my rage break on him.

ZERLINA: Ye gods! how did that rogue get away?

DONNA ELVIRA: His wicked master must have set him free.

ZERLINA: It was undoubtedly he: let's tell Don Ottavio about this, too: he is supposed to act for all of us or to demand vengeance!

All leave except Donna Elvira.

DONNA ELVIRA: In quali eccessi, o Numi, in quai misfatti orribili, tremendi è avvolto il sciagurato! Ah no! non puote tardar l'ira del cielo, la giustizia tardar. Sentir già parmi la fatale saetta, che gli piomba sul capo! aperto veggio il baratro mortal! Misera Elvira! che contrasto d'affetti in sen ti nasce! Perchè questi sospiri? e quest'ambascie?

Mi tradì quell'alma ingrata, quell'alma ingrata, infelice, o Dio! mi fa, infelice, o Dio, mi fa, infelice, o Dio! o Dio! mi fa! Ma tradita e abbandonata provo ancor per lui pietà, provo ancor per lui pietà, provo ancor per lui, per lui, per lui pietà. Mi tradì quell'alma ingrata, quell'alma ingrata, infelice, o Dio! mi fa, infelice, o Dio! mi fa,

DONNA ELVIRA: In what excesses, o Gods, in what horrible, tremendous misdeeds the villain is involved! Ah no! heaven's wrath, justice, cannot be delayed, cannot be delayed. I think I already sense the fatal thunderbolt that will fall on his head! I see the deadly chasm opening! Wretched Elvira! what conflicting emotions arise in your breast! why these sighs? and these pangs?
That thankless spirit betrayed me, that thankless spirit makes me miserable, o God! makes me miserable, o God! makes me miserable, o God! o God! But betrayed and abandoned, I still feel pity for him, I still feel pity for him, I still feel pity for him, for him, for him. That thankless spirit betrayed me, that thankless spirit makes me miserable, o God! makes

infelice, o Dio! o Dio! mi fa! Quando sento il mio tormento, il mio tormento, di vendetta il cor favella, ma se guardo il suo cimento, palpitando il cor mi va, palpitando il cor, il cor mi va, il cor mi va. Mi tradì quell'alma ingrata, quell'alma ingrata, infelice, o Dio! mi fa, infelice, o Dio! mi fa! infelice, o Dio! o Dio! mi fa! Ma tradita e abbandonata, provo ancor per lui pietà, per lui pietà, provo ancor per lui pietà, provo ancor per lui pietà, per lui pietà, per lui pietà!

me miserable, o God! makes me miserable, o God! o God! When I feel my torment, my torment, my heart speaks of revenge, but if I consider his peril, my heart goes throbbing, my heart, my heart goes, my heart goes throbbing. That thankless spirit betrayed me, that thankless spirit makes me miserable, o God! makes me miserable, o God! makes me miserable, o God! o God! But betrayed and abandoned, I still feel pity for him, pity for him, I still feel pity for him, I still feel pity for him, pity for him, pity for him!

Scene Four ✦

A graveyard in Seville, later that same night. The graveyard is enclosed by a low wall. Grouped about are several monuments and statues, including one of the Commendatore. (This is designated as an equestrian statue, but the horse is often omitted in performance.) Don Giovanni, still attired in Leporello's cloak, leaps over the wall, laughing. He does not notice Leporello, who is crouched in the shadow of the wall, waiting for him.

DON GIOVANNI: Ah, ah, ah, ah, questa è buona, or lasciala cercar; che bella notte! è più chiara del giorno, sembra fatta per gir a zonzo a caccia di ragazze. È tardi? Oh, ancor non sono due della notte;

DON GIOVANNI: Ha, ha, ha, ha, that's good, now let her search; what a lovely night! it's lighter than day, it seems made for strolling about on a girl-hunt. Is it late? Oh, it's not yet two o'clock at night:

avrei voglia un po' di saper come è finito l'affar tra Leporello e Donn'Elvira: s'egli ha avuto giudizio!

I'd like to know a little about how the affair of Leporello and Donna Elvira ended: whether he has been discreet!

LEPORELLO: (Alfin vuole ch'io faccia un precipizio.)

LEPORELLO: *To himself.* To top it off, he wants me to be ruined.

DON GIOVANNI: È desso; oh Leporello!

DON GIOVANNI: It's he; oh Leporello!

LEPORELLO: Chi mi chiama?

LEPORELLO: Who's calling me?

DON GIOVANNI: Non conosci il padron?

DON GIOVANNI: Don't you recognize your master?

LEPORELLO: Così nol conoscessi!

LEPORELLO: I wish I didn't recognize him!

DON GIOVANNI: Come, birbo?

DON GIOVANNI: What, rogue?

Leporello, feigning great surprise, steps from the shadows.

LEPORELLO: Ah, siete voi? scusate!

LEPORELLO: Oh, is it you? pardon me!

DON GIOVANNI: Cosa è stato?

DON GIOVANNI: What's happened?

LEPORELLO: Per cagion vostra io fui quasi accoppato.

LEPORELLO: Because of you, I was practically beaten to death.

DON GIOVANNI: Ebben, non era questo un onore per te?

DON GIOVANNI: Well, wasn't that an honor for you?

LEPORELLO: Signor, vel dono.

LEPORELLO: Sir, I give it to you.

DON GIOVANNI: Via, via, vien quà, vien quà! che belle cose ti deggio dir.

DON GIOVANNI: Now, now, come here, come here! what fine things I must tell you.

LEPORELLO: Ma cosa fate qui?

LEPORELLO: But what are you doing here?

DON GIOVANNI: Vien dentro, e lo saprai: diverse istorielle che accadute mi son dacchè partisti, ti dirò un'altra volta: or la più bella ti vo' solo narrar.

LEPORELLO: Donnesca, al certo?

DON GIOVANNI: C'è dubbio? una fanciulla, bella giovin galante, per la strada incontrai; le vado appresso, la prendo per la man, fuggir mi vuole; dico poche parole, ella mi piglia—sai per chi?

LEPORELLO: Non lo sò.

DON GIOVANNI: Per Leporello.

LEPORELLO: Per me?

DON GIOVANNI: Per te.

LEPORELLO: Va bene.

DON GIOVANNI: Per la mano essa allora mi prende—

LEPORELLO: Ancora meglio.

DON GIOVANNI: M'accarezza, mi abbraccia: "Caro il mio Leporello! Leporello, mio caro!" allor m'accorsi ch'era qualche tua bella.

LEPORELLO: Oh, maledetto!

DON GIOVANNI: Dell' inganno approfitto; non sò come mi riconosce, grida: sento gente, a fuggire mi metto, e pronto,

DON GIOVANNI: Come inside, and you'll find out: another time I'll tell you various little tales about what happened to me since you left: now I just want to tell you the prettiest one.

LEPORELLO: Concerning women, certainly?

DON GIOVANNI: Why, of course! I met a beautiful, young, elegant girl on the street; I went up to her, I took her by the hand, she wanted to run away from me: I spoke a few words, she mistook me —for whom do you think?

LEPORELLO: I don't know.

DON GIOVANNI: For Leporello.

LEPORELLO: For me?

DON GIOVANNI: For you.

LEPORELLO: That's fine.

DON GIOVANNI: So then she took me by the hand—

LEPORELLO: Better yet.

DON GIOVANNI: She caressed me, she embraced me: "My dear Leporello! Leporello, my dear!" so then it occurred to me that she was one of your pretty ladies.

LEPORELLO: Oh, damn!

DON GIOVANNI: I made the most of the deception; I don't know how she recognized me, she shouted: I heard people, I

Act 2, Scene 4. The graveyard scene. Decor by Joseph Quaglio for performances at Mannheim in September, 1789—the oldest known setting for *Don Giovanni*.

(Courtesy San Francisco Opera Company, photo by Carolyn Mason Jones)

Act 2, Scene 4. Taking refuge in the graveyard, Don Giovanni removes Leporello's cloak and hat and appears once more *in propria persona*. Behind him looms the statue of the Commendatore. Giorgio Tozzi is Don Giovanni.

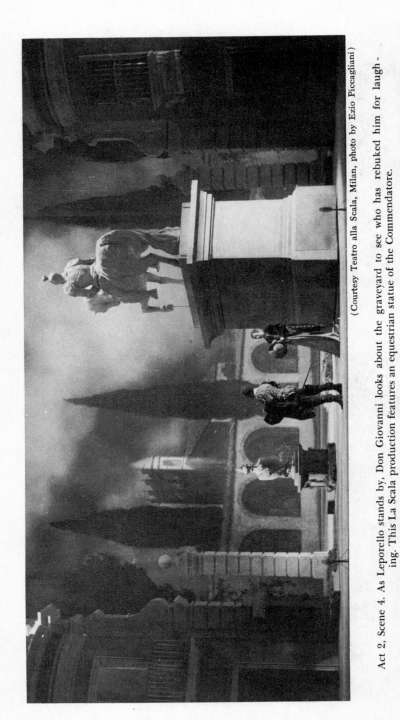

(Courtesy Teatro alla Scala, Milan, photo by Ezio Piccagliani)

Act 2, Scene 4. As Leporello stands by, Don Giovanni looks about the graveyard to see who has rebuked him for laughing. This La Scala production features an equestrian statue of the Commendatore.

pronto per quel muretto in questo loco io monto.

ran away, and quickly, quickly I climbed over that little wall here.

LEPORELLO: E mi dite la cosa con tale indifferenza?

LEPORELLO: And you tell me the thing so casually?

DON GIOVANNI: Perchè no?

DON GIOVANNI: Why not?

LEPORELLO: Ma se fosse costei stata mia moglie?

LEPORELLO: But what if she had been my wife?

Don Giovanni bursts out laughing.

DON GIOVANNI: Meglio ancora!

DON GIOVANNI: Better yet!

STATUE: Di rider finirai pria dell'aurora!

STATUE: You will cease laughing before dawn!

DON GIOVANNI: Chi ha parlato?

DON GIOVANNI: *Surprised.* Who spoke?

LEPORELLO: Ah, qualche anima sarà dell'altro mondo, che vi conosce a fondo.

LEPORELLO: Ah, it must be some spirit in the other world who knows you through and through.

Don Giovanni looks around and prepares to draw his sword.

DON GIOVANNI: Taci, sciocco! chi va là? chi va là?

DON GIOVANNI: Be quiet, stupid! who goes there? who goes there?

STATUE: Ribaldo audace! Lascia a'morti la pace!

STATUE: Brazen jester! Leave the dead in peace!

LEPORELLO: Ve l'ho detto!

LEPORELLO: I told you so!

DON GIOVANNI: Sarà qualcun di fuori che si burla di noi! Ehi, del Commendatore non è questa la statua? leggi un poco quella iscrizion.

DON GIOVANNI: It must be someone outside who's making fun of us! Hey, isn't this the Commendatore's statue? read off that inscription.

LEPORELLO: Scusate, non ho imparato a leggere a'raggi della luna.

LEPORELLO: *Nervously.* Pardon me, I've not learned to read by moonlight.

DON GIOVANNI: Leggi, dico!

DON GIOVANNI: *Threateningly.* Read it, I say!

Leporello reads the inscription in a shaky voice.

LEPORELLO: "Dell'empio, che mi trasse al passo estremo, qui attendo la vendetta." Udiste? io tremo!

LEPORELLO: "Here I await vengeance on the wicked man who brought me to my death." Did you hear? I'm trembling!

DON GIOVANNI: O vecchio buffonissimo! digli che questa sera l'attendo a cenar meco!

DON GIOVANNI: O great old clown! tell him that I'll expect him to dine with me this evening!

LEPORELLO: Che pazzia! ma mi par, oh Dei, mirate, che terribili occhiate egli ci dà! par vivo! par che senta, e che voglia parlar!

LEPORELLO: What madness! but I think, oh Gods, look, that he is giving us a terrible stare! he seems alive! as if he were listening and wanted to speak!

DON GIOVANNI: Orsù, va là, o qui t'ammazzo, e poi ti seppellisco!

DON GIOVANNI: *More threateningly.* Hurry up, go over there, or I'll murder you right here and then bury you!

LEPORELLO: Piano, piano, Signore, ora ubbidisco.

LEPORELLO: *Quavering.* Softly, softly, Sir, I'll obey now.

Trembling, Leporello goes to the Commendatore's statue.

O statua gentilissima del gran Commendatore—Padron! mi trema il core, non posso, non posso terminar!

O most noble statue of the great Commendatore—Master! my very heart is trembling, I can't, I can't finish!

DON GIOVANNI: Finiscila, o nel petto ti metto questo acciar, ti metto questo acciar!

DON GIOVANNI: Stop that, or I'll stick this sword in your breast, I'll stick this sword in you!

LEPORELLO: (Che impiccio, che capriccio!)

LEPORELLO: *To himself.* What a scrape, what a whim!

DON GIOVANNI: (Che gusto! che spassetto!)

LEPORELLO: (Io sentomi gelar, io sentomi gelar!)

DON GIOVANNI: (Lo voglio far tremar, lo voglio far tremar!)

LEPORELLO: O statua gentilissima, benchè di marmo siate—Ah, padron! Padron mio! mirate, mirate! che seguita a guardar, che seguita a guardar!

Don Giovanni makes a threatening movement toward Leporello.

DON GIOVANNI: Mori, mori!

LEPORELLO: No, no, no, no, attendete, attendete! Signor, il padron mio—badate ben, non io—vorria con voi cenar!

To Leporello's horror, the statue nods its head.

Ah! ah! ah! che scena è questa! ah, ah, ah—che scena è questa! o ciel! chinò la testa!

DON GIOVANNI: Va là, che sei un buffone, va là, che sei un buffone, un buffone, un buffone!

LEPORELLO: Guardate, guardate, guardate ancor, padrone!

DON GIOVANNI: *To himself.* What fun! what a joke!

LEPORELLO: (I feel myself turning to ice, I feel myself turning to ice.)

DON GIOVANNI: (I'll make him tremble, I'll make him tremble!)

LEPORELLO: *To the statue.* O most noble statue, although you're made of marble—Ah, master! My master! look, look! how he seems to go on staring, how he seems to go on staring!

DON GIOVANNI: Die, die!

LEPORELLO: No, no, no, no, wait, wait! *To the statue.* His Lordship, my master—mark you, not I—would like to dine with you!

Oh! oh! oh! what a scene this is! oh, oh, oh—what a scene this is! o heavens! he nodded his head!

DON GIOVANNI: Go on, what a clown you are, go on, what a clown you are, a clown, a clown!

LEPORELLO: Look, look, look again, master!

DON GIOVANNI: E che deggio guardar, deggio guardar, deggio guardar?

DON GIOVANNI: And what should I look at, should I look at, should I look at?

LEPORELLO: Colla marmorea testa ei fa così, così.

LEPORELLO: With his marble head he goes like this, like this.

DON GIOVANNI AND LEPORELLO: Colla marmorea testa ei fa così, così.

DON GIOVANNI AND LEPORELLO: With his marble head he goes like this, like this.

Don Giovanni steps forward and addresses the statue.

DON GIOVANNI: Parlate! se potete. Verrete a cena? verrete a cena?

DON GIOVANNI: Speak! if you are able. Will you come to dinner? will you come to dinner?

STATUE: Sì!

STATUE: Yes!

LEPORELLO: Mover mi posso appena, mi manca, o Dei, la lena! mi manca, o Dei, la lena! Per carità, partiamo, per carità, partiamo, andiamo via di quà! andiamo, andiamo via di quà! per carità, partiamo, andiamo via di quà, per carità, partiamo, andiamo via di quà, andiamo via di quà! andiamo via di quà, andiamo, andiamo via di quà, andiamo, andiamo via di quà, via di quà, via di quà, via di quà, di quà, di quà, di quà!

LEPORELLO: I can hardly stir, o Gods, my breath fails me! For pity's sake, let's leave, for pity's sake, let's leave, let's get away from here! let's go, let's get away from here! for pity's sake, let's leave, let's get away from here, for pity's sake, let's leave, let's get away from here, let's get away from here! let's get away from here, let's go, let's get away from here, let's go, away from here, away from here, from here, from here, from here!

DON GIOVANNI: Bizarra è inver la scena, verrà il buon vecchio, il buon vecchio a cena. A prepararla andiamo, a prepararla andiamo, partiamo via di quà! Bizarra è inver la

DON GIOVANNI: This scene is truly weird, the good old man, the good old man will come to dinner. Let us go to prepare it, let us go to prepare it, let's get away from here! This scene is

scena, verrà il buon vecchio a cena; a prepararla andiamo, partiamo via di quà, partiamo via di quà.

truly weird, the good old man will come to dinner; let us go to prepare it, let's get away from here, let's get away from here.

They leave—Don Giovanni swaggering, and Leporello cowering.

Scene Five

The following day, in a sitting room of Donna Anna. She and Don Ottavio are present.

DON OTTAVIO: Calmatevi, idol mio! di quel ribaldo vedrem puniti in breve i gravi eccessi, vendicati sarem.

DON OTTAVIO: Calm yourself, my idol. In a short time we shall see that profligate's terrible crimes punished, we shall be avenged.

DONNA ANNA: Ma il padre, o Dio!

DONNA ANNA: But my father, o God!

DON OTTAVIO: Convien chinare il ciglio al volere del ciel. Respira, o cara! di tua perdita amara fia domani, se vuoi, dolce compenso questo cor, questa mano, che il mio tenero amor . . .

DON OTTAVIO: One must bow one's head before the wish of heaven. Take heart, o dear! if you will it, your bitter loss can be sweetly recompensed tomorrow with this heart, this hand, which my tender love . . .

DONNA ANNA: O Dei! che dite in sì tristi momenti.

DONNA ANNA: O Gods! how can you speak at such a sad time.

DON OTTAVIO: E che? vorresti con indugi novelli accrescer le mie pene? crudele!

DON OTTAVIO: And what? would you increase my sorrows with fresh delays? Cruel woman!

DONNA ANNA: Crudele? Ah no, mio bene! Troppo mi spiace allontanarti un ben che lun-

DONNA ANNA: Cruel? Ah no, my dear! It makes me very unhappy to delay the reward

gamente la nostr'alma desia.
Ma il mondo, o Dio! non
sedur la costanza del sensibil
mio core; abbastanza per te
mi parla amore!
Non mi dir, bell'idol mio,
che son io crudel con te, tu
ben sai quant'io t'amai, tu
conosci la mia fè, tu conosci
la mia fè. Calma, calma il
tuo tormento, se di duol non
vuoi ch'io mora, se di duol
non vuoi ch'io mora, non
vuoi ch'io mora. Non mi dir,
bell'idol mio, che son io crudel con te; calma, calma il
tuo tormento, se di duol non
vuoi ch'io mora, non vuoi
ch'io mora!

Forse, forse un giorno il cielo
ancora sentirà, sentirà pietà
di me! forse un giorno il cielo
ancora sentirà pietà di me,
sentirà pietà, pietà di me,
sentirà pietà di me, forse,
forse il cielo un giorno sentirà pietà di me, sentirà pietà
di me, pietà di me.

that our soul has long desired.
But the world, o God!* do not
tempt the constancy of my
sensitive heart; love speaks
sufficiently in your favor!
Do not tell me, my handsome
idol, that I am cruel to you,
you well know how much I did
love you, you know my faithfulness, you know my faithfulness. Calm, calm your torment, if you don't want me to
die of sorrow, if you don't
want me to die of sorrow, if
you don't want me to die. Do
not tell me, my handsome
idol, that I am cruel to you;
calm, calm your torment, if
you don't want me to die of
sorrow, if you don't want me
to die!
Perhaps, perhaps one day
heaven will yet feel, feel pity
for me! perhaps one day heav-
en will yet feel pity for me, feel
pity, pity for me, feel pity for
me, perhaps, perhaps heaven
one day will feel pity for me,
feel pity for me, pity for me.

Sadly Donna Anna sweeps out.

DON OTTAVIO:† Ah, si segua il
suo passo: io vo' con lei divi-
dere i martiri; saran meco
men gravi i suoi sospiri.

DON OTTAVIO: Ah, I must follow her steps: I wish to share
her torments with her; with
me, her sighs will be less
heavy.

He follows Donna Anna.

* I.e. "what will people say?"
† These lines are often cut, so that the scene ends with Donna Anna's exit.

Scene Six

*Don Giovanni's banquet-hall, on the following even-
ing. Two doors to the rear of the stage, one on either
side; a table laden with wines and delicacies; an
alcove for musicians. Pretty girls flit about; Don
Giovanni enters and surveys the scene with pleasure.*

DON GIOVANNI: Già la mensa è preparata. Voi suonate, amici cari! Giacchè spendo i miei danari, io mi voglio divertir. Leporello, presto in tavola.

DON GIOVANNI: The table is already prepared. *To musicians.* Play, dear friends! As long as I'm spending my money, I want to amuse myself. Leporello, serve quickly.

LEPORELLO: Son prontissimo a servir, son prontissimo a servir.

LEPORELLO: I'm very ready to serve, I'm very ready to serve.

DON GIOVANNI: Giacchè spendo i miei danari, io mi voglio divertir. Voi suonate, amici cari! Giacchè spendo i miei danari, io mi voglio divertir, io mi voglio divertir.

DON GIOVANNI: As long as I'm spending my money, I want to amuse myself. *To musicians.* Play, dear friends! As long as I'm spending my money, I want to amuse myself, I want to amuse myself.

*The stage orchestra plays a selection from Vicente
Martín y Solar's opera* Una Cosa Rara, *a very
popular work of Mozart's day. (Da Ponte wrote
the libretto.)*

LEPORELLO: Bravi! "Cosa Rara."

LEPORELLO: Good men! "Cosa Rara."

DON GIOVANNI: Che ti par del bel concerto?

DON GIOVANNI: What do you think of the pretty concert?

LEPORELLO: È conforme, è conforme al vostro merto.

LEPORELLO: It's fitting, it's fitting to your worth!

DON GIOVANNI: Ah che piatto saporito! Ah che piatto saporito! Ah che piatto saporito!

LEPORELLO: Ah che barbaro appetito! che bocconi da gigante! mi par proprio di svenir, mi par proprio di svenir.

DON GIOVANNI: Nel veder i miei bocconi, gli par proprio di svenir, gli par proprio di svenir.

LEPORELLO: Ah che barbaro appetito! che bocconi da gigante!

DON GIOVANNI: Nel veder i miei bocconi gli par proprio di svenir, di svenir.

LEPORELLO: Ah che barbaro appetito!

DON GIOVANNI: Gli par proprio di svenir.

LEPORELLO: Che bocconi da gigante!

DON GIOVANNI: Gli par proprio di svenir, gli par proprio di svenir, gli par proprio di svenir.

LEPORELLO: Mi par proprio di svenir, mi par proprio di svenir.

DON GIOVANNI: Piatto!

LEPORELLO: Servo!

DON GIOVANNI: Ah, what a savory dish! Ah, what a savory dish! Ah, what a savory dish!

LEPORELLO: *To himself.* Ah, what a monstrous appetite! what giant mouthfuls! I'll die if I don't get some, I'll die if I don't get some.

DON GIOVANNI: *Chuckling to himself.* He's watching my mouthfuls, he'll die if he doesn't get some, he'll die if he he doesn't get some.

LEPORELLO: Ah what a monstrous appetite! what giant mouthfuls!

DON GIOVANNI: He's watching my mouthfuls, he'll die, he'll die if he doesn't get some.

LEPORELLO: Ah what a monstrous appetite!

DON GIOVANNI: He'll die if he doesn't get some.

LEPORELLO: What giant mouthfuls!

DON GIOVANNI: He'll die if he doesn't get some, he'll die if he doesn't get some, he'll die if he doesn't get some.

LEPORELLO: I'll die if I don't get some, I'll die if I don't get some.

DON GIOVANNI: Next course!

LEPORELLO: Coming!

The stage orchestra plays a selection from Giuseppe Sarti's Fra i Due Litiganti il Terzo Gode, *another very popular opera of Mozart's time.*

LEPORELLO: Evvivano i litiganti!

LEPORELLO: Hurray for the
Litiganti!

DON GIOVANNI: Versa il vino!
Eccellente marzimino!

DON GIOVANNI: Now for the
wine! Excellent *marzimino*!*

LEPORELLO: Questo pezzo di
fagiano, piano, piano, piano,
piano, piano vo' inghiottir.

LEPORELLO: *To himself.* I'll
swallow this piece of pheasant
quietly, quietly, quietly, quietly, quietly.

DON GIOVANNI: Sta mangiando
quel marrano! fingerò di non
capir.

DON GIOVANNI: *Mischievously to
himself.* That boor is eating!
I'll pretend not to catch on.

*The stage orchestra plays the "Non più andrai" from
Mozart's own* Le Nozze di Figaro, *another current
favorite.*

LEPORELLO: Questa poi la co-
nosco pur troppo.

LEPORELLO: This I also know
too well.

*Don Giovanni carefully averts
his glance from Leporello.*

DON GIOVANNI: Leporello!

DON GIOVANNI: Leporello!

LEPORELLO: Padron mio!

LEPORELLO: Master!

DON GIOVANNI: Parla schietto,
parla schietto, mascalzone.

DON GIOVANNI: Speak up,
speak up, scoundrel.

Leporello hastily gulps down the food.

LEPORELLO: Non mi lascia una
flussione le parole proferir, le
parole proferir.

LEPORELLO: My catarrh
doesn't permit me to enunciate the words, enunciate the
words.

DON GIOVANNI: Mentre io
mangio, fischia un poco.

DON GIOVANNI: Whistle a bit
while I eat.

LEPORELLO: Non sò far.

LEPORELLO: I can't do it.

Don Giovanni stares at him with great mock surprise.

DON GIOVANNI: Cos'è?

DON GIOVANNI: What's the
matter?

* A kind of grape and wine.

LEPORELLO: Scusate! scusate! sì eccellente è'l vostro cuoco, sì eccellente, sì eccellente è'l vostro cuoco, che lo volli anch'io provar, che lo volli anch'io provar—

DON GIOVANNI: Sì eccellente è il cuoco mio, che lo volle anch'ei provar.

LEPORELLO: —sì eccellente, che lo volli anch'io provar.

LEPORELLO: Pardon! pardon! your cook is so excellent, your cook is so excellent, so excellent, that I wanted to try some too, I wanted to try some too—

DON GIOVANNI: My cook is so excellent that he wanted to try some too.

LEPORELLO: —so excellent, that I wanted to try some too.

The stage orchestra finishes playing. The girls depart, and Donna Elvira rushes in.

DONNA ELVIRA: L'ultima prova dell'amor mio ancor vogl'io fare con te. Più non rammento gl'inganni tuoi, gl'inganni tuoi, pietade io sento!

DONNA ELVIRA: I want to prove my love for you one last time. I no longer remember your deceits, your deceits, I feel pity!

Don Giovanni waves away the musicians.

DON GIOVANNI AND LEPORELLO: Cos'è? Cos'è?

DON GIOVANNI AND LEPORELLO: What's the matter? What's the matter?

Donna Elvira kneels pleadingly.

DONNA ELVIRA: Da te non chiede quest'alma oppressa della sua fede qualche mercè.

DON GIOVANNI: Mi maraviglio! cosa volete? cosa volete? Se non sorgete, non resto in piè, non resto in piè.

DONNA ELVIRA: This oppressed soul asks no thanks for its faithfulness to you.

DON GIOVANNI: How wonderful! what do you want? what do you want? If you don't get up, *I* won't stay on my feet, *I* won't stay on my feet.

He too kneels.

DONNA ELVIRA: Ah non deridere gli affanni miei!

DONNA ELVIRA: Ah, don't mock my sorrows!

LEPORELLO: Quasi di piangere mi fa costei, quasi di piangere mi fa costei!

LEPORELLO: She's almost making me cry, she's almost making me cry!

Don Giovanni gets to his feet and pulls Donna Elvira up too.

DON GIOVANNI: Io te deridere!

DON GIOVANNI: I, mock you!

DONNA ELVIRA: Ah, non deridere!

DONNA ELVIRA: Ah, don't mock!

DON GIOVANNI: Io te deridere?

DON GIOVANNI: I, mock you?

DONNA ELVIRA: Ah, non deridere!

DONNA ELVIRA: Ah, don't mock!

DON GIOVANNI: Cielo! perchè? Che vuoi, mio bene?

DON GIOVANNI: Heavens! why? What do you want, my dear?

DONNA ELVIRA: Che vita cangi!

DONNA ELVIRA: That you change your life!

DON GIOVANNI: Brava!

DON GIOVANNI: Good girl!

DONNA ELVIRA: Cor perfido!

DONNA ELVIRA: Faithless scoundrel!

DON GIOVANNI: Brava!

DON GIOVANNI: Good girl!

DONNA ELVIRA: Cor perfido!

DONNA ELVIRA: Faithless scoundrel!

DONNA ELVIRA AND LEPORELLO: Cor perfido!

DONNA ELVIRA AND LEPORELLO: Faithless scoundrel!

Don Giovanni laughs and sits down at the table again.

DON GIOVANNI: Lascia ch'io mangi, lascia ch'io mangi, e se ti piace, mangia con me!

DON GIOVANNI: Let me eat, let me eat, and if you like, eat with me!

DONNA ELVIRA: Restati, barbaro! nel lezzo immondo esempio orribile d'iniquità!

DONNA ELVIRA: Remain, cruel man! a dreadful example of evil in your filthy stench!

LEPORELLO: Se non si muove del suo dolore, di sasso ha il core, o cor non ha!

LEPORELLO: If her sorrow doesn't move him, he has a heart of stone, or he hasn't got a heart!

Don Giovanni lifts his glass in a toast.

DON GIOVANNI: Vivan le femmine, viva il buon vino! sostegno e gloria d'umanità, sostegno e gloria d'umanità!

DON GIOVANNI: Long live women, long live good wine! sustenance and glory of humankind, sustenance and glory of humankind!

DONNA ELVIRA: Restati, barbaro! nel lezzo immondo, restati barbaro! nel lezzo immondo! esempio orribile d'iniquità! esempio orribile d'iniquità, d'iniquità, d'iniquità, esempio orribile d'iniquità!

DONNA ELVIRA: Remain, cruel man! remain, cruel man, in your filthy stench! in your filthy stench! a dreadful example of evil! a dreadful example of evil, of evil, of evil, a dreadful example of evil.

LEPORELLO: Se non si muove del suo dolore, di sasso ha il core, di sasso ha il core, o cor non ha. Di sasso ha il core, o cor non ha! o cor non ha, o cor non ha, di sasso ha il core, o cor non ha!

LEPORELLO: If her sorrow doesn't move him, he has a heart of stone, he has a heart of stone, or he hasn't got a heart. He has a heart of stone, or he hasn't got a heart! or he hasn't got a heart, or he hasn't got a heart, he has a heart of stone, or he hasn't got a heart!

DON GIOVANNI: Vivan le femmine, viva il buon vino! vivan le femmine, viva il buon vino! sostegno e gloria d'umanità, sostegno e gloria d'umanità, sostegno e gloria d'umanità, d'umanità, d'umanità, sostegno e gloria d'umanità!

DON GIOVANNI: Long live women, long live good wine! long live women, long live good wine! sustenance and glory of humankind, sustenance and glory of humankind, sustenance and glory of humankind, of humankind, of humankind, sustenance and glory of humankind!

Donna Elvira rushes out one of the doors, starts back with a terrified scream, turns, and rushes out the other door.

DONNA ELVIRA: Ah!

DONNA ELVIRA: *Screaming.* Ah!

DON GIOVANNI: Che grido è questo mai? che grido, che grido è questo mai?

LEPORELLO: Che grido è questo mai! che grido è questo mai?

DON GIOVANNI: Va a veder, va a veder che cosa è stato.

DON GIOVANNI: Whatever is that scream? Whatever is that scream, that scream?

LEPORELLO: Whatever is that scream! whatever is that scream?

DON GIOVANNI: *To Leporello.* Go to see, go to see what's happened.

Leporello goes to the first door, looks out, screams, and returns.

LEPORELLO: Ah!

DON GIOVANNI: Che grido indiavolato! che grido indiavolato! Leporello, che cos'è? che cos'è? che cos'è?

LEPORELLO: Ah! Signor! per carità! non andate fuor di quà! l'uom di sasso, l'uomo bianco, ah! padrone! io gelo, io manco. Se vedeste che figura, se sentiste come fa ta, ta, ta, ta!

DON GIOVANNI: Non capisco niente affatto.

LEPORELLO: Ta, ta, ta, ta!

DON GIOVANNI: Tu sei matto in verità, in verità, in verità!

LEPORELLO: *Screaming.* Ah!

DON GIOVANNI: What a devilish scream! what a devilish scream! Leporello, what is it? what is it? what is it?

LEPORELLO: *Eyes bulging.* Ah! Sir! for pity's sake! don't go out of here! the man of stone, the white man, ah! master! I'm freezing, I'm faltering. If you had seen that form, if you had heard how it goes, ta, ta, ta, ta!

DON GIOVANNI: I don't understand anything at all.

LEPORELLO: *Imitating the statue.* Ta, ta, ta, ta!

DON GIOVANNI: In truth, in truth, in truth, you're crazy!

A hollow knock sounds on the door.

LEPORELLO: Ah! sentite!

DON GIOVANNI: Qualcun batte! Apri!

LEPORELLO: Io tremo!

LEPORELLO: Ah! do you hear!

DON GIOVANNI: *Impatiently.* Someone is knocking! Open!

LEPORELLO: I'm trembling!

DON GIOVANNI: Apri, dico!

DON GIOVANNI: Open, I say!

LEPORELLO: Ah!

LEPORELLO: *Pleading, terrified.* Ah!

DON GIOVANNI: Apri!

DON GIOVANNI: Open!

LEPORELLO: Ah!

LEPORELLO: Ah!

DON GIOVANNI: Matto! Per togliermi d'intrico ad aprir io stesso andrò, io stesso andrò.

DON GIOVANNI: Madman! In order to clear up this mess, I'll go myself to open, I'll go myself.

Don Giovanni takes one of the candelabra from the table and goes to the door. Leporello crawls underneath the table and cowers there.

LEPORELLO: Non vo' più veder l'amico, pian, pianin m'asconderò, m'asconderò!

LEPORELLO: I don't want to see my friend again, quietly, very quietly I'll hide myself, I'll hide myself!

With a rumbling of tympani, the marble statue of the Commendatore enters the room.

STATUE: Don Giovanni! a cenar teco m'invitasti! e son venuto!

STATUE: Don Giovanni! you invited me to dine with you! and I have arrived!

Don Giovanni is somewhat startled but conceals his surprise under an air of bravado.

DON GIOVANNI: Non l'avrei giammai creduto; ma farò quel che potrò. Leporello! un'altra cena! fa che subito si porti!

DON GIOVANNI: I should never have believed it; but I'll do what I can. Leporello! another dinner! have it brought immediately!

Leporello peers dazedly out from under the table.

LEPORELLO: Ah, padron, ah, padron, ah, padron! siam tutti morti!

LEPORELLO: Ah, master, ah, master, ah, master! we're all dead!

DON GIOVANNI: Vanne, dico!

DON GIOVANNI: Go to it, I say!

Leporello begins to crawl out.

(Courtesy Teatro alla Scala, Milan, photo by Ezio Piccagliani)

Act 2, Scene 6. The statue comes to dine. Don Giovanni stands his ground, while Leporello hides under the table.

Act 2, Scene 6. The statue, gripping Don Giovanni's hand, asks him to repent. In this 1953 production of the Städtische Oper, Berlin, Dietrich Fischer-Dieskau is Don Giovanni and Otto von Rohr is the Commendatore.

Donna Anna discovers her father's body.

Leporello exhibits the catalogue.

Scenes from *Don Giovanni*. Engravings by J. H. Ramberg published in the *Almanach Orphea* of 1825.

Don Giovanni proposes to Zerlina.

Masetto upbraids Zerlina for infidelity.

Leporello sheds his Don Giovanni disguise.

Don Giovanni invites the statue to dinner.

Scenes from *Don Giovanni*. Engravings by J. H. Ramberg published in the *Almanach Orphea* of 1825.

The statue calls upon Don Giovanni to repent.

Don Giovanni plunges down to Hell.

Mozart's monument in St. Marx's Cemetery in Vienna, set up in 1902 on the supposed site of his burial.

The Rauhensteingasse, Vienna, about 1820. On the left is the house in which Mozart died.

STATUE: Ferma un po'! non si pasce di cibo mortale, chi si pasce di cibo celeste! Altre cure più gravi di queste, altra brama quaggiù mi guidò.

STATUE: Wait a bit! one who partakes of celestial food does not partake of mortal food. Other matters more serious than these, another desire brought me down here.

Leporello crawls back under the table.

LEPORELLO: La terzana d'avere mi sembra, e le membra fermar più non sò, la terzana d'avere mi sembra, e le membra fermar più non sò.

DON GIOVANNI: Parla dunque! che chiedi? che vuoi?

LEPORELLO: I seem to have the ague, and I can't stop shaking, I seem to have the ague, and I can't stop shaking.

DON GIOVANNI: *To Statue.* Speak, then! what do you ask? what do you want?

STATUE: Parlo: ascolta! più tempo non ho.

DON GIOVANNI: Parla, parla, ascoltando ti sto.

LEPORELLO: Ah le membra fermar più non sò; la terzana d'avere mi sembra, la terzana d'avere mi sembra, e le membra fermar più non sò!

STATUE: Parlo: ascolta! più tempo non ho!

STATUE: I speak: listen! I have not much time.

DON GIOVANNI: Speak, speak, I am listening to you.

LEPORELLO: Ah, I can't stop shaking; I seem to have the ague, I seem to have the ague, and I can't stop shaking!

STATUE: I speak: listen! I have not much time!

Don Giovanni becomes more defiant.

DON GIOVANNI: Parla, parla, ascoltando ti sto.

STATUE: Tu m'invitasti a cena, il tuo dover or sai, rispondimi, rispondimi, verrai tu a cenar meco?

DON GIOVANNI: Speak, speak, I am listening to you.

STATUE: You invited me to dinner, you know your obligation now, answer me, answer me, will you come to dine with me?

Leporello quavers from beneath the table.

LEPORELLO: Oibò, oibò; tempo non ha, scusate.

LEPORELLO: Oh, oh; he hasn't got time, sorry.

DON GIOVANNI: A torto di viltate tacciato mai sarò.

DON GIOVANNI: *Icily.* I shall never be accused of cowardice.

STATUE: Risolvi!

STATUE: Decide!

DON GIOVANNI: Ho già risolto!

DON GIOVANNI: I have already decided!

STATUE: Verrai?

STATUE: You will come?

LEPORELLO: Dite di no, dite di no!

LEPORELLO: Say no, say no!

DON GIOVANNI: Ho fermo il core in petto, non ho timor, verrò!

DON GIOVANNI: My heart is steady in my breast, I am not afraid, I shall come!

The Statue extends a hand toward Don Giovanni.

STATUE: Dammi la mano in pegno!

STATUE: Give me your hand as pledge!

Still defiant, Don Giovanni gives the Statue his hand.

DON GIOVANNI: Eccola! Ohimè!

DON GIOVANNI: Here it is! Ah!

STATUE: Cos'hai?

STATUE: What is the matter?

DON GIOVANNI: Che gelo è questo mai?

DON GIOVANNI: How freezing cold it is!

STATUE: Pentiti, cangia vita, è l'ultimo momento!

STATUE: Repent, change your life, it is your last moment!

Don Giovanni tries to withdraw his hand.

DON GIOVANNI: No, no, ch'io non mi pento, vanne lontan da me!

DON GIOVANNI: No, no, I do not repent, get you far away from me!

STATUE: Pentiti, scellerato!

STATUE: Repent, villain!

DON GIOVANNI: No, vecchio infatuato!

DON GIOVANNI: No, stupid old man!

STATUE: Pentiti!

STATUE: Repent!

DON GIOVANNI: No!

DON GIOVANNI: No!

STATUE: Pentiti!

DON GIOVANNI: No!

STATUE: Sì!

DON GIOVANNI: No!

STATUE: Sì!

DON GIOVANNI: No!

STATUE: Repent!

DON GIOVANNI: No!

STATUE: Yes!

DON GIOVANNI: No!

STATUE: Yes!

DON GIOVANNI: No!

*With a desperate effort, he wrests his hand
away from the Statue.*

STATUE: Sì! Sì!

DON GIOVANNI: No! No!

STATUE: Yes! Yes!

DON GIOVANNI: No! No!

*The Commendatore's Statue begins to move toward the
door whence it entered. Roaring flames begin to sur-
round Don Giovanni.*

STATUE: Ah! tempo più non v'è!

DON GIOVANNI: Da qual tremore insolito sento assalir gli spiriti! dond'escono quei vortici di foco pien d'orror?

STATUE: Ah! there is no more time!

DON GIOVANNI: I feel my strength gripped by such unwonted trembling! whence come those horror-filled whirlpools of fire?

A chorus of ghostly demon voices sounds from below.

DEMON VOICES: Tutto a tue colpe è poco! vieni! c'è un mal peggior!

DON GIOVANNI: Chi l'anima mi lacera? Chi m'agita le viscere? Che strazio, ohimè, che smania! Che inferno, che terror!

LEPORELLO: Che ceffo disperato! Che gesti da dannato! che gridi! che lamenti! come mi fa terror, mi fa terror!

DEMON VOICES: All is as nothing compared to your crimes! come! worse is in store for you!

DON GIOVANNI: Who tears my spirit? who shakes my innards? what twisting, alas, what frenzy! what hell, what terror!

LEPORELLO: What a despairing grimace! What gestures of a damned soul! what shouts! what wails! how terrified it makes me, terrified it makes me!

DEMON VOICES: Tutto a tue colpe è poco!

DON GIOVANNI: Chi l'anima mi lacera?

LEPORELLO: Che ceffo disperato!

DEMON VOICES: Vieni! c'è un mal peggior!

DON GIOVANNI: Chi m'agita le viscere? che strazio, ohimè, che smania! Ah! che inferno! che terror!

LEPORELLO: Che gesti da dannato! che gridi! che lamenti! che gridi! che lamenti! Come mi fa terror!

DEMON VOICES: Vieni! vieni! vieni! c'è un mal peggior!

DON GIOVANNI: Ah!

DEMON VOICES: All is as nothing compared to your crimes!

DON GIOVANNI: Who tears my spirit?

LEPORELLO: What a despairing grimace!

DEMON VOICES: Come! worse is in store for you!

DON GIOVANNI: Who shakes my innards? what twisting, alas, what frenzy! Ah! what hell! what terror!

LEPORELLO: What gestures of a damned soul! what shouts! what wails! what shouts! what wails! How terrified it makes me!

DEMON VOICES: Come! come! come! worse is in store for you!

DON GIOVANNI: *Screaming*. Ah!

Don Giovanni utters his final cry, is enveloped by flames and sinks to hell. Leporello echoes the Don's shout.

LEPORELLO: Ah!

LEPORELLO: *Screaming*. Ah!

Epilogue

The same setting as before, a few minutes later. Leporello is still crouched under the table. Donna Anna, Don Ottavio, Donna Elvira, Zerlina and Masetto enter, accompanied by minions of the law.

DONNA ELVIRA, ZERLINA, DON OTTAVIO AND MASETTO: Ah! dov'è il perfido? dov'è l'indegno? tutto il mio sdegno

DONNA ELVIRA, ZERLINA, DON OTTAVIO AND MASETTO: Ah! where is the liar? where is the worthless man? I want to pour

sfogar io vo', sfogar io vo'.

DONNA ANNA: Solo mirandolo, stretto in catene, alle mie pene calma darò.

Leporello emerges from hiding, somewhat shaken.

LEPORELLO: Più non sperate di ritrovarlo, più non cercate— lontano andò, lontano andò.

DONNA ANNA, DONNA ELVIRA, ZERLINA, DON OTTAVIO AND MASETTO: Cos'è? favella! cos'è? favella! Via presto, sbrigati! via presto, sbrigati!

LEPORELLO: Venne un colosso, venne un colosso—Ma se non posso, ma se non posso, ma se non posso, ma se non posso, ma se non posso—

DONNA ANNA, DONNA ELVIRA, ZERLINA, DON OTTAVIO AND MASETTO: Presto favella, sbrigati!

LEPORELLO: Tra fumo e fuoco —badate un poco—l'uomo di sasso—fermate il passo— giusto là sotto—diede il gran botto—giusto là il diavolo sel trangugiò.

DONNA ANNA, DONNA ELVIRA, ZERLINA, DON OTTAVIO AND MASETTO: Stelle, che sento!

LEPORELLO: Vero è l'evento.

forth, I want to pour forth all my indignation.

DONNA ANNA: Only seeing him bound in chains will ease my pain.

LEPORELLO: Don't ever hope to see him again, don't look for him any more—he went far away, he went far away.

DONNA ANNA, DONNA ELVIRA, ZERLINA, DON OTTAVIO AND MASETTO: What is it? speak! what is it? speak! Be quick, hurry up, be quick, hurry up!

LEPORELLO: Along came a colossus, along came a colossus—but if I can't, but if I can't, but if I can't, but if I can't—

DONNA ANNA, DONNA ELVIRA, ZERLINA, DON OTTAVIO AND MASETTO: Speak quickly, hurry up!

LEPORELLO: Mid smoke and fire—wait a bit—the stone man—block the passage— right down there—gave the final blow—right over there the devil swallowed him up.

DONNA ANNA, DONNA ELVIRA, ZERLINA, DON OTTAVIO AND MASETTO: Ye gods! what do I hear!

LEPORELLO: It really happened.

DONNA ELVIRA: Ah, certo è l'ombra che m'incontrò, ah! certo è l'ombra che m'incontrò, ah! certo è l'ombra, ah, certo, ah! certo è l'ombra che m'incontrò!

DONNA ANNA: Ah, certo è l'ombra che l'incontrò, ah! certo è l'ombra che l'incontrò, ah! certo è l'ombra, ah, certo, certo è l'ombra che l'incontrò.

ZERLINA: Ah, certo è l'ombra, ah! certo è l'ombra che m'incontrò, ah! certo è l'ombra, ah, certo, certo è l'ombra che m'incontrò.

DON OTTAVIO: Ah! certo è l'ombra, ah! certo è l'ombra che m'incontrò, ah! certo è l'ombra, ah! certo è l'ombra che m'incontrò.

MASETTO: Ah! certo è l'ombra, è l'ombra che m'incontrò, ah! certo è l'ombra, ah! certo è l'ombra che m'incontrò!

DONNA ELVIRA: Ah, it surely was the shade that met me, ah! it surely was the shade that met me, ah! it surely was the shade, ah, it surely, surely was the shade that met me!

DONNA ANNA: Ah, it surely was the shade that met her, ah! it surely was the shade that met her, ah! it surely was the shade, ah, it surely, surely was the shade that met her.

ZERLINA: Ah, it surely was the shade, ah! it surely was the shade that met me, ah! it surely was the shade, ah, it surely, surely was the shade that met me.

DON OTTAVIO: Ah! it surely was the shade, ah! it surely was the shade that met me, ah! it surely was the shade, ah! it surely was the shade that met me.

MASETTO: Ah! it surely was the shade, it was the shade that met me, ah! it surely was the shade, ah! it surely was the shade that met me!

Don Ottavio turns to Donna Anna.

DON OTTAVIO: Or che tutti, o mio tesoro! vendicati siam dal cielo, porgi, porgi a me un ristoro, non mi far languire ancor.

DONNA ANNA: Lascia, o caro! un anno ancora, allo sfogo del mio cor.

DON OTTAVIO: Now that we all have been avenged by heaven, o my treasure! offer, offer to me some relief, do not make me suffer any longer.

DONNA ANNA: Let there be, o my dear! one year still for the relief of my heart.

DON OTTAVIO: Al desio di chi m'adora—

DONNA ANNA: Al desio di chi t'adora—

DON OTTAVIO: —ceder deve un fido amor,—

DONNA ANNA: —ceder deve un fido amor—

DONNA ANNA AND DON OTTAVIO: —ceder deve, ceder deve un fido amor—

DONNA ANNA: —Al desio di chi t'adora—

DON OTTAVIO: —Al desio di chi m'adora—

DONNA ANNA: —ceder deve un fido amor—

DON OTTAVIO: —ceder deve un fido amor—

DONNA ANNA AND DON OTTAVIO: —ceder deve, ceder deve un fido amor, un fido, un fido amor.

DONNA ELVIRA: Io men vado in un ritiro a finir la vita mia!

ZERLINA: Noi, Masetto, a casa andiamo! a cenar in compagnia.

MASETTO: Noi, Zerlina, a casa andiamo! a cenar in compagnia.

LEPORELLO: Ed io vado all'osteria a trovar padron miglior.

ZERLINA, MASETTO AND LEPORELLO: Resti dunque quel bir-

DON OTTAVIO: To the wish of her who adores me—

DONNA ANNA: To the wish of her who adores you—

DON OTTAVIO: —a faithful love must yield—

DONNA ANNA: —a faithful love must yield—

DONNA ANNA AND DON OTTAVIO: —a faithful love must yield, must yield—

DONNA ANNA: —To the wish of her who adores you—

DON OTTAVIO: —To the wish of her who adores me—

DONNA ANNA: —a faithful love must yield—

DON OTTAVIO: —a faithful love must yield—

DONNA ANNA AND DON OTTAVIO: — faithful love, a faithful love, a faithful love must yield, must yield.

DONNA ELVIRA: *To the others.* I shall go away to end my days in a cloister!

ZERLINA: We, Masetto, are going home! to dine together.

MASETTO: We, Zerlina, are going home! to dine together.

LEPORELLO: And I'm going to the inn to find a better master.

ZERLINA, MASETTO AND LEPORELLO: May that rogue remain

bon con Proserpina e Pluton, con Proserpina e Pluton. E noi tutti, o buona gente, ripetiam allegramente l'antichissima canzon, l'antichissima canzon, l'antichissima canzon:

then with Proserpine and Pluto, with Proserpine and Pluto. And let us all, o good people, happily repeat the very ancient song, the very ancient song, the very ancient song:

DONNA ANNA: Questo è il fin di chi fa mal, di chi fa mal—

DONNA ANNA: This is the end of the evil-doer, of the evil-doer—

DONNA ELVIRA, DON OTTAVIO, MASETTO AND LEPORELLO: Questo è il fin—

DONNA ELVIRA, DON OTTAVIO, MASETTO AND LEPORELLO: This is the end—

ZERLINA: Questo è il fin di chi fa mal, di chi fa mal.

ZERLINA: This is the end of the evil-doer, of the evil-doer.

DONNA ANNA, DONNA ELVIRA, ZERLINA AND DON OTTAVIO: Questo è il fin, questo è il fin di chi fa mal, di chi fa mal, di chi fa mal, questo è il fin di chi fa mal, di chi fa mal.

DONNA ANNA, DONNA ELVIRA, ZERLINA AND DON OTTAVIO: This is the end, this is the end of the evil-doer, of the evil-doer, of the evil-doer, this is the end of the evil-doer, of the evil-doer.

LEPORELLO AND MASETTO: Questo è il fin di chi fa mal, di chi fa mal, di chi fa mal, questo è il fin di chi fa mal, di chi fa mal.

LEPORELLO AND MASETTO: This is the end of the evil-doer, of the evil-doer, of the evil-doer, this is the end of the evil-doer, of the evil-doer.

ALL: E de'perfidi la morte—

ALL: And the death of wicked men—

DONNA ANNA, DONNA ELVIRA, ZERLINA, DON OTTAVIO AND MASETTO: —all vita è sempre, è sempre ugual, è sempre ugual.

DONNA ANNA, DONNA ELVIRA, ZERLINA, DON OTTAVIO AND MASETTO: —is always, is always just like, is always just like their life.

LEPORELLO: —alla vita è sempre ugual, è sempre ugual.

LEPORELLO: —is always just like, is always just like their life.

ALL: E de'perfidi la morte—

DONNA ANNA AND DONNA ELVIRA: —alla vita è sempre, è sempre, è sempre ugual—

ZERLINA: —alla vita è sempre ugual, è sempre ugual—

DON OTTAVIO: —alla vita è sempre, è sempre, è sempre ugual—

MASETTO: —alla vita è sempre, è sempre ugual—

LEPORELLO: —alla vita è sempre ugual—

ALL: —alla vita è sempre ugual, alla vita è sempre ugual, è sempre ugual, è sempre ugual, sempre ugual.

ALL: And the death of wicked men—

DONNA ANNA AND DONNA ELVIRA: —is always, is always, is always just like their life—

ZERLINA: —is always just like, is always just like their life—

DON OTTAVIO: —is always, is always, is always just like their life—

MASETTO: —is always, is always just like their life—

LEPORELLO: —is always just like their life—

ALL: —is always just like their life, is always just like their life, is always just like it, is always just like it, always just like it.

End of Libretto

BIBLIOGRAPHY
AND CRITICAL COMMENTS

Biographies of Mozart and studies of *Don Giovanni* are many, and considerable care in selection is needed. For the purposes of this bibliography only the major sources of information have been presented; the list does not include many reference works, encyclopedias, periodical articles, and histories which the reader will find useful.

SOURCE OF ITALIAN LIBRETTO:

Don Giovanni: An Opera in Two Acts. Vocal Score, including the Secco Recitatives. New York: G. Schirmer, Inc.

MOZART:

Jahn, Otto, *The Life of Mozart*. 3 Volumes. Translated from the German by Pauline Townsend. London: Novello, Ewer and Co., 1891. The parent of modern Mozart biographies. One may quibble with its Victorian reticence about the composer's earthier aspects (the whole "Bäsle" interlude is omitted), but its detailed wealth of facts and documented sources is indisputable.

Hussey, Dyneley, *Wolfgang Amade Mozart*. New York and London: Harper & Brothers, 1928. A readable, carefully factual biography. Speculation is always labelled as such.

Turner, W. J., *Mozart, the Man and His Works*. New York: Alfred A. Knopf, Inc., 1938. A more leisurely and philosophical sort of biography than Jahn or Hussey. Its chronological documentation is very useful.

Blom, Eric, *Mozart*. Translated from English to German by Irma Silzer. Zurich: Büchergilde Gutenberg, 1954. Originally published in England in 1935, and in the United States in 1949. The style of the German version is coy, but its facts are accurate.

Einstein, Alfred, *Mozart, His Character, His Work*. Translated from the German by Arthur Mendel and Nathan Broder. New York: Oxford University Press, 1945.

Abert, Hermann, *W. A. Mozart*. 2 Volumes. 1919–21; 7th ed., 1955–56. Issued as a revised edition of Jahn, but practically a new book.

Wyzewa, T. de, and Saint-Foix, G. de, *W. A. Mozart, sa vie musicale et son œuvre*. 5 Volumes. 1912–1946. The first book to investigate thoroughly the sources and development of Mozart's style, and probably the best guide to the music.

The Mozart Companion. Edited by H. C. Robbins Landon and Donald Mitchell. New York: Oxford University Press, 1956.

Letters of Mozart and His Family. Edited by Emily Anderson and Cecil B. Oldham. 3 Volumes. New York: St. Martin's Press.

Mozarts Briefe. Selected by Dr. Karl Storck. Stuttgart: Greiner & Pfeiffer, 1906. Contains an incomplete but representative selection of Mozart's correspondence, 1770–*ca.* 1790. Excerpted translations have been made by the author.

Mozart's Letters. Edited and introduced by Eric Blom. Selected from *The Letters of Mozart and His Family*, translated and annotated by Emily Anderson. London: Penguin Books, 1956.

Mozart's Letters. 2 Volumes. Translated from the Collection of Ludwig Nohl by Lady Wallace. New York and Philadelphia: Frederick Leypoldt, 1866.

The Mozart Handbook. Edited by Louis Biancolli. Cleveland and New York: World Publishing Company, 1954. A nice "browsing book," with selections from many studies of Mozart and his music. A handy guide to the better-known sources, with an appendix listing all the composer's works.

DA PONTE:

The Memoirs of Lorenzo Da Ponte. Translated by Elisabeth Abbott from the Italian. Edited and annotated by Arthur Livingston. Philadelphia and London: J. B. Lippincott, 1929. A complete translation containing much supplementary information in frequently amusing footnotes. (The excerpted translation from Da Ponte's *Memoirs* is the author's; the source was an older Italian edition of the *Memoirs*.)

Memoirs of Lorenzo Da Ponte. Translated with an introduction and notes by L. A. Sheppard. London: George Routledge & Sons, 1929. A more readable translation than Abbott's but unfortunately abridged.

Russo, Joseph Louis, *Lorenzo Da Ponte, Poet and Adventurer.* New York: Columbia University Press, 1922.

Nettl, Paul, *The Other Casanova.* New York: Philosophical Library, 1950. Draws interesting parallels between the careers of Casanova and Da Ponte.

THE OPERA AND ITS BACKGROUND:

Tirso de Molina, *El Burlador de Sevilla y Convidado de Piedra.* Cambridge: Cambridge University Press, 1954. (A good translation of this play can be found in Volume 3 of *The Classic Theater*, edited by Eric Bentley, Garden City: Anchor Books, 1959. The translation, called *The Trickster of Seville*, is by Roy Campbell.)

The Dramatic Works of Molière. 3 Volumes. Translated by Charles Heron Wall. New York: G. P. Putnam's Sons, 1879.

Dent, Edward J., *Mozart's Operas*, 2nd ed. London and New York: Oxford University Press, 1947. A well-written, informative scholarly book.

Hughes, Patrick, *Famous Mozart Operas.* New York: Citadel Press, 1958. Neither as scholarly nor as packed with information as the Dent work, but offering much that is worthwhile.

Haas, Robert, *Wolfgang Amadeus Mozart.* Potsdam: Akademische Verlagsgesellschaft, Athenaion, 1933. A study in comparative musicology with much background information.

Grout, Donald J., *A Short History of Opera.* 2 Volumes. New York: Columbia University Press, 1947.

Tales of Hoffmann. Edited by Christopher Lazare. New York: A. A. Wyn, 1946.

Tiersot, Julien, *Don Juan de Mozart. Étude historique et critique, analyse musicale.* Paris: Mellettee, 1933.

Paul, Stefan, *Don Giovanni: Die Opernlegende von Don Juan dem Versucher und Sucher.* Vienna: Reichner, 1938.

Rank, Otto, *Don Juan [et] Une Étude sur le Double.* Paris: Denoël et Steele, 1932.

CATALOG OF DOVER BOOKS

Books Explaining Science and Mathematics

Books Explaining Science and Mathematics

WHAT IS SCIENCE?, N. Campbell. The role of experiment and measurement, the function of mathematics, the nature of scientific laws, the difference between laws and theories, the limitations of science, and many similarly provocative topics are treated clearly and without technicalities by an eminent scientist. "Still an excellent introduction to scientific philosophy," H. Margenau in PHYSICS TODAY. "A first-rate primer . . . deserves a wide audience," SCIENTIFIC AMERICAN. 192pp. 5⅜ x 8.   S43 Paperbound **$1.25**

THE NATURE OF PHYSICAL THEORY, P. W. Bridgman. A Nobel Laureate's clear, non-technical lectures on difficulties and paradoxes connected with frontier research on the physical sciences. Concerned with such central concepts as thought, logic, mathematics, relativity, probability, wave mechanics, etc. he analyzes the contributions of such men as Newton, Einstein, Bohr, Heisenberg, and many others. "Lucid and entertaining . . . recommended to anyone who wants to get some insight into current philosophies of science," THE NEW PHILOSOPHY. Index. xi + 138pp. 5⅜ x 8.   S33 Paperbound **$1.25**

EXPERIMENT AND THEORY IN PHYSICS, Max Born. A Nobel Laureate examines the nature of experiment and theory in theoretical physics and analyzes the advances made by the great physicists of our day: Heisenberg, Einstein, Bohr, Planck, Dirac, and others. The actual process of creation is detailed step-by-step by one who participated. A fine examination of the scientific method at work. 44pp. 5⅜ x 8.   S308 Paperbound **75¢**

THE PSYCHOLOGY OF INVENTION IN THE MATHEMATICAL FIELD, J. Hadamard. The reports of such men as Descartes, Pascal, Einstein, Poincaré, and others are considered in this investigation of the method of idea-creation in mathematics and other sciences and the thinking process in general. How do ideas originate? What is the role of the unconscious? What is Poincaré's forgetting hypothesis? are some of the fascinating questions treated. A penetrating analysis of Einstein's thought processes concludes the book. xiii + 145pp. 5⅜ x 8.   T107 Paperbound **$1.25**

THE NATURE OF LIGHT AND COLOUR IN THE OPEN AIR, M. Minnaert. Why are shadows sometimes blue, sometimes green, or other colors depending on the light and surroundings? What causes mirages? Why do multiple suns and moons appear in the sky? Professor Minnaert explains these unusual phenomena and hundreds of others in simple, easy-to-understand terms based on optical laws and the properties of light and color. No mathematics is required but artists, scientists, students, and everyone fascinated by these "tricks" of nature will find thousands of useful and amazing pieces of information. Hundreds of observational experiments are suggested which require no special equipment. 200 illustrations; 42 photos. xvi + 362pp. 5⅜ x 8.   T196 Paperbound **$1.95**

THE UNIVERSE OF LIGHT, W. Bragg. Sir William Bragg, Nobel Laureate and great modern physicist, is also well known for his powers of clear exposition. Here he analyzes all aspects of light for the layman: lenses, reflection, refraction, the optics of vision, x-rays, the photoelectric effect, etc. He tells you what causes the color of spectra, rainbows, and soap bubbles, how magic mirrors work, and much more. Dozens of simple experiments are described. Preface. Index. 199 line drawings and photographs, including 2 full-page color plates. x + 283pp. 5⅜ x 8.   T538 Paperbound **$1.85**

SOAP-BUBBLES: THEIR COLOURS AND THE FORCES THAT MOULD THEM, C. V. Boys. For continuing popularity and validity as scientific primer, few books can match this volume of easily-followed experiments, explanations. Lucid exposition of complexities of liquid films, surface tension and related phenomena, bubbles' reaction to heat, motion, music, magnetic fields. Experiments with capillary attraction, soap bubbles on frames, composite bubbles, liquid cylinders and jets, bubbles other than soap, etc. Wonderful introduction to scientific method, natural laws that have many ramifications in areas of modern physics. Only complete edition in print. New Introduction by S. Z. Lewin, New York University. 83 illustrations; 1 full-page color plate. xii + 190pp. 5⅜ x 8½.   T542 Paperbound **95¢**

CATALOGUE OF DOVER BOOKS

THE STORY OF X-RAYS FROM RONTGEN TO ISOTOPES, A. R. Bleich, M.D. This book, by a member of the American College of Radiology, gives the scientific explanation of x-rays, their applications in medicine, industry and art, and their danger (and that of atmospheric radiation) to the individual and the species. You learn how radiation therapy is applied against cancer, how x-rays diagnose heart disease and other ailments, how they are used to examine mummies for information on diseases of early societies, and industrial materials for hidden weaknesses. 54 illustrations show x-rays of flowers, bones, stomach, gears with flaws, etc. 1st publication. Index. xix + 186pp. 5⅜ x 8.   T622 Paperbound **$1.35**

SPINNING TOPS AND GYROSCOPIC MOTION, John Perry. A classic elementary text of the dynamics of rotation — the behavior and use of rotating bodies such as gyroscopes and tops. In simple, everyday English you are shown how quasi-rigidity is induced in discs of paper, smoke rings, chains, etc., by rapid motions; why a gyrostat falls and why a top rises; precession; how the earth's motion affects climate; and many other phenomena. Appendix on practical use of gyroscopes. 62 figures. 128pp. 5⅜ x 8.   T416 Paperbound **$1.00**

SNOW CRYSTALS, W. A. Bentley, M. J. Humphreys. For almost 50 years W. A. Bentley photographed snow flakes in his laboratory in Jericho, Vermont; in 1931 the American Meteorological Society gathered together the best of his work, some 2400 photographs of snow flakes, plus a few ice flowers, windowpane frosts, dew, frozen rain, and other ice formations. Pictures were selected for beauty and scientific value. A very valuable work to anyone in meteorology, cryology; most interesting to layman; extremely useful for artist who wants beautiful, crystalline designs. All copyright free. Unabridged reprint of 1931 edition. 2453 illustrations. 227pp. 8 x 10½.   T287 Paperbound **$2.95**

A DOVER SCIENCE SAMPLER, edited by George Barkin. A collection of brief, non-technical passages from 44 Dover Books Explaining Science for the enjoyment of the science-minded browser. Includes work of Bertrand Russell, Poincaré, Laplace, Max Born, Galileo, Newton; material on physics, mathematics, metallurgy, anatomy, astronomy, chemistry, etc. You will be fascinated by Martin Gardner's analysis of the sincere pseudo-scientist, Moritz's account of Newton's absentmindedness, Bernard's examples of human vivisection, etc. Illustrations from the Diderot Pictorial Encyclopedia and De Re Metallica. 64 pages.   **FREE**

THE STORY OF ATOMIC THEORY AND ATOMIC ENERGY, J. G. Feinberg. A broader approach to subject of nuclear energy and its cultural implications than any other similar source. Very readable, informal, completely non-technical text. Begins with first atomic theory, 600 B.C. and carries you through the work of Mendelejeff, Röntgen, Madame Curie, to Einstein's equation and the A-bomb. New chapter goes through thermonuclear fission, binding energy, other events up to 1959. Radioactive decay and radiation hazards, future benefits, work of Bohr, moderns, hundreds more topics. "Deserves special mention . . . not only authoritative but thoroughly popular in the best sense of the word," Saturday Review. Formerly, "The Atom Story." Expanded with new chapter. Three appendixes. Index. 34 illustrations. vii + 243pp. 5⅜ x 8.   T625 Paperbound **$1.45**

THE STRANGE STORY OF THE QUANTUM, AN ACCOUNT FOR THE GENERAL READER OF THE GROWTH OF IDEAS UNDERLYING OUR PRESENT ATOMIC KNOWLEDGE, B. Hoffmann. Presents lucidly and expertly, with barest amount of mathematics, the problems and theories which led to modern quantum physics. Dr. Hoffmann begins with the closing years of the 19th century, when certain trifling discrepancies were noticed, and with illuminating analogies and examples takes you through the brilliant concepts of Planck, Einstein, Pauli, Broglie, Bohr, Schroedinger, Heisenberg, Dirac, Sommerfeld, Feynman, etc. This edition includes a new, long postscript carrying the story through 1958. "Of the books attempting an account of the history and contents of our modern atomic physics which have come to my attention, this is the best," H. Margenau, Yale University, in "American Journal of Physics." 32 tables and line illustrations. Index. 275pp. 5⅜ x 8.   T518 Paperbound **$1.45**

SPACE AND TIME, E. Borel. Written by a versatile mathematician of world renown with his customary lucidity and precision, this introduction to relativity for the layman presents scores of examples, analogies, and illustrations that open up new ways of thinking about space and time. It covers abstract geometry and geographical maps, continuity and topology, the propagation of light, the special theory of relativity, the general theory of relativity, theoretical researches, and much more. Mathematical notes. 2 Indexes. 4 Appendices. 15 figures. xvi + 243pp. 5⅜ x 8.   T592 Paperbound **$1.45**

FROM EUCLID TO EDDINGTON: A STUDY OF THE CONCEPTIONS OF THE EXTERNAL WORLD, Sir Edmund Whittaker. A foremost British scientist traces the development of theories of natural philosophy from the western rediscovery of Euclid to Eddington, Einstein, Dirac, etc. The inadequacy of classical physics is contrasted with present day attempts to understand the physical world through relativity, non-Euclidean geometry, space curvature, wave mechanics, etc. 5 major divisions of examination: Space; Time and Movement; the Concepts of Classical Physics; the Concepts of Quantum Mechanics; the Eddington Universe. 212pp. 5⅜ x 8.   T491 Paperbound **$1.35**

Nature, Biology

NATURE RECREATION: Group Guidance for the Out-of-doors, William Gould Vinal. Intended for both the uninitiated nature instructor and the education student on the college level, this complete "how-to" program surveys the entire area of nature education for the young. Philosophy of nature recreation; requirements, responsibilities, important information for group leaders; nature games; suggested group projects; conducting meetings and getting discussions started; etc. Scores of immediately applicable teaching aids, plus completely updated sources of information, pamphlets, field guides, recordings, etc. Bibliography. 74 photographs. + 310pp. 5⅜ x 8½.　　　　　　　　　　　　　　T1015 Paperbound **$1.75**

HOW TO KNOW THE WILD FLOWERS, Mrs. William Starr Dana. Classic nature book that has introduced thousands to wonders of American wild flowers. Color-season principle of organization is easy to use, even by those with no botanical training, and the genial, refreshing discussions of history, folklore, uses of over 1,000 native and escape flowers, foliage plants are informative as well as fun to read. Over 170 full-page plates, collected from several editions, may be colored in to make permanent records of finds. Revised to conform with 1950 edition of Gray's Manual of Botany. xlii + 438pp. 5⅜ x 8½.　　　T332 Paperbound **$1.85**

HOW TO KNOW THE FERNS, F. T. Parsons. Ferns, among our most lovely native plants, are all too little known. This classic of nature lore will enable the layman to identify almost any American fern he may come across. After an introduction on the structure and life of ferns, the 57 most important ferns are fully pictured and described (arranged upon a simple identification key). Index of Latin and English names. 61 illustrations and 42 full-page plates. xiv + 215pp. 5⅜ x 8.　　　　　　　　　　　　　　　　　　　　T740 Paperbound **$1.25**

MANUAL OF THE TREES OF NORTH AMERICA, Charles Sprague Sargent. Still unsurpassed as most comprehensive, reliable study of North American tree characteristics, precise locations and distribution. By dean of American dendrologists. Every tree native to U.S., Canada, Alaska, 185 genera, 717 species, described in detail—leaves, flowers, fruit, winterbuds, bark, wood, growth habits etc. plus discussion of varieties and local variants, immaturity variations. Over 100 keys, including unusual 11-page analytical key to genera, aid in identification. 783 clear illustrations of flowers, fruit, leaves. An unmatched permanent reference work for all nature lovers. Second enlarged (1926) edition. Synopsis of families. Analytical key to genera. Glossary of technical terms. Index. 783 illustrations, 1 map. Two volumes. Total of 982pp. 5⅜ x 8.　　　　　　　　　　　T277 Vol. I Paperbound **$2.00**
　　　　　　　　　　　　　　　　　　　　　T278 Vol. II Paperbound **$2.00**
　　　　　　　　　　　　　　　　　　　　　　　　　The set **$4.00**

TREES OF THE EASTERN AND CENTRAL UNITED STATES AND CANADA, W. M. Harlow. A revised edition of a standard middle-level guide to native trees and important escapes. More than 140 trees are described in detail, and illustrated with more than 600 drawings and photographs. Supplementary keys will enable the careful reader to identify almost any tree he might encounter. xiii + 288pp. 5⅜ x 8.　　　　　　　　　　T395 Paperbound **$1.35**

GUIDE TO SOUTHERN TREES, Ellwood S. Harrar and J. George Harrar. All the essential information about trees indigenous to the South, in an extremely handy format. Introductory essay on methods of tree classification and study, nomenclature, chief divisions of Southern trees, etc. Approximately 100 keys and synopses allow for swift, accurate identification of trees. Numerous excellent illustrations, non-technical text make this a useful book for teachers of biology or natural science, nature lovers, amateur naturalists. Revised 1962 edition. Index. Bibliography. Glossary of technical terms. 920 illustrations; 201 full-page plates. ix + 709pp. 4⅝ x 6⅜.　　　　　　　　　　　　　　T945 Paperbound **$2.25**

FRUIT KEY AND TWIG KEY TO TREES AND SHRUBS, W. M. Harlow. Bound together in one volume for the first time, these handy and accurate keys to fruit and twig identification are the only guides of their sort with photographs (up to 3 times natural size). "Fruit Key": Key to over 120 different deciduous and evergreen fruits. 139 photographs and 11 line drawings. Synoptic summary of fruit types. Bibliography. 2 Indexes (common and scientific names). "Twig Key": Key to over 160 different twigs and buds. 173 photographs. Glossary of technical terms. Bibliography. 2 Indexes (common and scientific names). Two volumes bound as one. Total of xvii + 126pp. 5⅝ x 8⅜.　　　　　　　　　　　　　　　　　T511 Paperbound **$1.25**

INSECT LIFE AND INSECT NATURAL HISTORY, S. W. Frost. A work emphasizing habits, social life, and ecological relations of insects, rather than more academic aspects of classification and morphology. Prof. Frost's enthusiasm and knowledge are everywhere evident as he discusses insect associations and specialized habits like leaf-rolling, leaf-mining, and case-making, the gall insects, the boring insects, aquatic insects, etc. He examines all sorts of matters not usually covered in general works, such as: insects as human food, insect music and musicians, insect response to electric and radio waves, use of insects in art and literature. The admirably executed purpose of this book, which covers the middle ground between elementary treatment and scholarly monographs, is to excite the reader to observe for himself. Over 700 illustrations. Extensive bibliography. x + 524pp. 5⅜ x 8.　　T517 Paperbound **$2.45**

CATALOGUE OF DOVER BOOKS

COMMON SPIDERS OF THE UNITED STATES, J. H. Emerton. Here is a nature hobby you can pursue right in your own cellar! Only non-technical, but thorough, reliable guide to spiders for the layman. Over 200 spiders from all parts of the country, arranged by scientific classification, are identified by shape and color, number of eyes, habitat and range, habits, etc. Full text, 501 line drawings and photographs, and valuable introduction explain webs, poisons, threads, capturing and preserving spiders, etc. Index. New synoptic key by S. W. Frost. xxiv + 225pp. 5⅜ x 8. T223 Paperbound **$1.35**

THE LIFE STORY OF THE FISH: HIS MANNERS AND MORALS, Brian Curtis. A comprehensive, non-technical survey of just about everything worth knowing about fish. Written for the aquarist, the angler, and the layman with an inquisitive mind, the text covers such topics as evolution, external covering and protective coloration, physics and physiology of vision, maintenance of equilibrium, function of the lateral line canal for auditory and temperature senses, nervous system, function of the air bladder, reproductive system and methods—courtship, mating, spawning, care of young—and many more. Also sections on game fish, the problems of conservation and a fascinating chapter on fish curiosities. "Clear, simple language . . . excellent judgment in choice of subjects . . . delightful sense of humor," New York Times. Revised (1949) edition. Index. Bibliography of 72 items. 6 full-page photographic plates. xii + 284pp. 5⅜ x 8. T929 Paperbound **$1.50**

BATS, Glover Morrill Allen. The most comprehensive study of bats as a life-form by the world's foremost authority. A thorough summary of just about everything known about this fascinating and mysterious flying mammal, including its unique location sense, hibernation and cycles, its habitats and distribution, its wing structure and flying habits, and its relationship to man in the long history of folklore and superstition. Written on a middle-level, the book can be profitably studied by a trained zoologist and thoroughly enjoyed by the layman. "An absorbing text with excellent illustrations. Bats should have more friends and fewer thoughtless detractors as a result of the publication of this volume," William Beebe, Books. Extensive bibliography. 57 photographs and illustrations. x + 368pp. 5⅜ x 8½. T984 Paperbound **$2.00**

BIRDS AND THEIR ATTRIBUTES, Glover Morrill Allen. A fine general introduction to birds as living organisms, especially valuable because of emphasis on structure, physiology, habits, behavior. Discusses relationship of bird to man, early attempts at scientific ornithology, feathers and coloration, skeletal structure including bills, legs and feet, wings. Also food habits, evolution and present distribution, feeding and nest-building, still unsolved questions of migrations and location sense, many more similar topics. Final chapter on classification, nomenclature. A good popular-level summary for the biologist; a first-rate introduction for the layman. Reprint of 1925 edition. References and index. 51 illustrations. viii + 338pp. 5⅜ x 8½. T957 Paperbound **$1.85**

LIFE HISTORIES OF NORTH AMERICAN BIRDS, Arthur Cleveland Bent. Bent's monumental series of books on North American birds, prepared and published under auspices of Smithsonian Institute, is the definitive coverage of the subject, the most-used single source of information. Now the entire set is to be made available by Dover in inexpensive editions. This encyclopedic collection of detailed, specific observations utilizes reports of hundreds of contemporary observers, writings of such naturalists as Audubon, Burroughs, William Brewster, as well as author's own extensive investigations. Contains literally everything known about life history of each bird considered: nesting, eggs, plumage, distribution and migration, voice, enemies, courtship, etc. These not over-technical works are musts for ornithologists, conservationists, amateur naturalists, anyone seriously interested in American birds.

BIRDS OF PREY. More than 100 subspecies of hawks, falcons, eagles, buzzards, condors and owls, from the common barn owl to the extinct caracara of Guadaloupe Island. 400 photographs. Two volume set. Index for each volume. Bibliographies of 403, 520 items. 197 full-page plates. Total of 907pp. 5⅜ x 8½.
Vol. I T931 Paperbound **$2.35**
Vol. II T932 Paperbound **$2.35**

WILD FOWL. Ducks, geese, swans, and tree ducks—73 different subspecies. Two volume set. Index for each volume. Bibliographies of 124, 144 items. 106 full-page plates. Total of 685pp. 5⅜ x 8½.
Vol. I T285 Paperbound **$2.35**
Vol. II T286 Paperbound **$2.35**

SHORE BIRDS. 81 varieties (sandpipers, woodcocks, plovers, snipes, phalaropes, curlews, oyster catchers, etc.). More than 200 photographs of eggs, nesting sites, adult and young of important species. Two volume set. Index for each volume. Bibliographies of 261, 188 items. 121 full-page plates. Total of 860pp. 5⅜ x 8½.
Vol. I T933 Paperbound **$2.35**
Vol. II T934 Paperbound **$2.35**

THE LIFE OF PASTEUR, R. Vallery-Radot. 13th edition of this definitive biography, cited in Encyclopaedia Britannica. Authoritative, scholarly, well-documented with contemporary quotes, observations; gives complete picture of Pasteur's personal life; especially thorough presentation of scientific activities with silkworms, fermentation, hydrophobia, inoculation, etc. Introduction by Sir William Osler. Index. 505pp. 5⅜ x 8. T632 Paperbound **$2.00**

Puzzles, Mathematical Recreations

SYMBOLIC LOGIC and THE GAME OF LOGIC, Lewis Carroll. "Symbolic Logic" is not concerned with modern symbolic logic, but is instead a collection of over 380 problems posed with charm and imagination, using the syllogism, and a fascinating diagrammatic method of drawing conclusions. In "The Game of Logic" Carroll's whimsical imagination devises a logical game played with 2 diagrams and counters (included) to manipulate hundreds of tricky syllogisms. The final section, "Hit or Miss" is a lagniappe of 101 additional puzzles in the delightful Carroll manner. Until this reprint edition, both of these books were rarities costing up to $15 each. Symbolic Logic: Index. xxxi + 199pp. The Game of Logic: 96pp. 2 vols. bound as one. 5⅜ x 8.   **T492 Paperbound $1.50**

PILLOW PROBLEMS and A TANGLED TALE, Lewis Carroll. One of the rarest of all Carroll's works, "Pillow Problems" contains 72 original math puzzles, all typically ingenious. Particularly fascinating are Carroll's answers which remain exactly as he thought them out, reflecting his actual mental process. The problems in "A Tangled Tale" are in story form, originally appearing as a monthly magazine serial. Carroll not only gives the solutions, but uses answers sent in by readers to discuss wrong approaches and misleading paths, and grades them for insight. Both of these books were rarities until this edition, "Pillow Problems" costing up to $25, and "A Tangled Tale" $15. Pillow Problems: Preface and Introduction by Lewis Carroll. xx + 109pp. A Tangled Tale: 6 illustrations. 152pp. Two vols. bound as one. 5⅜ x 8.   **T493 Paperbound $1.50**

AMUSEMENTS IN MATHEMATICS, Henry Ernest Dudeney. The foremost British originator of mathematical puzzles is always intriguing, witty, and paradoxical in this classic, one of the largest collections of mathematical amusements. More than 430 puzzles, problems, and paradoxes. Mazes and games, problems on number manipulation, unicursal and other route problems, puzzles on measuring, weighing, packing, age, kinship, chessboards, joiners', crossing river, plane figure dissection, and many others. Solutions. More than 450 illustrations. vii + 258pp. 5⅜ x 8.   **T473 Paperbound $1.25**

THE CANTERBURY PUZZLES, Henry Dudeney. Chaucer's pilgrims set one another problems in story form. Also Adventures of the Puzzle Club, the Strange Escape of the King's Jester, the Monks of Riddlewell, the Squire's Christmas Puzzle Party and others. All puzzles are original, based on dissecting plane figures, arithmetic, algebra, elementary calculus and other branches of mathematics, and purely logical ingenuity. "The limit of ingenuity and intricacy," The Observer. Over 110 puzzles. Full Solutions. 150 illustrations. vii + 225pp. 5⅜ x 8.
T474 Paperbound $1.25

MATHEMATICAL EXCURSIONS, H. A. Merrill. Even if you hardly remember your high school math, you'll enjoy the 90 stimulating problems contained in this book and you will come to understand a great many mathematical principles with surprisingly little effort. Many useful shortcuts and diversions not generally known are included: division by inspection, Russian peasant multiplication, memory systems for pi, building odd and even magic squares, square roots by geometry, dyadic systems, and many more. Solutions to difficult problems. 50 illustrations. 145pp. 5⅜ x 8.   **T350 Paperbound $1.00**

MAGIC SQUARES AND CUBES, W. S. Andrews. Only book-length treatment in English, a thorough non-technical description and analysis. Here are nasik, overlapping, pandiagonal, serrated squares; magic circles, cubes, spheres, rhombuses. Try your hand at 4-dimensional magical figures! Much unusual folklore and tradition included. High school algebra is sufficient. 754 diagrams and illustrations. viii + 419pp. 5⅜ x 8.   **T658 Paperbound $1.85**

CALIBAN'S PROBLEM BOOK: MATHEMATICAL, INFERENTIAL AND CRYPTOGRAPHIC PUZZLES, H. Phillips (Caliban), S. T. Shovelton, G. S. Marshall. 105 ingenious problems by the greatest living creator of puzzles based on logic and inference. Rigorous, modern, piquant; reflecting their author's unusual personality, these intermediate and advanced puzzles all involve the ability to reason clearly through complex situations; some call for mathematical knowledge, ranging from algebra to number theory. Solutions. xi + 180pp. 5⅜ x 8.
T736 Paperbound $1.25

MATHEMATICAL PUZZLES FOR BEGINNERS AND ENTHUSIASTS, G. Mott-Smith. 188 mathematical puzzles based on algebra, dissection of plane figures, permutations, and probability, that will test and improve your powers of inference and interpretation. The Odic Force, The Spider's Cousin, Ellipse Drawing, theory and strategy of card and board games like tit-tat-toe, go moku, salvo, and many others. 100 pages of detailed mathematical explanations. Appendix of primes, square roots, etc. 135 illustrations. 2nd revised edition. 248pp. 5⅜ x 8.
T198 Paperbound $1.00

MATHEMAGIC, MAGIC PUZZLES, AND GAMES WITH NUMBERS, R. V. Heath. More than 60 new puzzles and stunts based on the properties of numbers. Easy techniques for multiplying large numbers mentally, revealing hidden numbers magically, finding the date of any day in any year, and dozens more. Over 30 pages devoted to magic squares, triangles, cubes, circles, etc. Edited by J. S. Meyer. 76 illustrations. 128pp. 5⅜ x 8.   **T110 Paperbound $1.00**

CATALOGUE OF DOVER BOOKS

THE BOOK OF MODERN PUZZLES, G. L. Kaufman. A completely new series of puzzles as fascinating as crossword and deduction puzzles but based upon different principles and techniques. Simple 2-minute teasers, word labyrinths, design and pattern puzzles, logic and observation puzzles — over 150 braincrackers. Answers to all problems. 116 illustrations. 192pp. 5⅜ x 8.
T143 Paperbound **$1.00**

NEW WORD PUZZLES, G. L. Kaufman. 100 ENTIRELY NEW puzzles based on words and their combinations that will delight crossword puzzle, Scrabble and Jotto fans. Chess words, based on the moves of the chess king; design-onyms, symmetrical designs made of synonyms; rhymed double-crostics; syllable sentences; addle letter anagrams; alphagrams; linkograms; and many others all brand new. Full solutions. Space to work problems. 196 figures. vi + 122pp. 5⅜ x 8.
T344 Paperbound **$1.00**

MAZES AND LABYRINTHS: A BOOK OF PUZZLES, W. Shepherd. Mazes, formerly associated with mystery and ritual, are still among the most intriguing of intellectual puzzles. This is a novel and different collection of 50 amusements that embody the principle of the maze: mazes in the classical tradition; 3-dimensional, ribbon, and Möbius-strip mazes; hidden messages; spatial arrangements; etc.—almost all built on amusing story situations. 84 illustrations. Essay on maze psychology. Solutions. xv + 122pp. 5⅜ x 8.
T731 Paperbound **$1.00**

MAGIC TRICKS & CARD TRICKS, W. Jonson. Two books bound as one. 52 tricks with cards, 37 tricks with coins, bills, eggs, smoke, ribbons, slates, etc. Details on presentation, misdirection, and routining will help you master such famous tricks as the Changing Card, Card in the Pocket, Four Aces, Coin Through the Hand, Bill in the Egg, Afghan Bands, and over 75 others. If you follow the lucid exposition and key diagrams carefully, you will finish these two books with an astonishing mastery of magic. 106 figures. 224pp. 5⅜ x 8. T909 Paperbound **$1.00**

PANORAMA OF MAGIC, Milbourne Christopher. A profusely illustrated history of stage magic, a unique selection of prints and engravings from the author's private collection of magic memorabilia, the largest of its kind. Apparatus, stage settings and costumes; ingenious ads distributed by the performers and satiric broadsides passed around in the streets ridiculing pompous showmen; programs; decorative souvenirs. The lively text, by one of America's foremost professional magicians, is full of anecdotes about almost legendary wizards: Dede, the Egyptian; Philadelphia, the wonder-worker; Robert-Houdin, "the father of modern magic;" Harry Houdini; scores more. Altogether a pleasure package for anyone interested in magic, stage setting and design, ethnology, psychology, or simply in unusual people. A Dover original. 295 illustrations; 8 in full color. Index. viii + 216pp. 8⅜ x 11¼.
T774 Paperbound **$2.25**

HOUDINI ON MAGIC, Harry Houdini. One of the greatest magicians of modern times explains his most prized secrets. How locks are picked, with illustrated picks and skeleton keys; how a girl is sawed into twins; how to walk through a brick wall — Houdini's explanations of 44 stage tricks with many diagrams. Also included is a fascinating discussion of great magicians of the past and the story of his fight against fraudulent mediums and spiritualists. Edited by W.B. Gibson and M.N. Young. Bibliography. 155 figures, photos. xv + 280pp. 5⅜ x 8.
T384 Paperbound **$1.25**

MATHEMATICS, MAGIC AND MYSTERY, Martin Gardner. Why do card tricks work? How do magicians perform astonishing mathematical feats? How is stage mind-reading possible? This is the first book length study explaining the application of probability, set theory, theory of numbers, topology, etc., to achieve many startling tricks. Non-technical, accurate, detailed! 115 sections discuss tricks with cards, dice, coins, knots, geometrical vanishing illusions, how a Curry square "demonstrates" that the sum of the parts may be greater than the whole, and dozens of others. No sleight of hand necessary! 135 illustrations. xii + 174pp. 5⅜ x 8.
T335 Paperbound **$1.00**

EASY-TO-DO ENTERTAINMENTS AND DIVERSIONS WITH COINS, CARDS, STRING, PAPER AND MATCHES, R. M. Abraham. Over 300 tricks, games and puzzles will provide young readers with absorbing fun. Sections on card games; paper-folding; tricks with coins, matches and pieces of string; games for the agile; toy-making from common household objects; mathematical recreations; and 50 miscellaneous pastimes. Anyone in charge of groups of youngsters, including hard-pressed parents, and in need of suggestions on how to keep children sensibly amused and quietly content will find this book indispensable. Clear, simple text, copious number of delightful line drawings and illustrative diagrams. Originally titled "Winter Nights Entertainments." Introduction by Lord Baden Powell. 329 illustrations. v + 186pp. 5⅜ x 8½.
T921 Paperbound **$1.00**

STRING FIGURES AND HOW TO MAKE THEM, Caroline Furness Jayne. 107 string figures plus variations selected from the best primitive and modern examples developed by Navajo, Apache, pygmies of Africa, Eskimo, in Europe, Australia, China, etc. The most readily understandable, easy-to-follow book in English on perennially popular recreation. Crystal-clear exposition; step-by-step diagrams. Everyone from kindergarten children to adults looking for unusual diversion will be endlessly amused. Index. Bibliography. Introduction by A. C. Haddon. 17 full-page plates. 960 illustrations. xxiii + 401pp. 5⅜ x 8½.
T152 Paperbound **$2.00**

Entertainments, Humor

ODDITIES AND CURIOSITIES OF WORDS AND LITERATURE, C. Bombaugh, edited by M. Gardner.
The largest collection of idiosyncratic prose and poetry techniques in English, a legendary work in the curious and amusing bypaths of literary recreations and the play technique in literature—so important in modern works. Contains alphabetic poetry, acrostics, palindromes, scissors verse, centos, emblematic poetry, famous literary puns, hoaxes, notorious slips of the press, hilarious mistranslations, and much more. Revised and enlarged with modern material by Martin Gardner. 368pp. 5⅜ x 8. T759 Paperbound **$1.50**

A NONSENSE ANTHOLOGY, collected by Carolyn Wells. 245 of the best nonsense verses ever written, including nonsense puns, absurd arguments, mock epics and sagas, nonsense ballads, odes, "sick" verses, dog-Latin verses, French nonsense verses, songs. By Edward Lear, Lewis Carroll, Gelett Burgess, W. S. Gilbert, Hilaire Belloc, Peter Newell, Oliver Herford, etc., 83 writers in all plus over four score anonymous nonsense verses. A special section of limericks, plus famous nonsense such as Carroll's "Jabberwocky" and Lear's "The Jumblies" and much excellent verse virtually impossible to locate elsewhere. For 50 years considered the best anthology available. Index of first lines specially prepared for this edition. Introduction by Carolyn Wells. 3 indexes: Title, Author, First lines. xxxiii + 279pp. T499 Paperbound **$1.25**

THE BAD CHILD'S BOOK OF BEASTS, MORE BEASTS FOR WORSE CHILDREN, and A MORAL ALPHABET, H. Belloc. Hardly an anthology of humorous verse has appeared in the last 50 years without at least a couple of these famous nonsense verses. But one must see the entire volumes—with all the delightful original illustrations by Sir Basil Blackwood—to appreciate fully Belloc's charming and witty verses that play so subacidly on the platitudes of life and morals that beset his day—and ours. A great humor classic. Three books in one. Total of 157pp. 5⅜ x 8. T749 Paperbound **$1.00**

THE DEVIL'S DICTIONARY, Ambrose Bierce. Sardonic and irreverent barbs puncturing the pomposities and absurdities of American politics, business, religion, literature, and arts, by the country's greatest satirist in the classic tradition. Epigrammatic as Shaw, piercing as Swift, American as Mark Twain, Will Rogers, and Fred Allen, Bierce will always remain the favorite of a small coterie of enthusiasts, and of writers and speakers whom he supplies with "some of the most gorgeous witticisms of the English language" (H. L. Mencken). Over 1000 entries in alphabetical order. 144pp. 5⅜ x 8. T487 Paperbound **$1.00**

THE PURPLE COW AND OTHER NONSENSE, Gelett Burgess. The best of Burgess's early nonsense, selected from the first edition of the "Burgess Nonsense Book." Contains many of his most unusual and truly awe-inspiring pieces: 36 nonsense quatrains, the Poems of Patagonia, Alphabet of Famous Goops, and the other hilarious (and rare) adult nonsense that place him in the forefront of American humorists. All pieces are accompanied by the original Burgess illustrations. 123 illustrations. xiii + 113pp. 5⅜ x 8. T772 Paperbound **$1.00**

MY PIOUS FRIENDS AND DRUNKEN COMPANIONS and MORE PIOUS FRIENDS AND DRUNKEN COMPANIONS, Frank Shay. Folksingers, amateur and professional, and everyone who loves singing: here, available for the first time in 30 years, is this valued collection of 132 ballads, blues, vaudeville numbers, drinking songs, sea chanties, comedy songs. Songs of pre-Beatnik Bohemia; songs from all over America, England, France, Australia; the great songs of the Naughty Nineties and early twentieth-century America. Over a third with music. Woodcuts by John Held, Jr. convey perfectly the brash insouciance of an era of rollicking unabashed song. 12 illustrations by John Held, Jr. Two indexes (Titles and First lines and Choruses). Introductions by the author. Two volumes bound as one. Total of xvi + 235pp. 5⅜ x 8½. T946 Paperbound **$1.00**

HOW TO TELL THE BIRDS FROM THE FLOWERS, R. W. Wood. How not to confuse a carrot with a parrot, a grape with an ape, a puffin with nuffin. Delightful drawings, clever puns, absurd little poems point out far-fetched resemblances in nature. The author was a leading physicist. Introduction by Margaret Wood White. 106 illus. 60pp. 5⅜ x 8. T523 Paperbound **75¢**

PECK'S BAD BOY AND HIS PA, George W. Peck. The complete edition, containing both volumes, of one of the most widely read American humor books. The endless ingenious pranks played by bad boy "Hennery" on his pa and the grocery man, the outraged pomposity of Pa, the perpetual ridiculing of middle class institutions, are as entertaining today as they were in 1883. No pale sophistications or subtleties, but rather humor vigorous, raw, earthy, imaginative, and, as folk humor often is, sadistic. This peculiarly fascinating book is also valuable to historians and students of American culture as a portrait of an age. 100 original illustrations by True Williams. Introduction by E. F. Bleiler. 347pp. 5⅜ x 8. T497 Paperbound **$1.35**

CATALOGUE OF DOVER BOOKS

THE HUMOROUS VERSE OF LEWIS CARROLL. Almost every poem Carroll ever wrote, the largest collection ever published, including much never published elsewhere: 150 parodies, burlesques, riddles, ballads, acrostics, etc., with 130 original illustrations by Tenniel, Carroll, and others. "Addicts will be grateful . . . there is nothing for the faithful to do but sit down and fall to the banquet," N. Y. Times. Index to first lines. xiv + 446pp. 5⅜ x 8.

T654 Paperbound **$1.85**

DIVERSIONS AND DIGRESSIONS OF LEWIS CARROLL. A major new treasure for Carroll fans! Rare privately published humor, fantasy, puzzles, and games by Carroll at his whimsical best, with a new vein of frank satire. Includes many new mathematical amusements and recreations, among them the fragmentary Part III of "Curiosa Mathematica." Contains "The Rectory Umbrella," "The New Belfry," "The Vision of the Three T's," and much more. New 32-page supplement of rare photographs taken by Carroll. x + 375pp. 5⅜ x 8.

T732 Paperbound **$1.65**

THE COMPLETE NONSENSE OF EDWARD LEAR. This is the only complete edition of this master of gentle madness available at a popular price. A BOOK OF NONSENSE, NONSENSE SONGS, MORE NONSENSE SONGS AND STORIES in their entirety with all the old favorites that have delighted children and adults for years. The Dong With A Luminous Nose, The Jumblies, The Owl and the Pussycat, and hundreds of other bits of wonderful nonsense. 214 limericks, 3 sets of Nonsense Botany, 5 Nonsense Alphabets, 546 drawings by Lear himself, and much more. 320pp. 5⅜ x 8.

T167 Paperbound **$1.00**

THE MELANCHOLY LUTE, The Humorous Verse of Franklin P. Adams ("FPA"). The author's own selection of light verse, drawn from thirty years of FPA's column, "The Conning Tower," syndicated all over the English-speaking world. Witty, perceptive, literate, these ninety-six poems range from parodies of other poets, Millay, Longfellow, Edgar Guest, Kipling, Masefield, etc., and free and hilarious translations of Horace and other Latin poets, to satiric comments on fabled American institutions—the New York Subways, preposterous ads, suburbanites, sensational journalism, etc. They reveal with vigor and clarity the humor, integrity and restraint of a wise and gentle American satirist. Introduction by Robert Hutchinson. vi + 122pp. 5⅜ x 8½.

T108 Paperbound **$1.00**

SINGULAR TRAVELS, CAMPAIGNS, AND ADVENTURES OF BARON MUNCHAUSEN, R. E. Raspe, with 90 illustrations by Gustave Doré. The first edition in over 150 years to reestablish the deeds of the Prince of Liars exactly as Raspe first recorded them in 1785—the genuine Baron Munchausen, one of the most popular personalities in English literature. Included also are the best of the many sequels, written by other hands. Introduction on Raspe by J. Carswell. Bibliography of early editions. xliv + 192pp. 5⅜ x 8.

T698 Paperbound **$1.00**

THE WIT AND HUMOR OF OSCAR WILDE, ed. by Alvin Redman. Wilde at his most brilliant, in 1000 epigrams exposing weaknesses and hypocrisies of "civilized" society. Divided into 49 categories—sin, wealth, women, America, etc.—to aid writers, speakers. Includes excerpts from his trials, books, plays, criticism. Formerly "The Epigrams of Oscar Wilde." Introduction by Vyvyan Holland, Wilde's only living son. Introductory essay by editor. 260pp. 5⅜ x 8.

T602 Paperbound **$1.00**

MAX AND MORITZ, Wilhelm Busch. Busch is one of the great humorists of all time, as well as the father of the modern comic strip. This volume, translated by H. A. Klein and other hands, contains the perennial favorite "Max and Moritz" (translated by C. T. Brooks), Plisch and Plum, Das Rabennest, Eispeter, and seven other whimsical, sardonic, jovial, diabolical cartoon and verse stories. Lively English translations parallel the original German. This work has delighted millions, since it first appeared in the 19th century, and is guaranteed to please almost anyone. Edited by H. A. Klein, with an afterword. x + 205pp. 5⅞ x 8½.

T181 Paperbound **$1.00**

HYPOCRITICAL HELENA, Wilhelm Busch. A companion volume to "Max and Moritz," with the title piece (Die Fromme Helena) and 10 other highly amusing cartoon and verse stories, all newly translated by H. A. Klein and M. C. Klein: Adventure on New Year's Eve (Abenteuer in der Neujahrsnacht), Hangover on the Morning after New Year's Eve (Der Katzenjammer am Neujahrsmorgen), etc. English and German in parallel columns. Hours of pleasure, also a fine language aid. x + 205pp. 5⅞ x 8½.

T184 Paperbound **$1.00**

THE BEAR THAT WASN'T, Frank Tashlin. What does it mean? Is it simply delightful wry humor, or a charming story of a bear who wakes up in the midst of a factory, or a satire on Big Business, or an existential cartoon-story of the human condition, or a symbolization of the struggle between conformity and the individual? New York Herald Tribune said of the first edition: ". . . a fable for grownups that will be fun for children. Sit down with the book and get your own bearings." Long an underground favorite with readers of all ages and opinions. v + 51pp. Illustrated. 5⅜ x 8½.

T939 Paperbound **75¢**

RUTHLESS RHYMES FOR HEARTLESS HOMES and MORE RUTHLESS RHYMES FOR HEARTLESS HOMES, Harry Graham ("Col. D. Streamer"). Two volumes of Little Willy and 48 other poetic disasters. A bright, new reprint of oft-quoted, never forgotten, devastating humor by a precursor of today's "sick" joke school. For connoisseurs of wicked, wacky humor and all who delight in the comedy of manners. Original drawings are a perfect complement. 61 illustrations. Index. vi + 69pp. Two vols. bound as one. 5⅜ x 8½.

T930 Paperbound **75¢**

CATALOGUE OF DOVER BOOKS

Say It language phrase books

These handy phrase books (128 to 196 pages each) make grammatical drills unnecessary for an elementary knowledge of a spoken foreign language. Covering most matters of travel and everyday life each volume contains:

Over 1000 phrases and sentences in immediately useful forms — foreign language plus English.

Modern usage designed for Americans. Specific phrases like, "Give me small change," and "Please call a taxi."

Simplified phonetic transcription you will be able to read at sight.

The only completely indexed phrase books on the market.

Covers scores of important situations: — Greetings, restaurants, sightseeing, useful expressions, etc.

These books are prepared by native linguists who are professors at Columbia, N.Y.U., Fordham and other great universities. Use them independently or with any other book or record course. They provide a supplementary living element that most other courses lack. Individual volumes in:

Russian 75¢	Italian 75¢	Spanish 75¢	German 75¢
Hebrew 75¢	Danish 75¢	Japanese 75¢	Swedish 75¢
Dutch 75¢	Esperanto 75¢	Modern Greek 75¢	Portuguese 75¢
Norwegian 75¢	Polish 75¢	French 75¢	Yiddish 75¢
Turkish 75¢			English for German-speaking people 75¢
English for Italian-speaking people 75¢		English for Spanish-speaking people 75¢	

Large clear type. 128-196 pages each. 3½ x 5¼. Sturdy paper binding.

Listen and Learn language records

LISTEN & LEARN is the only language record course designed especially to meet your travel and everyday needs. It is available in separate sets for FRENCH, SPANISH, GERMAN, JAPANESE, RUSSIAN, MODERN GREEK, PORTUGUESE, ITALIAN and HEBREW, and each set contains three 33⅓ rpm long-playing records—1½ hours of recorded speech by eminent native speakers who are professors at Columbia, New York University, Queens College.

Check the following special features found only in LISTEN & LEARN:

- **Dual-language recording. 812 selected phrases and sentences, over 3200 words,** spoken first in English, then in their foreign language equivalents. A suitable pause follows each foreign phrase, allowing you time to repeat the expression. You learn by unconscious assimilation.

- **128 to 206-page manual** contains everything on the records, plus a simple phonetic pronunciation guide.

- **Indexed for convenience. The only set on the market** that is completely indexed. No more puzzling over where to find the phrase you need. Just look in the rear of the manual.

- **Practical.** No time wasted on material you can find in any grammar. LISTEN & LEARN covers central core material with phrase approach. Ideal for the person with limited learning time.

- **Living, modern expressions,** not found in other courses. Hygienic products, modern equipment, shopping—expressions used every day, like "nylon" and "air-conditioned."

- **Limited objective.** Everything you learn, no matter where you stop, is immediately useful. You have to finish other courses, wade through grammar and vocabulary drill, before they help you.

- **High-fidelity recording.** LISTEN & LEARN records equal in clarity and surface-silence any record on the market costing up to $6.

"Excellent . . . the spoken records . . . impress me as being among the very best on the market," **Prof. Mario Pei,** Dept. of Romance Languages, Columbia University. "Inexpensive and well-done . . . it would make an ideal present," CHICAGO SUNDAY TRIBUNE. "More genuinely helpful than anything of its kind which I have previously encountered," **Sidney Clark,** well-known author of "ALL THE BEST" travel books.

UNCONDITIONAL GUARANTEE. Try LISTEN & LEARN, then return it within 10 days for full refund if you are not satisfied.

Each set contains three twelve-inch 33⅓ records, manual, and album.

SPANISH	the set $5.95	GERMAN	the set $5.95
FRENCH	the set $5.95	ITALIAN	the set $5.95
RUSSIAN	the set $5.95	JAPANESE	the set $5.95
PORTUGUESE	the set $5.95	MODERN GREEK	the set $5.95
MODERN HEBREW	the set $5.95		

Americana

THE EYES OF DISCOVERY, J. Bakeless. A vivid reconstruction of how unspoiled America appeared to the first white men. Authentic and enlightening accounts of Hudson's landing in New York, Coronado's trek through the Southwest; scores of explorers, settlers, trappers, soldiers. America's pristine flora, fauna, and Indians in every region and state in fresh and unusual new aspects. "A fascinating view of what the land was like before the first highway went through," Time. 68 contemporary illustrations, 39 newly added in this edition. Index. Bibliography. x + 500pp. 5⅜ x 8. **T761 Paperbound $2.00**

AUDUBON AND HIS JOURNALS, J. J. Audubon. A collection of fascinating accounts of Europe and America in the early 1800's through Audubon's own eyes. Includes the Missouri River Journals —an eventful trip through America's untouched heartland, the Labrador Journals, the European Journals, the famous "Episodes", and other rare Audubon material, including the descriptive chapters from the original letterpress edition of the "Ornithological Studies", omitted in all later editions. Indispensable for ornithologists, naturalists, and all lovers of Americana and adventure. 70-page biography by Audubon's granddaughter. 38 illustrations. Index. Total of 1106pp. 5⅜ x 8.
T675 Vol I Paperbound **$2.00**
T676 Vol II Paperbound **$2.00**
The set **$4.00**

TRAVELS OF WILLIAM BARTRAM, edited by Mark Van Doren. The first inexpensive illustrated edition of one of the 18th century's most delightful books is an excellent source of first-hand material on American geography, anthropology, and natural history. Many descriptions of early Indian tribes are our only source of information on them prior to the infiltration of the white man. "The mind of a scientist with the soul of a poet," John Livingston Lowes. 13 original illustrations and maps. Edited with an introduction by Mark Van Doren. 448pp. 5⅜ x 8.
T13 Paperbound $2.00

GARRETS AND PRETENDERS: A HISTORY OF BOHEMIANISM IN AMERICA, A. Parry. The colorful and fantastic history of American Bohemianism from Poe to Kerouac. This is the only complete record of hoboes, cranks, starving poets, and suicides. Here are Pfaff, Whitman, Crane, Bierce, Pound, and many others. New chapters by the author and by H. T. Moore bring this thorough and well-documented history down to the Beatniks. "An excellent account," N. Y. Times. Scores of cartoons, drawings, and caricatures. Bibliography. Index. xxviii + 421pp. 5⅝ x 8⅜.
T708 Paperbound $1.95

THE EXPLORATION OF THE COLORADO RIVER AND ITS CANYONS, J. W. Powell. The thrilling first-hand account of the expedition that filled in the last white space on the map of the United States. Rapids, famine, hostile Indians, and mutiny are among the perils encountered as the unknown Colorado Valley reveals its secrets. This is the only uncut version of Major Powell's classic of exploration that has been printed in the last 60 years. Includes later reflections and subsequent expedition. 250 illustrations, new map. 400pp. 5⅝ x 8⅜.
T94 Paperbound $2.00

THE JOURNAL OF HENRY D. THOREAU, Edited by Bradford Torrey and Francis H. Allen. Henry Thoreau is not only one of the most important figures in American literature and social thought; his voluminous journals (from which his books emerged as selections and crystallizations) constitute both the longest, most sensitive record of personal internal development and a most penetrating description of a historical moment in American culture. This present set, which was first issued in fourteen volumes, contains Thoreau's entire journals from 1837 to 1862, with the exception of the lost years which were found only recently. We are reissuing it, complete and unabridged, with a new introduction by Walter Harding, Secretary of the Thoreau Society. Fourteen volumes reissued in two volumes. Foreword by Henry Seidel Canby. Total of 1888pp. 8⅜ x 12¼. **T312-3 Two volume set, Clothbound $20.00**

GAMES AND SONGS OF AMERICAN CHILDREN, collected by William Wells Newell. A remarkable collection of 190 games with songs that accompany many of them; cross references to show similarities, differences among them; variations; musical notation for 38 songs. Textual discussions show relations with folk-drama and other aspects of folk tradition. Grouped into categories for ready comparative study: Love-games, histories, playing at work, human life, bird and beast, mythology, guessing-games, etc. New introduction covers relations of songs and dances to timeless heritage of folklore, biographical sketch of Newell, other pertinent data. A good source of inspiration for those in charge of groups of children and a valuable reference for anthropologists, sociologists, psychiatrists. Introduction by Carl Withers. New indexes of first lines, games. 5⅜ x 8½. xii + 242pp. **T354 Paperbound $1.65**

Art, History of Art, Antiques, Graphic Arts, Handcrafts

ART STUDENTS' ANATOMY, E. J. Farris. Outstanding art anatomy that uses chiefly living objects for its illustrations. 71 photos of undraped men, women, children are accompanied by carefully labeled matching sketches to illustrate the skeletal system, articulations and movements, bony landmarks, the muscular system, skin, fasciae, fat, etc. 9 x-ray photos show movement of joints. Undraped models are shown in such actions as serving in tennis, drawing a bow in archery, playing football, dancing, preparing to spring and to dive. Also discussed and illustrated are proportions, age and sex differences, the anatomy of the smile, etc. 8 plates by the great early 18th century anatomic illustrator Siegfried Albinus are also included. Glossary. 158 figures, 7 in color. x + 159pp. 5⅝ x 8⅜. T744 Paperbound **$1.45**

AN ATLAS OF ANATOMY FOR ARTISTS, F Schider. A new 3rd edition of this standard text enlarged by 52 new illustrations of hands, anatomical studies by Cloquet, and expressive life studies of the body by Barcsay. 189 clear, detailed plates offer you precise information of impeccable accuracy. 29 plates show all aspects of the skeleton, with closeups of special areas, while 54 full-page plates, mostly in two colors, give human musculature as seen from four different points of view, with cutaways for important portions of the body. 14 full-page plates provide photographs of hand forms, eyelids, female breasts, and indicate the location of muscles upon models. 59 additional plates show how great artists of the past utilized human anatomy. They reproduce sketches and finished work by such artists as Michelangelo, Leonardo da Vinci, Goya, and 15 others. This is a lifetime reference work which will be one of the most important books in any artist's library. "The standard reference tool," AMERICAN LIBRARY ASSOCIATION. "Excellent," AMERICAN ARTIST. Third enlarged edition. 189 plates, 647 illustrations. xxvi + 192pp. 7⅞ x 10⅝. T241 Clothbound **$6.00**

AN ATLAS OF ANIMAL ANATOMY FOR ARTISTS, W. Ellenberger, H. Baum, H. Dittrich. The largest, richest animal anatomy for artists available in English. 99 detailed anatomical plates of such animals as the horse, dog, cat, lion, deer, seal, kangaroo, flying squirrel, cow, bull, goat, monkey, hare, and bat. Surface features are clearly indicated, while progressive beneath-the-skin pictures show musculature, tendons, and bone structure. Rest and action are exhibited in terms of musculature and skeletal structure and detailed cross-sections are given for heads and important features. The animals chosen are representative of specific families so that a study of these anatomies will provide knowledge of hundreds of related species. "Highly recommended as one of the very few books on the subject worthy of being used as an authoritative guide," DESIGN. "Gives a fundamental knowledge," AMERICAN ARTIST. Second revised, enlarged edition with new plates from Cuvier, Stubbs, etc. 288 illustrations. 153pp. 11⅜ x 9. T82 Clothbound **$6.00**

THE HUMAN FIGURE IN MOTION, Eadweard Muybridge. The largest selection in print of Muybridge's famous high-speed action photos of the human figure in motion. 4789 photographs illustrate 162 different actions: men, women, children—mostly undraped—are shown walking, running, carrying various objects, sitting, lying down, climbing, throwing, arising, and performing over 150 other actions. Some actions are shown in as many as 150 photographs each. All in all there are more than 500 action strips in this enormous volume, series shots taken at shutter speeds of as high as 1/6000th of a second! These are not posed shots, but true stopped motion. They show bone and muscle in situations that the human eye is not fast enough to capture. Earlier, smaller editions of these prints have brought $40 and more on the out-of-print market. "A must for artists," ART IN FOCUS. "An unparalleled dictionary of action for all artists," AMERICAN ARTIST. 390 full-page plates, with 4789 photographs. Printed on heavy glossy stock. Reinforced binding with headbands. xxi + 390pp. 7⅞ x 10⅝. T204 Clothbound **$10.00**

ANIMALS IN MOTION, Eadweard Muybridge. This is the largest collection of animal action photos in print. 34 different animals (horses, mules, oxen, goats, camels, pigs, cats, guanacos, lions, gnus, deer, monkeys, eagles—and 21 others) in 132 characteristic actions. The horse alone is shown in more than 40 different actions. All 3919 photographs are taken in series at speeds up to 1/6000th of a second. The secrets of leg motion, spinal patterns, head movements, strains and contortions shown nowhere else are captured. You will see exactly how a lion sets his foot down; how an elephant's knees are like a human's—and how they differ; the position of a kangaroo's legs in mid-leap; how an ostrich's head bobs; details of the flight of birds—and thousands of facets of motion only the fastest cameras can catch. Photographed from domestic animals and animals in the Philadelphia zoo, it contains neither semiposed artificial shots nor distorted telephoto shots taken under adverse conditions. Artists, biologists, decorators, cartoonists, will find this book indispensable for understanding animals in motion. "A really marvelous series of plates," NATURE (London). "The dry plate's most spectacular early use was by Eadweard Muybridge," LIFE. 3919 photographs; 380 full pages of plates. 440pp. Printed on heavy glossy paper. Deluxe binding with headbands. 7⅞ x 10⅝. T203 Clothbound **$10.00**

CATALOGUE OF DOVER BOOKS

THE AUTOBIOGRAPHY OF AN IDEA, Louis Sullivan. The pioneer architect whom Frank Lloyd Wright called "the master" reveals an acute sensitivity to social forces and values in this passionately honest account. He records the crystallization of his opinions and theories, the growth of his organic theory of architecture that still influences American designers and architects, contemporary ideas, etc. This volume contains the first appearance of 34 full-page plates of his finest architecture. Unabridged reissue of 1924 edition. New introduction by R. M. Line. Index. xiv + 335pp. 5⅜ x 8. **T281 Paperbound $2.00**

THE DRAWINGS OF HEINRICH KLEY. The first uncut republication of both of Kley's devastating sketchbooks, which first appeared in pre-World War I Germany. One of the greatest cartoonists and social satirists of modern times, his exuberant and iconoclastic fantasy and his extraordinary technique place him in the great tradition of Bosch, Breughel, and Goya, while his subject matter has all the immediacy and tension of our century. 200 drawings. viii + 128pp. 7¾ x 10¾. **T24 Paperbound $1.85**

MORE DRAWINGS BY HEINRICH KLEY. All the sketches from Leut' Und Viecher (1912) and Sammel-Album (1923) not included in the previous Dover edition of Drawings. More of the bizarre, mercilessly iconoclastic sketches that shocked and amused on their original publication. Nothing was too sacred, no one too eminent for satirization by this imaginative, individual and accomplished master cartoonist. A total of 158 illustrations. Iv + 104pp. 7¾ x 10¾. **T41 Paperbound $1.85**

PINE FURNITURE OF EARLY NEW ENGLAND, R. H. Kettell. A rich understanding of one of America's most original folk arts that collectors of antiques, interior decorators, craftsmen, woodworkers, and everyone interested in American history and art will find fascinating and immensely useful. 413 illustrations of more than 300 chairs, benches, racks, beds, cupboards, mirrors, shelves, tables, and other furniture will show all the simple beauty and character of early New England furniture. 55 detailed drawings carefully analyze outstanding pieces. "With its rich store of illustrations, this book emphasizes the individuality and varied design of early American pine furniture. It should be welcomed," ANTIQUES. 413 illustrations and 55 working drawings. 475. 8 x 10¾. **T145 Clothbound $10.00**

THE HUMAN FIGURE, J. H. Vanderpoel. Every important artistic element of the human figure is pointed out in minutely detailed word descriptions in this classic text and illustrated as well in 430 pencil and charcoal drawings. Thus the text of this book directs your attention to all the characteristic features and subtle differences of the male and female (adults, children, and aged persons), as though a master artist were telling you what to look for at each stage. 2nd edition, revised and enlarged by George Bridgman. Foreword. 430 illustrations. 143pp. 6⅛ x 9¼. **T432 Paperbound $1.50**

LETTERING AND ALPHABETS, J. A. Cavanagh. This unabridged reissue of LETTERING offers a full discussion, analysis, illustration of 89 basic hand lettering styles — styles derived from Caslons, Bodonis, Garamonds, Gothic, Black Letter, Oriental, and many others. Upper and lower cases, numerals and common signs pictured. Hundreds of technical hints on make-up, construction, artistic validity, strokes, pens, brushes, white areas, etc. May be reproduced without permission! 89 complete alphabets; 72 lettered specimens. 121pp. 9¾ x 8. **T53 Paperbound $1.25**

STICKS AND STONES, Lewis Mumford. A survey of the forces that have conditioned American architecture and altered its forms. The author discusses the medieval tradition in early New England villages; the Renaissance influence which developed with the rise of the merchant class; the classical influence of Jefferson's time; the "Mechanicsvilles" of Poe's generation; the Brown Decades; the philosophy of the Imperial facade; and finally the modern machine age. "A truly remarkable book," SAT. REV. OF LITERATURE. 2nd revised edition. 21 illustrations. xvii + 228pp. 5⅜ x 8. **T202 Paperbound $1.60**

THE STANDARD BOOK OF QUILT MAKING AND COLLECTING, Marguerite Ickis. A complete easy-to-follow guide with all the information you need to make beautiful, useful quilts. How to plan, design, cut, sew, appliqué, avoid sewing problems, use rag bag, make borders, tuft, every other aspect. Over 100 traditional quilts shown, including over 40 full-size patterns. At-home hobby for fun, profit. Index. 483 illus. 1 color plate. 287pp. 6¾ x 9½. **T582 Paperbound $2.00**

THE BOOK OF SIGNS, Rudolf Koch. Formerly $20 to $25 on the out-of-print market, now only $1.00 in this unabridged new edition! 493 symbols from ancient manuscripts, medieval cathedrals, coins, catacombs, pottery, etc. Crosses, monograms of Roman emperors, astrological, chemical, botanical, runes, housemarks, and 7 other categories. Invaluable for handicraft workers, illustrators, scholars, etc., this material may be reproduced without permission. 493 illustrations by Fritz Kredel. 104pp. 6½ x 9¼. **T162 Paperbound $1.00**

PRIMITIVE ART, Franz Boas. This authoritative and exhaustive work by a great American anthropologist covers the entire gamut of primitive art. Pottery, leatherwork, metal work, stone work, wood, basketry, are treated in detail. Theories of primitive art, historical depth in art history, technical virtuosity, unconscious levels of patterning, symbolism, styles, literature, music, dance, etc. A must book for the interested layman, the anthropologist, artist, handicrafter (hundreds of unusual motifs), and the historian. Over 900 illustrations (50 ceramic vessels, 12 totem poles, etc.). 376pp. 5⅜ x 8. **T25 Paperbound $1.95**

Fiction

FLATLAND, E. A. Abbott. A science-fiction classic of life in a 2-dimensional world that is also a first-rate introduction to such aspects of modern science as relativity and hyperspace. Political, moral, satirical, and humorous overtones have made FLATLAND fascinating reading for thousands. 7th edition. New introduction by Banesh Hoffmann. 16 illustrations. 128pp. 5⅜ x 8. T1 Paperbound **$1.00**

THE WONDERFUL WIZARD OF OZ, L. F. Baum. Only edition in print with all the original W. W. Denslow illustrations in full color—as much a part of "The Wizard" as Tenniel's drawings are of "Alice in Wonderland." "The Wizard" is still America's best-loved fairy tale, in which, as the author expresses it, "The wonderment and joy are retained and the heartaches and nightmares left out." Now today's young readers can enjoy every word and wonderful picture of the original book. New introduction by Martin Gardner. A Baum bibliography. 23 full-page color plates. viii + 268pp. 5⅜ x 8. T691 Paperbound **$1.45**

THE MARVELOUS LAND OF OZ, L. F. Baum. This is the equally enchanting sequel to the "Wizard," continuing the adventures of the Scarecrow and the Tin Woodman. The hero this time is a little boy named Tip, and all the delightful Oz magic is still present. This is the Oz book with the Animated Saw-Horse, the Woggle-Bug, and Jack Pumpkinhead. All the original John R. Neill illustrations, 10 in full color. 287 pp. 5⅜ x 8. T692 Paperbound **$1.45**

FIVE GREAT DOG NOVELS, edited by Blanche Cirker. The complete original texts of five classic dog novels that have delighted and thrilled millions of children and adults throughout the world with their stories of loyalty, adventure, and courage. Full texts of Jack London's "The Call of the Wild"; John Brown's "Rab and His Friends"; Alfred Ollivant's "Bob, Son of Battle"; Marshall Saunders's "Beautiful Joe"; and Ouida's "A Dog of Flanders." 21 Illustrations from the original editions. 495pp. 5⅜ x 8. T777 Paperbound **$1.50**

TO THE SUN? and OFF ON A COMET!, Jules Verne. Complete texts of two of the most imaginative flights into fancy in world literature display the high adventure that have kept Verne's novels read for nearly a century. Only unabridged edition of the best translation, by Edward Roth. Large, easily readable type. 50 illustrations selected from first editions. 462pp. 5⅜ x 8. T634 Paperbound **$1.75**

FROM THE EARTH TO THE MOON and ALL AROUND THE MOON, Jules Verne. Complete editions of 2 of Verne's most successful novels, in finest Edward Roth translations, now available after many years out of print. Verne's visions of submarines, airplanes, television, rockets, interplanetary travel; of scientific and not-so-scientific beliefs; of peculiarities of Americans; all delight and engross us today as much as when they first appeared. Large, easily readable type. 42 illus. from first French edition. 476pp. 5⅜ x 8. T633 Paperbound **$1.75**

THE CRUISE OF THE CACHALOT, Frank T. Bullen. Out of the experiences of many years on the high-seas, First Mate Bullen created this novel of adventure aboard an American whaler, shipping out of New Bedford, Mass., when American whaling was at the height of its splendor. Originally published in 1899, the story of the round-the-world cruise of the "Cachalot" in pursuit of the sperm whale has thrilled generations of readers. A maritime classic that will fascinate anyone interested in reading about the sea or looking for a solid old-fashioned yarn, while the vivid recreation of a brief but important chapter of Americana and the British author's often biting commentary on nineteenth-century Yankee mores offer insights into the colorful era of America's coming of age. 8 plates. xiii + 271pp. 5⅜ x 8½. T774 Paperbound **$1.00**

28 SCIENCE FICTION STORIES OF H. G. WELLS. Two full unabridged novels, MEN LIKE GODS and STAR BEGOTTEN, plus 26 short stories by the master science-fiction writer of all time! Stories of space, time, invention, exploration, future adventure—an indispensable part of the library of everyone interested in science and adventure. PARTIAL CONTENTS: Men Like Gods, The Country of the Blind, In the Abyss, The Crystal Egg, The Man Who Could Work Miracles, A Story of the Days to Come, The Valley of Spiders, and 21 more! 928pp. 5⅜ x 8. T265 Clothbound **$3.95**

DAVID HARUM, E. N. Westcott. This novel of one of the most lovable, humorous characters in American literature is a prime example of regional humor. It continues to delight people who like their humor dry, their characters quaint, and their plots ingenuous. First book edition to contain complete novel plus chapter found after author's death. Illustrations from first illustrated edition. 192pp. 5⅜ x 8. T580 Paperbound **$1.15**

GESTA ROMANORUM, trans. by Charles Swan, ed. by Wynnard Hooper. 181 tales of Greeks, Romans, Britons, Biblical characters, comprise one of greatest medieval story collections, source of plots for writers including Shakespeare, Chaucer, Gower, etc. Imaginative tales of wars, incest, thwarted love, magic, fantasy, allegory, humor, tell about kings, prostitutes, philosophers, fair damsels, knights, Noah, pirates, all walks, stations of life. Introduction. Notes. 500pp. 5⅜ x 8. T535 Paperbound **$1.85**

Music

A GENERAL HISTORY OF MUSIC, Charles Burney. A detailed coverage of music from the Greeks up to 1789, with full information on all types of music: sacred and secular, vocal and instrumental, operatic and symphonic. Theory, notation, forms, instruments, innovators, composers, performers, typical and important works, and much more in an easy, entertaining style. Burney covered much of Europe and spoke with hundreds of authorities and composers so that this work is more than a compilation of records . . . it is a living work of careful and first-hand scholarship. Its account of thoroughbass (18th century) Italian music is probably still the best introduction on the subject. A recent NEW YORK TIMES review said, "Surprisingly few of Burney's statements have been invalidated by modern research . . . still of great value." Edited and corrected by Frank Mercer. 35 figures. Indices. 1915pp. 5⅜ x 8. 2 volumes.
T36 The Set, Clothbound **$12.50**

A DICTIONARY OF HYMNOLOGY, John Julian. This exhaustive and scholarly work has become known as an invaluable source of hundreds of thousands of important and often difficult to obtain facts on the history and use of hymns in the western world. Everyone interested in hymns will be fascinated by the accounts of famous hymns and hymn writers and amazed by the amount of practical information he will find. More than 30,000 entries on individual hymns, giving authorship, date and circumstances of composition, publication, textual variations, translations, denominational and ritual usage, etc. Biographies of more than 9,000 hymn writers, and essays on important topics such as Christmas carols and children's hymns, and much other unusual and valuable information. A 200 page double-columned index of first lines — the largest in print. Total of 1786 pages in two reinforced clothbound volumes. 6¼ x 9¼.
The set, T333 Clothbound **$15.00**

MUSIC IN MEDIEVAL BRITAIN, F. Ll. Harrison. The most thorough, up-to-date, and accurate treatment of the subject ever published, beautifully illustrated. Complete account of institutions and choirs; carols, masses, and motets; liturgy and plainsong; and polyphonic music from the Norman Conquest to the Reformation. Discusses the various schools of music and their reciprocal influences; the origin and development of new ritual forms; development and use of instruments; and new evidence on many problems of the period. Reproductions of scores, over 200 excerpts from medieval melodies. Rules of harmony and dissonance; influence of Continental styles; great composers (Dunstable, Cornysh, Fairfax, etc.); and much more. Register and index of more than 400 musicians. Index of titles. General Index. 225-item bibliography. 6 Appendices. xix + 491pp. 5⅝ x 8¾.
T705 Clothbound **$10.00**

THE MUSIC OF SPAIN, Gilbert Chase. Only book in English to give concise, comprehensive account of Iberian music; new Chapter covers music since 1941. Victoria, Albéniz, Cabezón, Pedrell, Turina, hundreds of other composers; popular and folk music; the Gypsies; the guitar; dance, theatre, opera, with only extensive discussion in English of the Zarzuela; virtuosi such as Casals; much more. "Distinguished . . . readable," Saturday Review. 400-item bibliography. Index. 27 photos. 383pp. 5⅜ x 8.
T549 Paperbound **$2.00**

ON STUDYING SINGING, Sergius Kagen. An intelligent method of voice-training, which leads you around pitfalls that waste your time, money, and effort. Exposes rigid, mechanical systems, baseless theories, deleterious exercises. "Logical, clear, convincing . . . dead right," Virgil Thomson, N.Y. Herald Tribune. "I recommend this volume highly," Maggie Teyte, Saturday Review. 119pp. 5⅜ x 8.
T622 Paperbound **$1.25**

Dover publishes books on art, music, philosophy, literature, languages, history, social sciences, psychology, handcrafts, orientalia, puzzles and entertainments, chess, pets and gardens, books explaining science, intermediate and higher mathematics mathematical physics, engineering, biological sciences, earth sciences, classics of science, etc. Write to:

Dept. catrr.
Dover Publications, Inc.
180 Varick Street, N. Y. 14, N. Y.

MUSIC